SEARCHING FOR
AMERICA'S HEART

PETER EDELMAN

Searching for America's Heart

RFK AND THE RENEWAL OF HOPE

HOUGHTON MIFFLIN COMPANY

BOSTON NEW YORK

2001

For information about permission to reproduce selections from
this book, write to Permissions, Houghton Mifflin Company,
215 Park Avenue South, New York, New York 10003.

Visit our Web site: www.houghtonmifflinbooks.com.

Library of Congress Cataloging-in-Publication Data
Edelman, Peter B.
Searching for America's heart : RFK and the renewal of
hope / Peter Edelman.
p.   cm.
Includes index.
ISBN 0-395-89544-8
1. Poor children — Government policy — United States.
2. Kennedy, Robert, 1925–1968.   3. Clinton, Bill, 1946–   I. Title.
HV741 .E34   2001
362.7'8'0973 — dc21   00-040804

Printed in the United States of America

Book design by Victoria Hartman

QUM 10 9 8 7 6 5 4 3 2 1

To the women, and their children,
who have been pushed to the edge — or beyond

ACKNOWLEDGMENTS

THIS BOOK would not exist without Wendy Strothman, who, impelled by my resignation from the Clinton administration, suggested it. The marvelous coincidence was that it was the very idea I had in mind for a long time and never pursued. Wendy did a second terrific thing: assigning Eric Chinski to be my editor. Eric guided me through a process of turning a discursive draft into a finished product that could not have been what it is without his help. And then, at the end, Bill Whitworth was brought in for polish — like engaging Heifetz to give me violin lessons.

My wife, Marian, read the draft with loving care and gave me fabulous feedback, and our sons — Joshua, Jonah, and Ezra — were generous in taking the time to read and comment thoughtfully. Marian was wonderfully supportive through the whole endeavor. Then there were the friends who spent amazing amounts of time reading the book at various stages. Sam Smith, Dan Porterfield, and Elizabeth Drew were literally unbelievable in the amount of work they did, to say nothing of the major difference it made. I still don't understand how Paul Wellstone had the time to read an early draft and then sit with me going through it page by page. Michael Wald, Lee Schorr, Caitlin Halligan, Deepak

Bhargava, Corey Washington, and David Birenbaum also read the whole manuscript and provided valuable advice. Bill Ayers, John Bouman, Prue Brown, Marv Hoffman, and Wendell Primus read portions and made useful suggestions. Thanks also to my agent, Esther Newberg, for all her help.

My research assistants, a substantial group by now — Wataru Matsuyasu, Emily Johnson, Lisa Pritchard Bayley, Bill Lyons, and Candice Jones — were great. All of them worked hard and were fine colleagues in the effort. Lisa Pritchard Bayley was a special help, continuing to read successive drafts and make thoughtful comments long after she had stopped working for me.

Judy Areen, my colleague and dean at Georgetown University Law Center, helped materially with summer writing grants.

I especially cherish the help of the women who, struggling to cope in the wake of our national shift in welfare policy, took the time to tell me about their lives. I am also grateful for the time and conversations, some multiple, that so many people allowed me. The visits in Baltimore, Boston, Chicago, and New York were crucial. I talked, in person and by telephone, with dozens of people — some who played a role in the events of the sixties and since, and others who are involved now as advocates and organizers, experts and researchers, civic and political leaders, foundation and nonprofit executives, and, most important, people coping with poverty in their own lives.

Thank you to all of you who helped. I appreciate it more than I can say.

CONTENTS

INTRODUCTION

On AUGUST 22, 1996, President Bill Clinton signed, with great fanfare, a law radically restricting the aid America offers to poor families with children — a measure colloquially known as "welfare reform." The event was the culmination of a backlash that had been growing for three decades, and reflected an even deeper change in Americans' sense of communal responsibility and what it means to be an American. The long-building anger at some of our most powerless people had finally boiled over — ironically, on the watch of a Democratic president.

President Clinton buttressed his action with the words of Senator Robert F. Kennedy. "Work," RFK had said, "is the meaning of what this country is all about. We need it as individuals. We need to sense it in our fellow citizens. And we need it as a society and as a people."

I was then serving President Clinton as an assistant secretary of Health and Human Services, and had been Kennedy's legislative assistant. I knew both men well. I knew what Kennedy envisioned was a national investment to assure that people actually had jobs. I knew that he also wanted to assure a decent measure of help for people unable to find work, and especially for their children. He wanted concrete help for all those having trouble getting by. He wanted to do something serious about poverty.

President Clinton hijacked RFK's words and twisted them totally. Instead of assuring jobs and a safety net, Clinton and the Republican Congress invited states to order people to work or else, even if there are no jobs, and with no regard for what happens to them or their children. In the postwelfare world, no cash help has to be offered to parents who fail to find work, even when they are wholly without fault. By signing the bill Clinton signaled acquiescence in the conservative premise that welfare *is* the problem — the source of a "culture" of irresponsible behavior.

President Clinton's misuse of Robert Kennedy's words highlighted a stark difference between the two young leaders. One pressed for social justice whenever he could. The other, originally projecting a commitment to renewing national idealism, ended up governing mainly according to the lowest common denominator. A proper invocation of RFK would have brought us full circle to a new commitment. Instead we completed a U-turn.

I have watched the changing course of our attitudes from close range. In a small way, I have continued the journey Robert Kennedy was not allowed to finish. I had been headed to Wall Street before I went to work for him, but after he was assassinated that path no longer seemed right for me. Newly married to my wonderful wife, Marian, with her own passion for justice, which has brought her from the civil rights movement in Mississippi to the Children's Defense Fund, I decided to pursue my personal memorial to Robert Kennedy by carrying on in his spirit.

That my life should concern itself so much with the question of why we respond so unsatisfactorily to the poorest among us was unimaginable to me growing up in Minneapolis in the fifties. My father, whom I adored as a child, was a successful lawyer and a decent, community-spirited man, and my mother, who died of colon cancer when I was fifteen, was a smart, shy, musical woman who mistrusted country clubs and wealth. I had an instinctive but undeveloped liberalism derived from my father's Democratic-Farmer-Labor Party politics and from being Jewish in a historically anti-Semitic city. I went to public school and Hebrew school and heard often about the great-grandfather for whom I was named, a great rabbi and mystical healer in Russia. I no doubt knew poor people in school, but I didn't know they were poor. In a city that was then 3 percent black, the only people of color I met were my father's two black colleagues on the Mayor's Council on Human Relations and the black student who transferred into the class behind me at West High School (and was soon elected class president).

My parents encouraged me to get good grades and play the clarinet. My father occasionally took me to hearings and community meetings, but he never stressed much of anything besides getting all "A"s. (The clarinet part came from my mother.) I ran for student offices, but I think my main reason for doing so was to gain certification that I wasn't a nerd. When I went away to Harvard in 1954, my father's only advice was not to join anything, it being the heyday of Senator Joseph McCarthy.

I did get good grades, and ended up serving as a Supreme Court law clerk, which led to the Justice Department and to Robert Kennedy. Something besides career development must have driven me, but I wouldn't have been able to articulate it.

The almost four years that I worked for Robert Kennedy changed everything. This was the formative professional relationship of my life. Like many who experienced so much so quickly in the sixties, I was not the same person at age thirty that I had been at twenty-five. I had been shaped by witnessing injustice in the company of a man who constantly sought it out and tried to right it. His passion to make a difference left a permanent mark. If there was a specific time when the mark became indelible, it occurred a year before he was murdered, when, in Mississippi with him to build support for the War on Poverty, I saw children starving in this rich country and at the same time met my wife-to-be.

I've tried to keep at it. At the Robert F. Kennedy Memorial, where I was deputy director, we created a fellowship for young people to work in low-income communities. As a vice president at the University of Massachusetts I pressed for a College of Public and Community Service, university courses in the prisons, care by doctors from the medical school for mentally retarded people in state institutions, academic credit for students who did community service in poor neighborhoods, and admission of minority students to the medical school. As director of the New York State Division for Youth, my focus, which became controversial, was on improving the life chances of the disadvantaged young people enmeshed in the juvenile justice system. At Georgetown University Law Center my teaching and writing have mainly concentrated on poverty, as did my work in the Clinton administration and for Democratic candidates for office over the years.

When Bill Clinton was elected president I thought we had a chance to move forward. I had known him almost fifteen years and his wife, Hillary, almost twenty-five, and I thought I understood him. They were both friends (Hillary more than the President), and Hillary had chaired my wife Marian's board at the Children's Defense Fund. I knew his politics were more centrist than mine. Marian and I had seen him lobby to limit Medicaid expansion in the late eighties, increase state discretion in the welfare legislation of 1988, and weaken the child care legislation of 1990. I recognized that the times were more conservative, and that the deficit inherited from Presidents Reagan and Bush made money for new or expanded programs scarce.

Nonetheless, I thought this intelligent and articulate young man would project an idealism that would inspire the country, especially young people. Things started out pretty well. It was wonderful to see how many young people had worked in his campaign and then joined the administration, although their numbers had dwindled by the time he left office. And he did appoint, and keep, a number of top people who worked hard to be a good influence.

The day after Clinton was inaugurated, I found myself walking into the Old Executive Office Building for the first time in many years for a meeting of a small group charged with fleshing out Clinton's national-service proposal. It was exciting, and I was happy to accept a position as counselor to Donna Shalala, the secretary of Health and Human Services. When Clinton made some moves with which I disagreed, I initially accepted them as probably necessary if unfortunate exceptions to his prevailing direction. But during the first two years there were also many positive things. I had the privilege of working on some of them, and I felt good about it.

The second Clinton presidency began in 1995 after the Democrats lost Congress. The Clinton who emerged from the ashes of that disaster was different. He had already acquired a reputation for timidity and wobbling, especially in abandoning proposed appointees who ran into rough seas. He had already disappointed many by failing to persevere in some of his own positive efforts, as in the case of the health care fiasco. But the second Clinton acquired a deserved reputation for governing by polls, press releases, and Rose Garden events. The second Clinton told donors he thought he had raised their taxes too much. The second Clinton proved that his own political survival was more important to him than any substantive issue.

Clinton had a chance to make things better. He was a brilliant man in some ways. He was a gifted and inspiring speaker. Yet he never made full use of his many talents in a consistently positive direction, and brought obloquy on the presidency by his personal behavior.

I resigned from the administration to protest the new welfare law. I was shocked when Clinton decided to sign it. He had previously signaled a willingness to sign a bill freeing the states from any obligation to help anyone and imposing an arbitrary time limit on receiving welfare besides, but the version before him was even broader — especially in its failure to protect children, its harsh effects on legal immigrants, and its deep cuts in the food stamp program. I had thought he would seize on those features as the basis for a veto.

My decision to resign was easy in one way and difficult in others. My visceral reaction to this fundamental break with the long-standing commitment of the Democratic Party to protect poor children was the simple part. I didn't need a long analysis to figure out how I felt. But I had great respect for Secretary Shalala and my other colleagues at HHS who were not going to resign (although two others — Mary Jo Bane and Wendell Primus — did resign). And there is not much of a tradition in America of resigning in protest.

Wanting to make our point but not jeopardize Clinton's re-election, Mary Jo and I (Wendell had left a couple of weeks earlier) sought no publicity. I was astonished at the attention we received. Our action resonated with many people around the country, which made it seem all the more worthwhile.

I was out of the country when Clinton signed the bill, so I did not hear him quote Kennedy. I heard about it later from Rory Kennedy, Robert and Ethel Kennedy's last child, who was born after his death in 1968. She wrote me in outrage about Clinton's twisting of her father's meaning, which, she said, had the effect of "bastardizing, in my opinion, his name and legacy."

The irony is, Bill Clinton could have learned something real from Robert Kennedy. Robert Kennedy was the first "new" Democrat, the first to espouse values of grassroots empowerment and express doubts about big bureaucratic approaches, the first to call for partnerships between the private and public sectors and insist that what we now call civic renewal is essential, the first to put particular emphasis on personal responsibility. But Robert Kennedy differed from those who now call themselves "new" Democrats, because he also insisted on national policy, national leadership, and national funding to help empower people at the bottom and address other pressing issues. His work and his views were prescient. It is still not too late to learn from them.

Robert Kennedy was uncomfortable when anyone called him a liberal — in fact, when anyone tried to put any label on him. Yet his politics did not resemble the abdication of responsibility and commitment that characterizes too many of today's "new" Democrats. There could be no doubt of his passion for justice. This, combined with a commitment to results and a highly original mind, produced a view of government and of remedies for powerless people different from that of Bill Clinton.

RFK also rejected the liberal label because he saw what traditional liberalism had brought us: a domino-theory logic that, in the Vietnam War, killed tens of thousands of Americans and more than a million Asians for reasons that became harder to discern with each passing month; a paternalism toward the poor at home and poorer nations abroad that promoted neither individual strength nor national competence; and a rigidity in large institutions that closed ears and minds to fresh ideas and challenges.

What I would call Robert Kennedy's new progressivism is largely absent from our politics now. Even during a long period of aggregate prosperity (for which President Clinton deserves some credit), Americans have been deeply cynical. Our attitudes toward the most powerless reflect this. Richer than any nation in history, we think of the poor as culturally deficient and rush to blame them for the circumstances in which they find themselves. We jump to the conclusion that they could earn a reasonable share of the national pie if they would only try. We fail to challenge the amazing proposition, put forward by radicals of the Right, that if we would only stop helping the poor they would be better off.

America's poor are like the homeless man we pass sitting against a building. We give him our loose change but he is still there, every day. He looks no better off despite our largesse. Exasperated, we stop seeing him and step past as though he were not there, and we never ask why he was homeless in the first place. And, concentrating our enmity on those we classify as poor, we obscure the problems of millions of others who, working as hard as they can, continually fall short of making even a minimally adequate income.

The backdrop of the last thirty years features a vicious circle of injurious economic change, national tragedy, and negative politics. People were disillusioned by the additive effects of the assassinations of revered leaders, the Vietnam War, the Watergate scandal, and the changes in the economy. Many blamed government for not stemming the disappearance of good jobs and the damaging combination of inflation and high unemployment in the late seventies. Millions lost economic ground. People either stopped voting or voted for the candidate who said the best government was the one that was closest to no government, except for the military. With voters opting out in droves, special interests had even more power to use their money to get what they wanted. Gaps in wealth, income, and power widened. Spurts of positive policy, especially in the early seventies, brought strengthened protections without which those at the lower end would be in even deeper trouble today, but the declines in real wages and the failure of public policies to compensate nonetheless left the bottom worse off.

The public view of the poor turned nasty. People working two or three jobs to survive were told that their problems were caused by those below them on the economic ladder. Clinton could sign a bill endangering millions of children and still get re-elected handily, by a combination of people who agreed with him and people who didn't but thought the prospect of Bob Dole, Newt

Gingrich, and Trent Lott running the country was even worse. (I was a member of the latter group. Disappointed as I am in Clinton, I have never believed that worse is better. Clinton was always fortunate in the quality of the enemies he attracted.)

The welfare system we had in place until 1996 badly needed reform, just as Robert Kennedy had said thirty years earlier. It left too many on the welfare rolls for too long, and did not help people find jobs and escape poverty. It was never an antipoverty program, although it did assure some cash income for families with children. But the new law was not real reform. It did not remove the barriers to self-sufficiency and it did not protect children. It freed the states to push people off the welfare rolls regardless of the consequences. What President Clinton signed was not a responsible policy but an abdication of responsibility.

We have been told repeatedly, by the White House and others, that the new law is a smashing success. In fact, while a few states have used it positively and more people are working, many formerly on welfare are worse off, even during unprecedented prosperity. The welfare rolls have been cut in half, but that is less than half the story.

A few numbers reveal what the public relations juggernaut obscures. Of the 7-million-plus people who have left welfare, 2.5 million are adults, mostly women. Nationally, about 60 percent of those have jobs at any given time. This means that about 1.5 million have jobs and about 1 million don't. Those million people and their children add up to 3 million people. That is a big number.

Where are they? We don't know precisely. They are truly America's "disappeared." Why did they leave welfare without a job? Mostly because they were kicked off, and in some places because they hit time limits. Many left for a job, lost it, couldn't find another, reapplied for welfare, and were turned away because of Catch-22 policies that tell people to look for work that they were already unable to find. Large numbers have lost food stamps and health coverage erroneously, compounding the problem. Welfare-to-work programs, often contracted out to profit-making companies like Lockheed Martin, add little concrete help.

We can see all of this in the statistics. The poorest 10 percent of single mothers lost 14 percent of their income from 1996 through 1998. In simple English, they lost more in welfare and food stamps than they gained in earnings. This loss, with all the increased homelessness, hunger, and other misery that goes with it, is the story people are not hearing. Moreover, often people who get jobs do not escape poverty. In 1998 the number of family heads with full-time jobs who could not get their families out of poverty was the highest it had been in the twenty-four years that this statistic has been recorded. And this says nothing of the millions who are not "officially" poor but do not earn even a barely adequate income.

"Welfare" is the wrong issue anyway. Reducing the number of people on welfare is laudable only if it results in making people better off. Ending poverty and achieving a better shake for all of those in difficulty even amid record prosperity are the right goals. Welfare — cash assistance for people at the bottom — is only a small part of a strategy to pursue those goals. But it should not be a dirty word. We need it to help when the economy goes sour either nationally or locally, and for people who are not in a position to work outside the home. It should be a safety net.

The irony may be that we hit bottom with the welfare policy put into place on that August day in 1996. The coincidentally ensuing prosperity, the lancing of the boil of our anger, and the highlighted visibility of the continuing misery of some are ingredients for positive action. But major changes in policy have yet to occur. The cold fact is that nearly one child in five is still poor, and the percentage of children in poverty remains higher than it was for all of the seventies. But with a new president and a new

Congress and, more important, an increased commitment of people around the country, we may be able to turn the corner.

This book is about economic justice and what that means for our country. It is not just about welfare and it is not just a story about Bill Clinton. The America that permitted him to sign a law shredding the sixty-year-old safety net for children is different in many ways from the America of Robert Kennedy's time. We are far richer materially, but too much of the increased wealth has gone to those at the top. Our politics has been corrupted by money and suffused with meanness. Trust in government and public institutions has eroded. Voter participation in elections has gone from bad to worse than worse.

I offer here a look at our journey from idealism to cynicism through the experience of one who was there when we said we were fighting a war against poverty, and was there when times changed. I explore the antipoverty legacy of Robert Kennedy, what happened to that legacy, and what that legacy means today. I suggest a strategy for greater economic and social justice that is neither "neo," kneejerk, nor naive, but features a full measure of national policy while being rooted in a renewal of civic engagement by all of us.

Poverty Today:
What's Wrong with This Picture?

WHY DO SOME people have so little though we are vastly wealthier as a nation than even a generation ago?

Two stories vie for acceptance.

One — the truth — says that the labor market has been in trouble since about 1973 because of deindustrialization, globalization, and technological change. Even in our current prosperity there are large numbers of lousy jobs. These big changes have made it ever harder to earn a living wage, especially for African

Americans, Latinos, female single parents, and high school graduates. It is worse yet for high school dropouts, and worst of all for
those who combine these characteristics.

The other explanation is much simpler. It says the problem is
government programs, and especially "welfare." It says welfare
has produced dependency, unwillingness to work, increased nonmarital births, drug abuse, and crime. It especially emphasizes "illegitimacy," and says poverty is not an issue of money at all but
one of "culture," which has to be changed by sanctions to change
behavior. Since the 1994 Congressional elections, the second
story has held sway.

Nearly all the neglected and exploited groups that achieved
visibility in the sixties and earlier have been pushed back to the
margins. Michael Harrington wrote in 1962 that "poverty is often
off the beaten track." It still is, although so often it is right in
front of us. Seasonal farmworkers are still exploited, and people,
mainly recent immigrants, still work in sweatshop conditions
that should have ended after the infamous Triangle Shirtwaist
factory fire in 1911. A quarter of the poor are still in rural areas far
from jobs — former coal miners mired in the hollows of Appalachia, poor farmers and sharecroppers across the black belt in
the South, day laborers in the *colonias* of south Texas, and those
Native Americans not among the few enriched by casinos. A
third of the poor are scattered in suburbs, often employed but
still poor, and quite invisible.

The face of poverty has changed in important ways, some
positive and some negative. Most of the poor are still white,
but with recent immigration, more are Latino and Asian. The
increase in single-parent families means more of the poor are
women and children. Thanks to the cost-of-living indexing of
Social Security and other policy changes, far fewer of the poor are
elderly. Changes in residential patterns have produced more entrenched areas of poverty in inner cities and, less noticed, new
clusters of poverty in inner-ring suburbs. The huge migration of

people from rural areas has cut the rural portion of the poor in half, although changes in the agricultural economy and in farm policy have created a new cadre of poor farmers, especially in the Midwest. Regional differences have eased, with the South now having only slightly higher poverty than the rest of the country. Changes in housing and mental health policy have produced new cadres of urban homeless people. Changes in opportunity have produced a much larger African American middle class, even though the percent of African Americans who are poor remains high. Changes in policy and attitudes have brought more disabled people into the mainstream economy, even though their overall unemployment statistics have not changed much. Changes in the economy have enlarged the numbers of those who work as hard as they can but are still poor or close to it.

The poverty of the sixties was disproportionately rooted in the rural economy and in the continuing pervasive discrimination against blacks. Fewer jobs required a high school education. There were fewer single-parent families, and poverty among two-parent families was more prevalent. Now, with a more educated population and more jobs requiring education, those without a high school diploma are more likely to be poor. Minorities now are frozen out less by overt discrimination and more by a mixture of weak schooling, residual prejudice, and competition from immigrants. In an economy in which having two wage-earners in a household is often essential to make ends meet, the worst off are female-headed families of color with limited education.

The number of poor people concentrated in inner-city neighborhoods doubled between 1970 and 1990. Most of the middle class moved away from these places when they could. Their departure destroyed community cohesion and left those remaining even more isolated from the regional economy. Things fell apart. Welfare became a staple for too many of the women and prison the address for too many of the men. Too many unmarried young women had children. The children went to schools that did not teach, and later on ran the gauntlet of adolescence torn between the values their mothers tried to instill and those offered by the young men on the street. The high-rise public housing projects in large cities presented the most dramatic instances of the destruction of community. The most persistent poverty is among disorganized families in disorganized neighborhoods. Still, we might be surprised to discover that this sort of poverty that so drives our prejudices and our politics describes only 12 percent of the poverty in the nation.

What happened in inner-city neighborhoods is a story of economics as well as race. The past three decades have not been kind to the American central city and its poorest inhabitants. Especially the older cities of the Northeast and Midwest have seen a massive exodus of people and jobs, leaving behind those least able to get out, along with disastrously diminished tax bases. The conditions that produced five consecutive summers of urban unrest and conflagration more than thirty years ago have actually worsened in the ensuing years. The manufacturing jobs that had previously disappeared to the suburbs, to nonunion sites in the South, and to other rural areas have now moved offshore as well or have been replaced by technology. Millions of white central-city residents have moved to the suburbs and exurbs. African Americans, helped by new antidiscrimination laws, have moved out in considerable numbers, too. Even to discuss the idea that the ensuing pneumonia of the inner city (as in "when the economy catches cold, the poor get pneumonia") was caused by welfare would be ludicrous if it were not so ardently purveyed by the adherents of the "cultural" view.

The federal definition of poverty is grossly inadequate today, and it was none too generous to begin with. Since the official poverty line was established, in the sixties, the cost of living for the poor has risen much faster than the rate of inflation, especially for housing. The poverty line now exceeds thirteen thousand dollars a year for a family of three. But by the time one adds up the real cost of rent, food, clothing, transportation, and everything else, even a family earning half again as much would have a hard time making ends meet.

Nonetheless, the country is angry at the poor. Feeling insecure because of their own tough sledding, many voters bought the arguments of ideologues and demagogues and in recent years took a huge whack not only at welfare but at food stamps, disability, housing aid, state programs that help single adults, drug treatment, and assistance to legal immigrants.

The reductions in free legal services were especially crippling. Not only will we reduce benefits for the poor, the cutters said, we will constrain their capacity to challenge bureaucrats who push them around. You can still get a federally funded lawyer to challenge your eviction, they said, provided you can find one after we cut the already paltry budget by a third, but we will allow no class actions and no challenges to any welfare program. So in addition to declaring war on the poor Congress declared war on lawyering for the poor — to make sure no one would talk back in court.

Worst of all, children long ago became the poorest age group. The elderly are better off, and that is wonderful. But children are much poorer, because so many of their families have steadily lost economic ground. With more children in poverty, breaking the cycle becomes harder. And the policies encouraged by the new welfare law pose the question whether we really believe that raising children constitutes a contribution to society.

Facing the Tough Facts

WE HAVE TO face up to some unpleasant trends that make solutions much harder to come by.

There has, for example, been a major increase in the number of single-parent families, mainly headed by women. This trend runs across income lines, but it is more pronounced among the poor, especially the African American poor, with more than half of poor children living in families headed by a single parent. Women's average earnings are still only about three-quarters of men's. So the income of a typical one-parent family is less than half that of a two-parent family where both parents work. The children of these families lack not only a father (not that just any father is better than no father) but the money that father would earn.

Even more disturbing is the increased percentage of births to mothers who are not married, especially to unmarried teens. This, too, is a trend that cuts across class and race, but it is greater in low-income groups and most serious among poor African American teens, albeit with a slight but steady reversal over most of the last decade. (I am talking about trends in percentage rates, not absolute numbers. The total number of teen births has been decreasing for a long time.)

No one can deny the seriousness of these problems. But the answer is not punitive welfare policy and stern lectures. Nor will provision of contraceptives do the job by itself. My wife, who is wise about many things, once said that "hope is the best contraceptive." Her insight is where I would start.

A second disturbing set of facts is the huge increase in illegal drug use over the last thirty years. Robert Kennedy, introducing legislation on drug addiction (then mainly heroin), talked about fifty thousand to one hundred thousand addicts in the U.S. Now there are close to two million regular cocaine or heroin users, with cocaine far more prevalent and methamphetamine use on the rise. These numbers affect not only the inner city but also the suburbs and, increasingly, smaller cities and rural areas. And there is actually more drug and alcohol abuse on the job than on the street corner.

The crack-cocaine epidemic of the eighties has abated somewhat, but illegal drugs and alcohol are still pandemic in the inner city. They are destroying lives wholesale. The consequences are all over the place: crack babies, children with the even worse fetal-alcohol syndrome, learning-disabled children, unmanageable foster care caseloads, grandparents raising their grandchildren, and prisons chock full and overflowing.

Serious as this is, it does not describe everyone. Even in the poorest neighborhoods most adults have jobs. There are hard-working, decent people in every neighborhood. In every public housing project, too. There are young people who make it despite everything.

A third set of terrible facts involves guns and lethal violence, although the recent drop in homicides is a hopeful development. The drug boom may not have caused the guns to proliferate, but they coincided. In the mid-eighties there was a flood of cheap handguns and the new, high-tech guns that shoot lots of bullets very quickly — bigger, meaner bullets that don't make a clean wound but instead fragment on impact and tear jagged holes in people's bodies. The guns were used by drug dealers (and gangs, often the same thing) to stake out and protect turf. The drug dealers became role models, and the guns important symbols of status. Gangs not in the drug business still guarded turf, with sometimes lethal consequences. Fights that used to end in black eyes or sometimes a knife cut now ended in death.

America rightly grieves when white boys in rural areas and the suburbs amass arsenals and take twisted minds to school to mas-sacre their classmates. Yet Littleton and Paducah and Jonesboro happen on the streets of our cities every day, both literally with firearms and more slowly in other ways.

Finally, there is the massive increase in our prison population, disproportionately African American and Latino young men. This trend became more pronounced with the fading of military service as a means of transformation for young men of color.

We are so simplistic and negative in our responses. Too many women on welfare, especially women of color? Cut them off. Too many young men of color hanging out in the street, underskilled and pushed out of lousy schools, doing drugs, with bad attitudes, and not needed in the labor market? Put them in prison.

For African Americans and many Latinos, the problem of poverty is also one of pervasive, plain old garden-variety discrimination that confronts so many seeking jobs in the legal economy. For those getting out of jail it is even worse. The reality for too many young black men is not three strikes and you're out but one jail term and you're finished.

This is not a simple issue. Some young minority applicants are not prize-winning workers. They too often have bad attitudes and are otherwise poorly prepared for the labor market. But that does not mean they don't face racism when looking for work. Recently, as employers have had to reach further to get workers, it has been heartening to see the picture improve somewhat for young black men as well as for former welfare recipients, but we have a long way to go.

The job issue is complicated by the far-reaching changes in technology. This goes much beyond hooking every school to the Internet. With proper investment in the children as well as in the hardware and software, we could create a great democratizing force. While in theory employment in cyberspace is race blind, there are a lot of big ifs. As things stand, technology threatens to be yet another wedge dividing our society.

Conservatives have had more political success than they should have in painting liberals as indifferent to questions of personal responsibility. This has never been a fair charge, any more than there was merit to conservatives' claims to own the flag, opposition to crime, or true religion. Liberals need to make clearer their commitment to personal responsibility, although one might hope that conservatives would in return drop some of their preconceptions against the need for societal and governmental responsibility.

Values issues in the larger society add fuel to the fire. Nonmarital teen births among young African American women, for example, are just one face on an increase in the rate of nonmarital births generally. Violence is exacerbated by the violence in the media. More and more studies in recent years have found the connection. What moves so many children these days to pick up guns and kill their schoolmates and teachers? The most likely catalyst is the flood of violence in the media. Guns have always been accessible, although they are far more available and lethal now. And there have always been emotionally disturbed young people. So what plants the idea, what sets off the spark? Killer video games, killer rap lyrics, killer films in theaters, killer programs and films on television, especially cable (which is far worse than the traditional networks). Illegal drug use and underage alcohol use are also treated all too favorably in the media, especially in music, film, and (for beer) commercials. If the society sends a permissive or even an encouraging message about all this to young people, it has an unfortunate effect in both wealthy and low-income neighborhoods. No one should be afraid to say so.

A Vision for the New Century

THE NEW PROGRESSIVISM that I derive from Robert Kennedy emphasizes a fair measure of government responsibility in a world where too many see little or no role for public policy. It means a mixed economy based in the market but holding corporate predators to account. And it also means a robust role for the civic sector in solving our pressing problems, not instead of government but along with government. It is both/and, not either/or.

The strategies I advocate combine the here and now and the future: in the here and now, work equally offered that results in a decent income, and a humane safety net for those not in a position to work; for the future, schooling and child- and youth-development activities that produce adults who are good parents, good workers, and good citizens.

The strategy involves national solutions where appropriate, like managing the economy toward full employment, establishing national health insurance, and investing more federal money in workers' incomes and in human needs. We are, however temporarily, in an era of surplus. For a long time we heard the refrain that we could not afford whatever was being proposed. It was said that we might have the will but we did not have the wallet. That excuse is no longer available.

We also need a new (or, remembering RFK, a renewed) partnership of bottom and top, combining federal resources with grassroots design of both the vision and the details. Communities of all kinds — geographic (from the neighborhood out to the metropolitan region), business, religious, philanthropic, educational, and others — must take on greater responsibility. Personal responsibility is critical, too.

Civic and political energy have to focus on issues that transcend money: changing structures of all kinds, especially schools, that fail to serve low-income people well regardless of how much money pours through them. Places — both urban and rural — where too many people are poor need a special focus. What emanates from Washington often means little without local people committed to making it work. Much of what we need to do, in fact, has nothing at all to do with Washington, or with government at all. Private action is as much a part of the answer as public policy. For a portion of the challenge it does not matter who is president, or which party controls Congress.

Even as we remember that most of the poor are white, our engagement must include a determination to achieve racial, ethnic, and gender justice. African Americans and Latinos suffer poverty at nearly three times the rate of whites, and are disproportionately penned in high-poverty inner-city areas. Native Americans and certain groups of Asian Americans are disproportionately poor, too. Any African American of any economic stratum has

stories of overt disrespectful treatment, often including incidents fresh in memory. But much of America continues its self-
delusion that racism is a thing of the past. Continuing gender
discrimination makes things worse, too, since some poverty
stems from the way we treat women and what happens to them
when they enter the workplace.

Two broad groups need attention: the millions of working
people, extending well beyond those officially classified as poor,
who are on the short end of the widened economic gap of the
past three decades; and the much smaller group at the bottom,
not even all of the poor, who have attracted the virulent attacks
of those who speak of a culture of poverty. No strategy that anyone can imagine will enable all parents to succeed in supporting
their children through work, even at the top of the business cycle.
Some have good excuses, like living in rural areas far from jobs or
taking care of disabled children or relatives, and some frankly
don't. The ultimate measure of our decency is whether we provide cash help for those families whose children are at risk even
though they are neither abused nor neglected in a legal sense. We
have to have a safety net even when the economy is performing at
top speed.

The debate must address fathers and fatherhood, and families. The poverty of so many children is heavily connected to the
absence of a father. There is of course a double edge to this asser-
tion. No one should have to put up with fathers who hurt mothers or children. And there are large numbers of courageous single
mothers who send their children into the world as productive
and successful adults. But children tend to do better with two
parents. More parents would marry in the first place if there
were a context of serious economic opportunity, and more absent fathers could be reached, too. We need jobs programs for
men as well as women, and particularly for young men. Child-
support collection policies would be much more successful if

fewer fathers were broke, and if child support, once collected, were passed along to the children for whom it is intended. Without diminishing our recognition that families today come in many forms, we can develop economic incentives and supports that encourage marriage and make it more likely that both fathers and mothers take a full measure of responsibility for the nurturing of their children.

The widening income gap is permanently altering American society. Twenty years ago the late Brookings economist Arthur Okun was shocked to realize that the income of the top 1 percent of earners in the United States equaled the total income of the bottom 20 percent. The top 1 percent now have income equal to that of the 38 percent at the bottom. This means that the top 2.7 million people have a total income equal to that of the bottom 100 million. The disparities in wealth are even greater. Three American men now have combined wealth that exceeds the total gross national product of forty-three countries.

We have to create a framework of public opinion that is conducive to action. The stakes are enormous. The issue is no less than what kind of a country we are and want to be. More than 30 million Americans — more than the entire population of California — are counted as poor, and tens of millions more earn far less than a fair share in our country's prosperity. Thirteen million children are poor, which means close to a million reach adulthood each year with a stunted chance of success.

Why we tolerate such massive economic gaps amid such phenomenal prosperity is a great moral and political issue. It raises the deepest questions of how we treat our neighbors, of whom we consider a neighbor and who really is an American. Almost everyone would say they want the same opportunity for all children that their own children have, but what that means in practice is something else. What is the meaning of our democracy when millions find that citizenship is worth so little? What is wrong with our politics when we seem perfectly content to have a gravy train that does not stop at every station?

Nonetheless, even as the idealism of the sixties is gone, things are happening that are not on center stage. Out of the spotlight, people are building housing, organizing communities and workers, starting businesses, improving schools, working with young people, and making a difference. In some places, whole blocks, and in a few places, whole neighborhoods, school systems, cities, and states are changing how they do things. Most of this is small scale. Yet it contains the vision of what our country could stand for, as well as how to make it happen.

As America lost heart over the past third of a century, there have been people who kept at it — here, there, everywhere across the country. Some are veterans of the civil rights movement and the War on Poverty. More joined later, inspired by a mentor, by things they read, by religious teaching, or by an intuitive sense that something was wrong. They have been lonely at times, and victories sometimes have seemed few and far between. But they have persevered.

I believe we are in a better place now, with a renewed opportunity to move ahead, and a new possibility of attracting more people to the effort. The recent health of the economy is one reason, as is the irony that the new welfare law has made some of the problems more visible and energized many people to work on softening its impact. The details of what must be done are not precisely what they were in 1968, because we have learned a lot since then and some of the facts are different. But Robert Kennedy's vision is as true now as it was then. We can learn from it.

1

ROBERT KENNEDY

The Man Who Loved Children

T HE YEARS from the end of World War II to the middle of Lyndon Johnson's presidency were one of the most positive periods in American history. We were justly proud of having played a decisive role in defeating Hitler and his Axis. Returning GIs went to school and to work and added infectious energy to the hum of a confident nation. With the pain of the Great Depression still burning in the national consciousness, pent-up demand from years of war rationing exploded and our standard of living skyrocketed. The isolationism of the thirties was replaced by a commitment to help rebuild war-torn nations.

People trusted government. Even with the stalemate of the Korean War and the overreaching of Senator Joseph McCarthy, they were not cynical. The New Deal was remembered fondly for its contribution to putting millions of people back on their feet and establishing security against old age, fraudulent stock manipulators, rampant floods, and other ravages of life. We were on top of the world. "Onward and upward" were watchwords of the day.

Into this fifties world of burgeoning suburbs and gray flannel suits, of *Father Knows Best* and Beaver Cleaver, the American "other" — the people kept out and left out — began making an appearance. The New Deal had mainly helped white people.

Now, an emerging civil rights movement was teaching the country that American apartheid was still in place. The "discovery" that millions of white Americans were also excluded from the new prosperity was not far behind.

Who can say what was inevitable, what was accidental, and what was the result of strategic planning, but black America began to speak up. Men who had fought for their country found it unacceptable to come home to Jim Crow. The Supreme Court, responding to Thurgood Marshall and the NAACP, decided unanimously that legally mandated segregation was no longer permissible. And Rosa Parks created the opportunity the Montgomery NAACP had been seeking when she refused to yield her bus seat to a white man.

A next generation of black young people, seeing little change, began sitting in at lunch counters, riding interstate buses, and picketing segregated places, to a local response of murders, beatings, attack dogs, fire hoses, and arrests, and a national response of outrage. A cautious President John F. Kennedy found the political space to respond, and then, after he was assassinated, a deeply committed President Johnson won passage of historic legislation. Most Americans added progress on civil rights to their list of how well things were going.

If Bull Connor's dogs and fire hoses, shown nationally on the nightly news of our newly ubiquitous television sets, scandalized Americans by the millions in a way that print never could, Michael Harrington's book *The Other America,* telling of another "other," the American poor, reached a far smaller, but nonetheless influential, audience. Throughout John Kennedy's presidency a small group within the government was meeting, championed by Robert Kennedy, to think through what could be done to reduce the poverty that those who bothered to look could see was still palpably present. President Kennedy was doodling "poverty" on a yellow legal pad at the last cabinet meeting before he died.

Poverty in America is deeply intertwined with being a member of a racial minority or of any disadvantaged minority group. The new interest in poverty came partly from the civil rights movement, because assuring the right to eat at any lunch counter wouldn't do much good if a person didn't have the money to pay for a meal. But emphasizing poverty seemed like good politics, too. Census facts showed that poverty had a white face as well as a face of color, and the discovery of Appalachian poverty in particular opened the way to an effort encompassing all races.

So President Lyndon Johnson proposed a War on Poverty, with the hyperbole that was intrinsic to his Texas style. We now know that even an all-out attack would not have wiped out poverty completely, and what he proposed was far from that (although most parts of the War on Poverty are still operating along with other elements of Johnson's Great Society, and have had a positive effect). But talking of a War on Poverty created an opening for Ronald Reagan to suggest, with mirror-image hyperbole, that we had fought a War on Poverty and poverty had won. Some of today's cynicism about public policy to help the poor stems from the idea, so suggestive and seductive and so appealing and American, that we could declare war on poverty and win. We had beaten Hitler — why couldn't we beat poverty?

Lyndon Johnson's commitment was in fact much more far-reaching than the grab-bag of worthwhile but underfunded items called the War on Poverty. It was reflected in his much larger idea of a Great Society, extending to laws assuring equal opportunity, to health care for the elderly and the poor, to improving the education of poor children, and to supporting inner-city revitalization and low-income housing. But however deep his commitment, however vast his ambition, it lost momentum as he escalated the war in Vietnam and as the civil rights movement, so successful in dismantling legal apartheid, gave way to explosions of anger from those who saw no consequent changes in their own lives.

In truth, the idealism of the early sixties was in deep disarray even before Vietnam took its full toll. Barely two weeks after Johnson signed the Voting Rights Act in 1965, the Watts area of Los Angeles went up in flames. By then there had already been dozens of smaller incidents indicating that demands for change were outrunning accomplishments by an enormous margin. Calls for integration were shouted down with demands for Black Power. Outstretched hands were replaced by clenched fists. Gandhian nonviolence was eclipsed by violence, reinforced by new apostles intoning that violence is as American as cherry pie. City after city burned. Medgar Evers was murdered. Malcolm X was murdered. Martin Luther King, Jr. was murdered. Robert Kennedy was murdered.

The loss of Robert Kennedy hurt America in many ways, none more consequential than its effect on our precarious national effort to reduce poverty. No high public official was more at the forefront of thinking and action about poverty than Robert Kennedy. Lyndon Johnson declared war on poverty, but Robert Kennedy was a key force in laying the groundwork. Dozens and hundreds of people in poor communities, foundations, universities, and public agencies did the thinking and experimenting that came together in Washington in the early days of the New Frontier, but Robert Kennedy — busy as he was as the alter ego of his brother, the President — was a constant stimulus to the conversion of ideas into policy proposals. Thousands participated in running Head Start and community health centers and other programs created with the new federal funds, but Robert Kennedy was a visionary critic who continually proposed next steps and new approaches. Millions benefited from the initiatives of the time, but Robert Kennedy always expressed a passionate insistence that we could do better.

Why did this son of wealth care so much — much more than his brother the President? His own childhood had given him a special appreciation of what it was like to be an outsider. His father, serving as ambassador to Great Britain, took much more interest in RFK's two older brothers. RFK was sent to American boarding schools, where he had few friends and was seen by others as awkward and moralistic. The product was a young man with decidedly rough edges, but always interested in the excluded and the disempowered. Many people report a softer, more empathetic Robert Kennedy in the wake of his brother's death, but those who knew him before say the streak of caring was always there.

The sixties represent the zenith of American interest in reducing poverty, and Robert Kennedy was a major actor on the subject during that decade. That peak period did not come from thin air, of course. The New Deal had established a federal role in responding to the dispossessed, uneven and designedly temporary as much of it was. The civil rights activism of the late fifties helped set the stage for the realization that people other than those of color had been left behind. When Lyndon Johnson succeeded the slain John F. Kennedy, a political moment of special responsiveness about race, and to a lesser extent poverty, occurred, and was then enhanced by the large majorities accorded the Democrats in Congress in the 1964 elections. And Lyndon Johnson's commitment to reducing poverty was clearly genuine.

Between World War II and the sixties there had been very little that might be recognized as antipoverty policy. Slum clearance, urban renewal, public housing, and the depressed-areas legislation of the fifties made up a short list. Cash assistance to families with children and the elderly poor had been available since the New Deal. The sixties, with Michael Harrington's writing at the tip of the iceberg, brought a wider recognition that World War II and postwar prosperity had not wiped away all vestiges of the Depression. Robert Kennedy, ahead of most, understood this.

Where I Came In

I ARRIVED IN midstream. My personal discovery of poverty, and even of the larger spirit of the sixties, occurred because of Robert Kennedy, and only really began in the fall of 1964 when he ran for the Senate and I got involved in his campaign. He had been at it for the nearly four years he was attorney general, plus the lifelong instinctive identification with the underdog that he had brought to that job. I didn't know much, and I learned on the job as one of his legislative assistants in the Senate. Kennedy always treated me as though I knew something, and after a while maybe he was right. I traveled with him to places the vast majority of Americans never see, and talked with people — hundreds, if not thousands — whom most Americans never have the chance to meet. By the time he died, only three and a half years later, I knew a lot.

I was at Harvard Law School when the decade began, headed to a career in private law practice like my father's. My only clear ambition was to practice on a stage larger than my home city of Minneapolis, although I had a vague idea of doing periodic stints of government service, as many distinguished Harvard alumni had done in the past. I realized years later that my father's deep commitment to community service had inspired me subliminally, but in 1961 I just wanted to get my career started. The lunch-counter sit-ins in the South were a universe away. The closest I came to the action was being a witness to heated debates at the *Law Review* about whether civil disobedience was justifiable.

Two busy years of clerking for judges didn't get me any closer, although Arthur Goldberg, for whom I clerked at the Supreme Court, taught me more about justice than anybody at the Harvard Law School ever did. Also, Justice Goldberg caused me to go to the Justice Department, and if I hadn't done that, none of the rest of what has happened to me over the past thirty-five years would have taken place. I was supposed to clerk for Justice Felix

Frankfurter, but he had a stroke in the spring of 1962 and retired three days before I was to start working for him. Justice Goldberg was kind enough to keep me on. While Justice Frankfurter always told his law clerks to go home to where they had grown up, Justice Goldberg told me there would be few administrations like that of President Kennedy in my lifetime and recommended government service. This seemed odd, since to me respected presidents like FDR and Truman were the norm. I took his advice, though, and went to work at the Department of Justice in the fall of 1963 for John Douglas, RFK's assistant attorney general for the Civil Division (and son of the distinguished Illinois senator Paul Douglas), who has been my friend ever since.

The Justice Department began to involve me in the issues of the day, although not enough to keep me from accepting a job with a Wall Street firm that was to start in November 1964. I had spent a year learning from John Douglas and others how to be a lawyer, and had participated in some important litigation. The bigger change came because I went to work for Robert Kennedy in his campaign for the Senate in September 1964.

Kennedy — committed to a career in public service, driven by ambition instilled by his father, and feeling a responsibility to carry on for his fallen brother — had emerged from a winter and spring of grief following the assassination with a decision to run for the Senate in New York. There was nothing to run for in Massachusetts, and he could claim a small tie to New York, having lived there for the first five years of his life. He had no experience as a candidate, and was still carrying psychological baggage from the tragedy of less than a year earlier. At the outset he was not very good at campaigning on his own behalf.

I doubt that RFK would have put my face together with my name if we had run into one another in the corridor. We had met twice, in groups. After his brother's murder he was often absent from the department, and no longer wandered around the halls to see what his lawyers were up to.

I had no campaign experience, other than running, mostly without success, for student office in high school and college. But John Douglas had poked around the campaign and, finding it to be severely understaffed, had persuaded the notoriously penurious Kennedy to hire me and my Justice Department colleague Adam Walinsky. Walinsky became assistant speechwriter (under Milt Gwirtzman, a close associate of Ted Kennedy), and I was assistant to the research director, Bill vanden Heuvel. (The two of them later wrote a good book about RFK's Senate years, called *On His Own.*) I was excited about the job, but had no intention of remaining after the election. I was due on Wall Street, and the campaign seemed a good way to get to know more people in New York.

In the campaign I became the expert on the voting record of the incumbent, Senator Kenneth Keating. A kind looking, somewhat older (sixty-four, to be exact) man with white hair, Keating had a moderate voting record as a senator, following a much more conservative record as an upstate congressman. I looked through the vote tabulations in *Congressional Quarterly* and found a number of instances where Keating's Senate votes had diverged from those of his more liberal Republican colleague from New York, Jacob Javits, and others where his recent liberal position diverged from his own earlier stance.

We produced two full-page newspaper ads, one titled "Keating vs. Keating," and the other called "the box score." The latter showed a dozen or so issues on which Javits had voted identically with then-Senator Hubert Humphrey and Keating had voted the same as Senator Barry Goldwater. From the time the box score ad appeared until the end of the campaign, I would be summoned to Kennedy's suite in the Carlyle Hotel whenever he needed to be briefed on Keating's record for a debate or some other appearance. I had pasted my entire knowledge of Keating onto the box score ad so that it would unfold as a sort of Rube Goldberg contraption that I could use as a prop. I had found my niche. I was a pioneer in opposition research.

When the campaign was over, Ed Guthman, Kennedy's press secretary in the Justice Department, told me to expect a call after everyone returned from vacation. The Senator-elect might be interested in offering me a job in the Senate. In my twenty-six-year-old wisdom (another word for which might be arrogance), I worried about whether I would have to report to someone other than Kennedy. I went to see John Douglas to ask whether I should accept even a properly crafted offer. He said yes, but that I should not stay for more than two years, because by then I would be out of law school five years and should get on with law practice.

The call came. Meet Kennedy and Guthman at the White House. Why the White House? It turned out Kennedy had twisted his knee playing — what else? — touch football, and wanted it looked at by Dr. Janet Travell, who had ministered to JFK's bad back and was now serving President Johnson. Dr. Travell tapped here and there and told Kennedy everything was okay. We went out to the driveway between the White House and the Old Executive Office Building, where Kennedy perched on the fender of a car. The interview was about to start. He would undoubtedly ask me for my strengths and weaknesses, for the last three books I had read, things like that. I was ready.

"Are you going to come to work for me?" he said. I was speechless. I thought fast and stammered, "How much will you pay me?"

"You can work that out with Ed" was the reply.

"I have this problem," I heard myself saying. "I've been out of law school three and a half years and I haven't practiced law."

"I had that problem, too," Kennedy said. "I worked it out."

I took the job.

RFK as Attorney General —
The War on Poverty

FOUR YEARS EARLIER President Kennedy had taken the audacious step of naming his brother, barely thirty-five years old when confirmed by the Senate, as attorney general of the United States. RFK started to work on the problems of the excluded right away. Even before his brother was inaugurated, he asked his prep school friend David Hackett to start thinking about what the Justice Department could do to reduce juvenile delinquency and youth crime, and gave him a small office that opened directly into the AG's personal office. Hackett was neither a lawyer nor an expert on disadvantaged youth, but he proved to be a positive model of the frequent Kennedy practice of appointing people to take on important assignments based on trust rather than expertise.

RFK always saw poverty through the lens of children and young people, and he always saw the connection of race to poverty. He always looked for opportunities to learn by seeing and hearing firsthand. His understanding and commitment were as much in his gut and heart as in his intellect. Because so much of what he did was based on instinct, his interactions with people he met ranged from immediate bonding to downright rudeness. Children and grassroots activists were at one end of the spectrum (where there was also room for Russian poets and Hollywood stars) and evasive bureaucrats and the pompous of all stripes at the other. He was quite different from his cool, cerebral brother, the President, in his mode of thought and action.

Six weeks into the job as attorney general, Robert Kennedy walked to Harlem after appearing in midtown Manhattan on a CBS television panel on communism. There he met with gang members (some black, some Italian — the meetings were separate) to hear what they thought. Two months later, even though the Bay of Pigs had occurred in the interim and Soviet Premier

Nikita Khrushchev had started to test the new young American president — RFK spoke to a conference on out-of-school youth and said that the problem was "employment and education opportunities" as well as "moral discipline and control," and that the needed response "requires a broad concentrated effort to narrow the gap . . . a large-scale prevention effort" that "exceeds the unaided capacities of individual families or even local communities." He continued, "The effects of widespread changes in the social and economic life have had a tremendous impact on the unskilled and poor youth in the slum areas of our large cities," adding, prophetically, "Where aspirations outstrip opportunities, law-abiding society becomes the victim." The civil rights issue was becoming visible, but what RFK was talking about was nowhere near the front burner. If "juvenile delinquency" was to be an important issue, it would only be because RFK made it so.

The first fruit of David Hackett's work was new juvenile delinquency prevention legislation, to be funded at $30 million annually. The sixteen communities favored with planning grants were told to develop comprehensive plans that would attack the causes of delinquency across the board. The grants were pitifully small, but the idea of multifaceted activity to get at the underlying causes of delinquency was new. The intention was to follow the planning with larger-scale funding to implement the plans.

RFK as attorney general was able to exert effective leadership with a modest investment of time. It was he who, a year or so into the process, observed that what he and Hackett had really been talking about all along was poverty, and that their proposed strategy should explicitly tackle poverty. He was particularly interested in a national service corps in which young people could serve in their own communities, and in assuring that the poor themselves participated in planning and running new initiatives.

Kennedy met regularly with the guerrillas, as they called themselves — Hackett, Dick Boone, Len Duhl, Jule Sugarman, and others — people with day jobs in other agencies who came together under his patronage to put together a plan. He would spend an hour here, an hour there; an evening meeting when everyone else had long since left the office; a breakfast meeting at his house, with him hugging his various children while the conversation went on; always pushing the group toward the goals he favored.

Once in 1963, RFK invited the entire cabinet, except for Secretary of State Dean Rusk, to his office at the Justice Department to meet with the guerrillas. Kennedy locked the door, keeping them there for four hours to discuss doing something about poverty. The discussion ranged from community building to youth service to American Indians to Appalachia. The only one who responded with enthusiasm to the overall idea of attacking poverty was Robert McNamara, the secretary of defense, who said this was the most important issue facing the country. Kennedy remained deeply involved in the issue until JFK was murdered. After that he took little interest in any policy discussion, and LBJ transferred control over the planning to the Bureau of the Budget.

RFK traveled to learn, too, with trips to Los Angeles to visit black and Mexican American neighborhoods, to Appalachia, and elsewhere, always meeting with people, especially young people, to whom others in government never talked or listened. He had an intuitive ability to get to the heart of an issue almost instantly. He could be absent from a discussion for a month or two, and then re-enter in midsentence, in effect. I saw this repeatedly when I worked for him in the Senate.

The guerrillas, the other government officials, and involved outsiders argued about what to emphasize. Some said opportunity was the top priority — that better education and training and strong antidiscrimination policy would give everyone a fairer chance to compete. Others said job creation was also essential to provide work for people who couldn't find jobs on their own. A third focus was income for people not in a position to work, and especially for their children, and for people working but not earning enough to get by. A fourth camp was especially interested in the places where people live, stressing investment in housing and community. Fifth were those who argued that political empowerment and organizing efforts would have a multiplier effect in making government and other institutions more responsive. Finally, there were those who said families needed help with an array of services, from legal to medical to child care and more, if they were to do better for themselves.

The Economic Opportunity Act, to use the statutory name for the War on Poverty, was finally enacted in 1964 and was a combination of the radical, the timid (or parsimonious, anyway), and some sound ideas like Head Start, Job Corps, and VISTA that would stand the test of time. The strategy emphasized organizing, opportunity, and services. Secretary of Labor Willard Wirtz had pushed for significant job creation, but that would have been expensive, and President Johnson turned him down, opting instead for community action, which had the virtue of being relatively inexpensive, and for a series of items to help children and young adults be better prepared for the job market. Even though the package invested much more in the opportunity and services items than in the organizing, it was the organizing part of it that drew the flak.

The thing that caused most of the political trouble was community action, the idea of a new system of services for the poor that would be controlled by the poor themselves. There is no question that RFK's constant pushing for involvement of the poor was a major reason why Hackett's guerrillas put it front and center. Its immediate champion was Dick Boone, a former Ford Foundation program officer with a deep commitment to grassroots organizing as a key to social change, who became the first director of community action in the Office of Economic Opportunity, which was set up to run the War on Poverty.

The main point of community action was totally sensible —
an inventive response to the existing agencies that were supposed
to help poor families but were unfriendly to the new (or previously invisible) inner-city communities of color. The federal
money would build new local agencies to deliver or buy needed
services. Community residents would be hired to help do the
work. Boone's dogged insistence led to the insertion in the draft
legislation of the soon-to-be-controversial requirement of "maximum feasible participation" of the poor, including control over
where the new money went and whom it helped. With the new
service agencies not controlled by local government, a few of
them actually confronted city hall, often to sensationalized press
coverage. Even mayors who were not targets of confrontations
joined in complaining, because new federal money was coming
to town and they didn't control it. By 1966, with the charge led
by Mayor Richard Daley of Chicago (the original Mayor Daley),
the mayors gained control over the community action agencies.

I experienced Mayor Daley's view of community action firsthand. In the spring of 1967, we were in Chicago for Senate oversight hearings on the poverty program. The hearings were in city
hall and RFK asked me to set up a meeting with Mayor Daley. I
went to the Mayor's office and asked for his secretary. After a couple of minutes the receptionist said, "The Mayor will see you
now." I tried to say I wasn't the one who wanted to see the
Mayor, but got a blank look. So I went in. The Mayor's office was
cavernous. There wasn't a piece of paper anywhere on his enormous desk. There were fifty chairs set up in five rows in front of
his desk. He said, "What brings you here?" I explained that we
were having hearings on the poverty program. He paused for a
few seconds and said, "Oh yeah, that's that community action
thing, isn't it. I never understood that. The people of Chicago
elected me to be their mayor, and if they don't like what I'm
doing they can throw me out of office."

The War on Poverty was much more than the community action program that caused all the controversy, but even when the other extremely important elements of President Johnson's Great Society — the civil rights laws, Medicare and Medicaid, federal aid to education, housing programs, and all the rest — are added in, the strategies of the time did not sufficiently address the issues of education, employment, and low wages that have to be dealt with in a three-dimensional attack on persistent poverty. After the initial urban unrest in the summer of 1964, which was on a far smaller scale than that in Watts a year later, Attorney General Kennedy sent President Johnson a memorandum entitled "Racial Violence in Urban Centers," calling for years of sustained efforts on jobs and housing opportunities. It presaged RFK's Senate years. His thinking had already moved past the limited scope of the War on Poverty.

The Junior Senator from New York

IN 1965, ROBERT KENNEDY joined an 89th Congress with Democratic majorities that today's Democrats can only dream about. High on his agenda was the work to reduce poverty and powerlessness. He was not the only person in Washington who wanted to make progress in reducing poverty, but he quickly claimed a leadership role on these and other matters. His position was only strengthened as he came to be the leader of those Democrats who found themselves increasingly confronting the sitting President.

His antipoverty endeavors ranged far and wide. An early special priority was to improve education for poor children, perhaps on the assumption that the opportunities to work would present themselves to those who were prepared. As time passed, he became increasingly aware that even when unemployment is low nationally, jobs are not necessarily available to people isolated by reason of race or geography or both. By the end of his life his major focus was on jobs and economic development: public funding and tax incentives to create economic activity and jobs in areas of concentrated poverty. He had come to see that education was not sufficient by itself.

He always looked for ways to strengthen the political power of people at the grassroots. This drew him to Cesar Chavez and to people in eastern Kentucky and rural Mississippi trying to make headway against entrenched courthouse crowds and power structures. He came to realize that people at the bottom were not always going to be able to work and that a safety net to end hunger and assist in survival was essential. At the same time he believed in strong but fair law enforcement to assure community safety and promote personal responsibility. And more and more he saw the complexity of it all — that all the pieces had to be pursued if progress was to be made.

Kennedy hit the ground running. One advantage he had was staffers and senators who wanted to be helpful — out of respect and mourning for his brother, out of ambition for the future, because of past working relationships, or based on genuine feeling for RFK himself. There were people in the executive branch who felt the same way, although their number diminished as the bad blood between RFK and LBJ worsened.

He had been in the Senate only a few days when he succeeded in amending the Appalachian regional development legislation to pave the way for including thirteen quite poor New York counties along the Pennsylvania border. His poverty-related activity went from prenatal care and Head Start to amending Social Security to make its financing more equitable and its coverage more complete. His geographic focus went from the inner city to the isolated, powerless rural poor, to farm workers in California and Texas, to Native Americans on Indian reservations and in cities all over the country, as well as to the poor in Latin America and

South Africa. His work spanned every subject that would make a difference, from jobs and education and welfare to labor organizing and fairness in the criminal justice system and getting food to hungry people.

My journey of discovery cut across almost all of it. The beginning of 1965 was an amazing and exciting time in America. Between my work at the Court, in the Justice Department, and the campaign, I was now much more attuned to what was happening around me. In that two-and-a-half-year period President Kennedy had been assassinated, the civil rights movement had shaken America's conscience, President Johnson had surprised people by pressing for historic civil rights and antipoverty legislation, and the war in Vietnam had begun to be more than a local conflict involving American military advisers.

I still had no inkling of the role Kennedy would play in the next stages of these great matters. The dramatic escalation of the war had not occurred, the next phase of civil rights activity was not clearly delineated, and to all appearances Robert Kennedy's personal timetable was firmly focused on 1972, when LBJ was expected to have completed his second term.

I was in over my head at the beginning. I had never had a job where it wasn't possible to return all the phone calls and get all of the mail answered. Paper started piling up on my desk in a crazy-quilt way — not even neat piles, just a big heap of stuff sticking out in all directions. Finding any one thing would have been very hard, but I didn't have time to try, so it didn't matter. One day Kennedy walked by my desk and said, very quietly, "Is your mind like that?" I have kept my piles very neat ever since. And I did learn to keep up with the pace.

To say that Kennedy was ubiquitous would be pallid. He was busy both inside and outside the Senate, in Washington, all over New York State, around the country, and around the world. His interests were presidential in scope, perhaps from ambition, but more certainly from habit and experience. He had no interest in downsizing his perspective because of what had happened in Dallas, and no reason to.

He was conscientious about his conventional Senate work, attending hearings, introducing bills and amendments, and voting — all subject, of course, to competition from the other activities he undertook as part of his outsized definition of the job. His day-to-day Senate work has received little attention from biographers, because he was doing so many other things, and has even been belittled by some, but I can attest that he was more than fully attentive to the job as it is defined in the civics textbooks. Some have suggested that he was bored with the Senate. That misses the point. He wasn't the least bit uninterested. He was just interested in so much else at the same time.

The intense pace of events contributed to the breadth of Kennedy's focus — made it unavoidable, really. It affected not just our work but, gradually, the attention of the country. Nineteen sixty-five is indicative. President Johnson dramatically escalated the Vietnam War in February after the Viet Cong had mounted a major assault on an American barracks at Pleiku, and invaded the Dominican Republic in late April to undo a coup against the military regime. The Selma civil rights march in April intensified the drive to enact the Voting Rights Act. And the Watts rebellion in South Central Los Angeles occurred in early August. Kennedy was deeply involved, both publicly and privately, in trying to influence the direction of foreign policy, and maintained an equal intensity on the intertwined questions of race, poverty, and racial reconciliation. Pleiku was a first intimation of the distraction that would overtake concern for racial and economic justice at home and begin the fraying of our public life that has been going on ever since.

Cesar Chavez

EARLY IN 1966 I learned what Kennedy meant when he repeatedly said one person can make a difference. Some time in February, I received a call from Jack Conway, the head of the Industrial Union Department of the AFL-CIO and a top lieutenant to Walter Reuther of the United Auto Workers. He said there was a new farmworkers organizing effort going on in California, led by a man named Cesar Chavez. There had never been a successful effort to organize farmworkers in the United States, and there hadn't even been a serious attempt for years. Their wages were horribly low, working conditions terrible, housing awful, and coverage by the laws protecting other workers nonexistent.

Senator Harrison (Pete) Williams of New Jersey (later convicted in the Abscam bribery scandal but in other matters a caring, decent man and an effective senator) was going to take his Migratory Labor Subcommittee, on which Kennedy sat, to California to bring attention to Chavez's efforts. Conway said he and Walter Reuther would appreciate it if Kennedy would attend. Kennedy was a magnet for television cameras, and could elevate national consciousness of issues just by being there. In my innocence I took this for granted, but there have been few United States senators (Joe McCarthy was another) who could get national attention the way RFK could.

I was somewhat aware of Chavez because my friend Andrew Kopkind had written a favorable piece about him in the *New Republic*. I walked into Kennedy's office and told him of the call, and mentioned my slight familiarity with Chavez. He said sure, he'd be glad to go. This was how Kennedy ran his office. When he was in, his door was always open. And he operated in shorthand. You made your point concisely and he answered, equally tersely. We didn't deal much in memos, except when we wanted to say something that was too complicated for a conversation.

Kennedy detested long-winded people, and he himself rarely went on at great length about anything in private conversation. He never told jokes, although he was very funny with one-liners, usually at his own expense. He had an amazing capacity to grasp complicated ideas quickly. The downside was that if you didn't make your best case in your first shot, or if for some reason he didn't get it right away, you seldom got a second shot. Sometimes when he did say yes quickly to something I suggested, I was tempted to say, Wait a minute, have you really thought about this? It didn't take me long to learn that was unnecessary.

In February 1966 RFK decided he had to speak out for a negotiated settlement to the Vietnam war. He was increasingly worried that Johnson intended to pursue the war to unconditional surrender. He called for admitting the National Liberation Front — the political arm of the Viet Cong — to "a share of power and responsibility" in governing the country, evoking a firestorm of attack that was orchestrated by President Johnson, although he was supported by the eminent columnist Walter Lippmann and the *New York Times* editorial page. The war was beginning to drain hope and political will from the country. The developing divisions over both Vietnam and racial issues would erode the Democratic majorities in Congress in the fall of 1966 far more than anyone anticipated just a few months earlier.

In early March, we went to California. On the plane as we reached cruising altitude out of Dulles, Kennedy suddenly turned to me and said, in a rough tone, "Now why the hell am I dragging my ass all the way out to California?" Probably stammering a little, I repeated my initial report to him of Reuther's request and my own modestly documented validation of the cause. He seemed to accept this — at least, he moved the conversation on to another subject. When we arrived at Visalia, California, in the San Joaquin Valley, the hearings were already under way. The main focus was the attempt of the United Farm Workers to organize some vineyards owned by the Schenley Corporation.

The UFW figured that Schenley, as a major national corporation, wouldn't want the embarrassment of resisting an organizing effort and would cave fairly easily, laying the groundwork for actions against other growers.

As we walked into the hearing room, in a high school auditorium, it was about a half hour before lunch. The witness was the county sheriff. He was explaining how he had ordered the arrest of the pickets, who had all been on the highway and not on private property, because he was concerned about their safety and he wanted to protect them. Kennedy sat down and listened. After a few minutes, it was his turn to question. He pressed the sheriff on the fact that deputies had taken pictures of the pickets and then ascertained that people were being arrested even though they had not violated the law. He asked, "How can you go arrest somebody if they haven't violated the law?"

"They're ready to violate the law," the sheriff answered.

Kennedy, it now being time for lunch, replied, "Can I suggest in the interim period of time . . . that the sheriff and the district attorney read the Constitution of the United States?" The auditorium, packed with farmworkers and their supporters, erupted in applause.

In the parking lot Kennedy met Chavez. It was a riveting scene. The two men immediately bonded. Chavez, himself a child of poor farmworkers, had a mystical quality. He was a very quiet man, short in stature, with a face that was as purely kind in its appearance as that of any human being I have ever seen. The two of them stood talking, eye to eye, in a low conversational tone that was barely audible even to the first ring of people around them. A crowd gathered, two deep, then four deep, and finally ten or fifteen people deep. It went on for maybe five minutes, maybe even ten. I don't know what they said to each other. I do know that when it was over they were friends for life. Kennedy never asked me again why he was going there.

I had arranged for us to have lunch with Wendy Goepel, a

young aide to Chavez, and some farmworkers. Andy Kopkind had written about her and I had recognized her when we walked into the hearings, because she was wearing a monogrammed blouse. (She was an Anglo from New Jersey whose brother later had a brief stint as an NFL quarterback.) We sat at a Formica table in a local motel cafe, and RFK ordered a club sandwich. (He always had a club sandwich for lunch or a late evening meal.) Wendy started the conversation by saying she was glad that Kennedy had come because his father owned Schenley. He said his father never owned Schenley. She said, Well then he owns Cutty Sark. RFK said that whatever his father had owned he didn't own it anymore. I thought, Am I in trouble! Then I noticed that she was so nervous she was dropping food off her fork into her lap, and Kennedy, sitting next to her, was picking the food up and putting it back on her plate.

The next day the hearings shifted to Delano, where the headquarters of the union were located. Wendy drove me to the airport in her battered car to pick up Kennedy, who had flown to Los Angeles to have dinner with the singer Andy Williams. At the airport I found the best car among those that had come to meet Kennedy, a clean looking, blue, fairly late model Plymouth or Chevrolet, and arranged for him to ride to the hearing in it. He got off the plane and I started steering him to that car, and he said, "Where's Wendy? I want to ride with her." He had a tremendous respect for people who "made a difference," as he always said. She was one of them.

From that day on, Kennedy was the farmworkers union's best friend in Washington, and I was the union's contact in Kennedy's office. Kennedy became active in trying to extend the minimum wage to farmworkers, which was accomplished on a limited basis later that year, and in trying to extend the National Labor Relations Act to protect the union organizing efforts of farmworkers, which has not been accomplished to this day.

Kennedy's immediate bonding with Cesar Chavez was typical of the intuitive, nonlinear, even existential way in which he operated. I saw no ulterior political motive in the instantaneous warmth of his response, although, since there were almost always unrevealed layers to his thinking, I am sure that a political thought or two crossed his mind. But his general way of operating was to ask the question of principle first and the question of politics second. The question of politics was, how do we do the politics to accomplish the maximum on the principle? That is an approach that seems rare today. It turned out that Kennedy's fervent support of Chavez paid off politically. Chavez organized Mexican Americans to register and vote in the presidential primary in California in 1968, and contributed very substantially to Kennedy's winning margin in the state.

The fortunes of the farmworkers have ebbed and flowed since. Governor Jerry Brown was a big supporter, and created a state farm-labor board, which gave them the legal framework that other workers have nationally. The backlash from powerful agribusiness interests in the state would help elect Republican governors for sixteen years thereafter.

The local details of poverty are tied to local economics and politics. The continuing marginality of the people who pick the crops is a prototypical example. In some ways the idea of a disposable labor force, which is exemplified by the farmworkers — part-year, part-time, without benefits — has spread in recent years, as more and more companies use workers on a contingent basis. The new fluid economy of part-time and even itinerant work was prefigured by the classic disparities of power that have long characterized the world of farm labor.

I had been working in the Senate for a little over a year when we met Chavez. In that time I had become deeply immersed in the great issues of the day. For me the Voting Rights Act meant representing Kennedy in Democratic staff meetings that were drafting alternatives to the administration's proposals, and working with Senator Javits' staff on an important amendment concerning the use of literacy tests. The escalation of the war meant helping strategize over Kennedy's remarks and his response to critics. The Watts rebellion meant assisting in thinking about what RFK should say and do, and going with him to the area a few months later to talk with people there. Representing New York meant going upstate with a friendly Department of Agriculture staffer to talk with rural poor people and develop legislative ideas to help them, and spending a week in Albany hanging out with the speaker of the assembly to stiffen his back in support of strong legislation to implement the new federal Medicaid law. By the time we met Cesar Chavez I was fully enrolled in a street university of American studies, beginning to understand through personal observation the hard reality of life for millions whom most of us never encounter, and learning what politics could and could not do to change that.

Hunger in Mississippi

A LITTLE MORE than a year later, I went to Mississippi in advance of hearings to be held by a subcommittee of which Kennedy was a member, concerning the reauthorization of the Economic Opportunity Act. The War on Poverty was by now quite controversial, and Pennsylvania Senator Joseph Clark, the subcommittee chair, thought it would help to hold field hearings highlighting some of the good things being accomplished. This was less than three years after the murders of three civil rights workers in Neshoba County and dozens of church burnings around the state. National civil rights legislation had been enacted, but Mississippi was barely beginning to change.

Mississippi was chosen because it was home to the largest multi-county Head Start program in the country, the Child

Development Group of Mississippi. CDGM had come under furious attack from the local political establishment, ostensibly because of alleged misuse of funds, but in fact because, in addition to employing many veterans of the civil rights movement, it had given thousands of black parents hope for their children and had helped them deal with elected officials on behalf of those children. CDGM was a political threat.

Kennedy's trip was hardly uncontroversial. He had just delivered a highly publicized speech calling for a halt in American bombing of North Vietnam, and no one had forgotten that, as attorney general, he had presided over the admission of James Meredith to the University of Mississippi. He was met at the Jackson airport by pickets carrying a Ku Klux Klan flag and signs saying, "LBJ — Send Bobby to Hanoi, Not Mississippi," "Race Mixers Go Home," and "American Soldiers' Blood on Bobby's Hands." Local officials were extremely nervous about security.

RFK sent me to do some advance scouting and to lay out some possible lines of questioning for the witnesses (which, in fact, he seldom used beyond the first couple of questions). I arrived in Jackson on a Friday, two days ahead of Kennedy, and called Marian Wright, the head of the NAACP Legal Defense Fund office in Mississippi and general counsel to CDGM. Then twenty-seven, she was the first black woman ever admitted to the bar in Mississippi and already the leading civil rights lawyer in the state. She was scheduled to testify at the hearings, and our mutual friend, Dick Boone, by then the head of a watchdog group called the Citizens Crusade Against Poverty, had told me she would be the best person to orient me.

She was reluctant to take the time, because she had a deadline on a brief, but we had dinner. It was a decidedly pleasant evening, even though the conversation was in large part about decidedly unpleasant subjects. I was extremely impressed. She was really smart and *really* good looking. The conversation went on until midnight, and we got together again the next day so she could give me some materials she thought might help the Senator at the hearings.

She had told me that widespread hunger and malnutrition were now occurring among poor blacks. Before the subcommittee, she laid out the problem in graphic terms. She said that while she knew the senators were expecting her to talk about CDGM, this was an emergency of overriding concern.

The gist of the story was this. Because of the civil rights movement the white establishment was eager to get as many blacks to leave the state as possible. Farm labor was no longer as necessary, because of the arrival of automated methods of picking cotton and the use of herbicides. The recent enactment of the agricultural minimum wage, which, while it applied to only the largest farms in the country, nonetheless applied to many large growers in Mississippi, had made farm labor more costly, and hastened mechanization and increased use of chemicals. People were being pushed off the plantations in large numbers and out of housing that had been a partial return for their work. Long stuck in poverty as sharecroppers and laborers, they were now even worse off.

Welfare in Mississippi was available only to one-parent families, and many of those being dispossessed were couples with children. Food had been available through the surplus commodities program, under which one went to a warehouse and received bulk sacks of surplus flour, bulgur, or other items. These were often partially spoiled or worm infested, but it was still food. Many Mississippi counties, however, had decided to switch from the commodities program to the new food stamp program, which was at the time a matter of local option. In theory this was better because with food stamps a family could go to the grocery store and choose what to buy. In practice, the food stamp office was open at odd and unpredictable hours. More important, the way the program was then structured (nationally as well as in Mississippi) was that one had to pay money for the stamps and then purchase food worth more than the cost of the stamps. But large numbers of families had no cash. The payment schedule provided that even people with no income had to pay fifty cents per family member per month for the food stamps.

Rural poverty in Mississippi was highly politicized — intimately connected to race and rooted in the nature of the local economy. We had seen a similar politics of poverty in Cesar Chavez's California, and would see it again in eastern Kentucky a few months later. We may think of the inner city when we speak of the geography of poverty, but in fact much of rural poverty, especially in places that are disproportionately poor, is also tied to local politics.

People were starving, Marian Wright said, and invited the subcommittee to see for itself. The visiting senators included not only Democrats Clark and Kennedy but also Republicans Javits and George Murphy of California, an arch-conservative former song-and-dance movie star who was a friend and political clone of Ronald Reagan.

The next day the entourage set out from Jackson. After visiting a job training program at the former Greenville Air Force Base (during which the mayor of Greenville declared, "A lot of people down here say federal money has a taint. I agree. 'Tain't enough"), we went to Cleveland, a town in Bolivar County. Amzie Moore, a local civil rights leader and post office worker, took us around. Kennedy, moved by Marian Wright's testimony, invited her to ride with us. He peppered her with questions about how she had accomplished so much at such a young age and about herself personally. She answered some of his questions and bluntly told him that others were none of his business.

Amzie Moore took us to a group of grim houses. Kennedy's presence had drawn network cameras, and in particular CBS, in the person of Daniel Schorr. What we saw that day was also seen by the rest of America on the evening news.

At one house all the children had been lined up outside with their mother to meet the visitors. There were visible swollen bellies and running sores on their arms and legs that appeared not to be healing. The refrigerator was empty. Kennedy asked the children when they had last eaten and how many meals they ate every day. They said that they usually had only one meal a day, and they had already eaten whatever they were going to eat that day. As we walked through a vacant lot to the next house, Kennedy said to me that these conditions were as bad as he had seen in Third World countries.

At the next house Kennedy went inside first. Marian Wright and I followed. Everyone else stayed outside. I don't think Kennedy was aware of our presence. There was a child on the floor, with a plate of something that looked from across the room like rice. Kennedy knelt down for perhaps five minutes, trying to get a response from the child. It appeared that the child could not stand up, even though he or she seemed old enough. Marian would later say that this was the moment she knew Robert Kennedy was for real.

For me the experience was so shocking it was hard to handle. With everything that had happened in the country and with my own experience working with the Senator, I had come to believe that nothing could surprise me. But I remember standing inside that house as though it happened yesterday, the same way I remember exactly where I was when the phone call came in 1953 saying my mother had died, or the way we all remember when and where we heard that President Kennedy had been murdered. It was one thing to say we needed more jobs or improvements in public education or a better welfare policy. It was something quite different to say we had near starvation in our rich country, and that we had to spend time and money to end that. Kennedy's children say he came home to dinner that night deeply shaken, and that he, a man of few words so much of the time, couldn't stop talking about what he had seen that day.

Not surprisingly, Kennedy wanted to follow up. The next day, back in Washington, we went with Senator Clark and his staff person, Bill Smith, to see Secretary of Agriculture Orville Freeman. Freeman was a former governor of Minnesota who had been instrumental in President Kennedy's nomination and election. Kennedy told Freeman what he had seen, as graphically as he could. He said, "Orville, you have got to get some food down there."

He explained to Freeman that we had met people with no income, and that the Agriculture Department's food-stamp purchase schedule, which could be changed just by rewriting the regulations, was keeping them from getting food stamps. Freeman said, "Bob, there isn't anybody in America who has no income." Kennedy said, "Yes there is. We met them. I'll tell you what. I'll send Peter here back down there with some of your people, and they'll retrace our route from the other day. Will you agree that you'll change the regulations if your people are convinced there really are people in Mississippi who have no income?" Freeman said he would.

I went back down, and drove around with Marian Wright in her car followed by a government vehicle carrying the USDA officials, Bill Seabron and Howard Davis. We introduced them to the families the subcommittee had met and convinced them that there were people with no income. As agreed, Secretary Freeman changed the policy. Providing free food stamps for people with zero income affected few people, but it was an important symbol, and it was the first in a string of policy changes that eventually made food stamps a national program that assured a baseline of nutritional adequacy for all Americans. A congressman from upstate New York named Joe Resnick had gone to Mississippi a year earlier and had come back with the same story of widespread hunger. No one had paid any attention. This time people paid attention.

I remember some not purely professional feelings when I called Marian to say I would be coming back with the USDA officials, and my sensing that her response was not purely professional, either. We found ourselves holding hands in the front seat of her car as we were driving along, with Seabron and Davis following. The hand holding led to romance and marriage and three wonderful sons and happiness. We were married in July 1968, five and a half weeks after Kennedy was murdered. Many of our friends and family said it was about the only good thing that happened in 1968.

The mixture of Marian, extreme hunger, and Robert Kennedy epitomized the intertwining of the personal and the professional that has characterized our lives ever since. Kennedy was very taken with her, and supportive of our romance. He was especially there for me when my father's initial reaction to the interracial relationship was less than enthusiastic. The three of us spent considerable time together over the next year, until he died.

Once, when we were having lunch together at his house, Marian told him she was going to see Dr. King in Atlanta the next day to talk with him about what the Southern Christian Leadership Conference should do next. Kennedy said, "Tell him to bring poor people to Washington to stay until Congress is so uncomfortable that it does what they want just to get them to go home." The advice inspired the Poor People's Campaign, which — after King's death, as it turned out — brought thousands of poor people of all races and ethnic backgrounds to Washington in the spring of 1968. Resurrection City, as their muddy encampment by the Lincoln Memorial was called, produced little response from a government preoccupied with the Vietnam War and a tightening budget, although a small cadre of senior black officials scattered across the executive branch were able to produce, quietly, a number of valuable changes in administrative policy.

In the thirty-plus years since, Marian and I have shared most of all our love and our commitment to our three sons, but also a continuing desire to act for social justice, advising each other as times, issues, and the two of us have evolved and changed.

The romance, like all romances, was personal above all, but for us the personal and professional have never been separated by a bright line.

Because of the efforts of Marian Wright and others, the Field Foundation was already working on the hunger issue. Its money came from the New York branch of the Marshall Field family, and it had been active in civil rights for some time. The foundation was run by a taciturn, deeply principled southerner named Leslie Dunbar, who before coming to New York had been the courageous head of the Southern Regional Council in Atlanta. Dunbar had already arranged for a group of physicians to go to Mississippi to examine large numbers of children and document more accurately the malnutrition. The six-physician team included the now renowned child psychiatrist Dr. Robert Coles, and, more important, a southerner: Dr. Raymond Wheeler, a white pediatrician from Charlotte, North Carolina.

The team went a few weeks after our visit. They examined hundreds of children, and found not only pernicious anemia but diseases like rickets, kwashiorkor, and marasmus that were thought to exist only in underdeveloped countries. Kennedy urged Joe Clark to convene the subcommittee to give their findings greater visibility, and to invite Senators James Eastland and John Stennis of Mississippi to the hearings. To their credit, the Mississippi senators came, with Eastland puffing on a huge cigar throughout the July day. The testimony was powerful, especially when, at the end, Dr. Wheeler described with strong emotion the shame he felt to find these conditions in his native and beloved South.

A couple of weeks later Senator Stennis proposed a $10 million fund to assist in hunger emergencies. Compared with the magnitude of the need, this was a joke. But Kennedy felt that we should take it as a good-faith gesture and support it, even as we said that more was needed. The hunger issue had gained great political strength. Stennis's response showed that it was perhaps an area where southern politicians could do the right thing with less fear of a backlash from their white constituents (and maybe even attract some votes from the blacks, who were registering in steadily increasing numbers because of the Voting Rights Act).

We decided to hold more field hearings on hunger. By then, though, the war in Vietnam had become even more enveloping and draining as a political issue. The country was deeply divided, and Kennedy was under relentless pressure from antiwar advocates to run for president. So we weren't able to get back to hunger until the beginning of 1968. Our first idea was to go to South Carolina, where a young OEO-financed physician named Donald Gatch, in Beaufort County, on the Atlantic Ocean, had documented severe malnutrition among his patients. We notified Senator Ernest Hollings of South Carolina, with whom Kennedy had a cordial relationship, and he begged Kennedy not to come, promising to do his own investigation. I was quite annoyed when Kennedy agreed, but he was proved right a little over a year later. Hollings announced that he had discovered widespread hunger in South Carolina, and became the first southerner to support broad expansion of the food stamp program.

We went to eastern Kentucky instead, the last visit we were able to make before Kennedy decided to run for president. Visiting families and holding community hearings in a school gymnasium, we documented the existence of serious hunger in that economically devastated former coal-mining area. The inquiry revealed not just the economic decline but the power disparities. In nearly every place, especially rural communities, where we found a severe unwillingness to help the poor, we also found, and not always because of ethnic differences, a pocket of feudalism in America: a local power structure committed to perpetuating itself at all costs and unwilling to countenance the slightest improvement in the lives of the excluded, for fear they would gain the confidence and the wherewithal to overturn the status quo at the ballot box. Elected officials, judges, police officers and sheriffs, and local bankers and business people were always ready to use any tool necessary to quash dissidence whenever it appeared. This was true in Cesar Chavez's world in California, in the Rio Grande valley in south Texas, in Mississippi, and in Appalachia.

I learned in eastern Kentucky that my true calling in this world was not as an advance person (or advance man, as it literally was then). Tom Johnston, from the Senator's New York office, who was a native Kentuckian, and I went down to Kentucky to advance the trip. We set up a good itinerary, with the help of Tom Gish, the editor and publisher of the *Mountain Eagle,* in Whitesburg, Kentucky; Milton Ogle, a terrific community organizer who was the head of the Appalachian Volunteers; and John Tiller, a former coal miner and a local activist.

What neither of us foresaw was the degree of press interest. It was the second week of February 1968, and speculation was rife about whether RFK would run for president, even though he had said just a few days earlier that he did not expect to be a candidate.

Tom and I hadn't rented a bus, assuming that whatever press we had would rent their own cars and form a caravan. The caravan turned out to be thirty or forty cars. This caused a general grumpiness and threw our timing out the window. Drive times between stops doubled. By the end of the first day we were three hours behind schedule. That was, most emphatically, not the way Robert Kennedy did business. We had arranged a number of chances for Kennedy to drop in on families. He would go in, have a conversation, and be ready to leave before the end of the caravan pulled up at the house. There were some really irritated reporters.

Much of what Kennedy started during these critical months came to fruition only after his death. For example, Kennedy had seen his friend Don Hewitt, a CBS news producer, at a social occasion, and told him he should do something about hunger. Hewitt began work on a documentary that finally aired in 1969.

It was after Kennedy's death but perfectly timed to support the developing politics of hunger. The documentary, by a young filmmaker-activist named Martin Carr, showed hunger in four regions of the country, including a newborn baby in San Antonio dying on camera as a consequence of its malnutrition during pregnancy. The powerful House Agricultural Appropriations Subcommittee chairman, Jamie Whitten of Mississippi, sent FBI agents to question the people who had appeared in the film, to find out who had manipulated them.

While Kennedy was still alive, the Senate authorized creation of a Select Committee on Hunger and Malnutrition, and after his death it started work, with Senator George McGovern of South Dakota as its chair. The committee continued the pattern of field hearings and other dramatizing steps, to the point where President Nixon sent the first-ever presidential message on hunger to Capitol Hill, in which he called for a vast expansion of the food stamp program. The House and Senate Agriculture Committees, bastions of the status quo, gradually softened, especially after agribusiness interests came to realize that they had a self-interest in an enlarged food stamp program.

By the time Richard Nixon left office the food stamp program had become national and the benefit structure had been reformed. It was the first time a national income floor, albeit at a minimal level, had been put into place. The program now reaches around 19 million people, down from a high of 28 million in 1994 — the result of the prosperity of the late nineties, the budget cuts of 1996, and bureaucratic confusion and meanness in the wake of the new welfare law. It is the subject of conservative attack and budget cuts from time to time, but it is in fact one of the important social-policy successes of the last thirty years. Too many people still lack adequate income to pay the rent, and food stamps routinely run out well before the end of the month, but widespread, severe malnutrition is now a thing of the past.

2

ROBERT KENNEDY'S LEGACY

The Inner City, Race, Jobs, and Welfare

THE INNER CITY was at the heart of Kennedy's interest in poverty. In his days as attorney general, he thought of the challenge in terms of preventing juvenile delinquency, and the particular human face he put on it was that of black teenagers in Harlem. In April 1965, with historic civil rights legislation recently signed into law and voting rights legislation on the way, he went to the National Conference of Christians and Jews to tell them that the battle for civil rights was not over but only shifting to a new battlefield of economic justice. He told them to beware of "the new voice of intolerance," which said that Negroes "have the same chance as anyone else [and] if they don't take advantage of what we offer, that's their responsibility."

The Watts rebellion in South Central Los Angeles in August 1965 drew him back to these issues. It was by far the largest, deadliest, and most destructive racial confrontation of the sixties, and commanded the attention of a horrified public for days. RFK addressed the issues in a speech to a white audience in upstate New York a few days later. Because of his extraordinary visibility as the bearer of the torch of the fallen President, speeches were a tool of exceptional power for him. In this one he spoke of the transcendent significance of work as affecting the quality of everything else in life, the anger that comes from enforced isolation in a slum, the necessity for law enforcement to keep order, the harm to the entire community from the perpetuation of problems, the need for the poor to have a voice, the responsibility of the black community to provide leadership, and the importance of understanding that people handed program funds they are unused to having will steal some and waste some.

The speech was a masterly piece of public education. He said, "Someone had neglected to tell the folks down home about one of the most important aspects of the promised land: it was a slum ghetto . . . [with] too many people full of hate and bitterness crowded into a dirty, stinky, uncared-for, closet-size section of a great city." He charged that "we have been strangely insensitive to the problems of the northern Negro . . . [which] unfortunately and dangerously . . . are the problems of everyday living, in jobs and housing and education."

These thoughts could not be pigeonholed. He insisted on law enforcement, on order, on individuals being held personally responsible for their acts, but there was an equal demand for community responsibility. There was a statement of urgent need for public action but also an implicit critique of the black community for not acting effectively on behalf of its own. The point about inevitable graft and waste was especially important, because, like Claude Rains in *Casablanca,* many politicians professed to be shocked when community groups misspent federal money, and then would call for shutting down all federal funding as a result. Kennedy was saying, Put the offenders in jail, but don't judge the whole program by a few bad actors.

The speech received a lot of attention. Kennedy wanted to follow up. He told Walinsky and me to think about what he could do. I started looking at strengthening existing civil rights laws in two areas: one, making it easier to prosecute police officers and sheriffs who engaged in brutality and to sue their departments, and two, enacting a strong federal fair-housing law. I wrote Kennedy a long memo on these items, but he was more interested in the agenda he had laid before the nation after the violence in Watts. Walinsky and I convinced him that a useful first step would be to set out our emerging thinking in a series of speeches.

This effort turned out to be three addresses, on which Walinsky and I worked extensively and which Kennedy delivered on successive days in January. The speeches made two big points: one, that there should be active efforts to promote complete freedom for people to choose where they would live in a metropolitan area; and two, that there should be immediate and intensive efforts to improve conditions in the inner-city areas in which blacks had been segregated.

The first idea was hardly popular. The Democratic Party has always had a split between its more suburban and middle-class constituency and its more urban and heavily minority constituency. Kennedy was definitely on the urban side of the fault line, although not without some suburban issues, particularly the war in Vietnam. Even within the urban wing of the party he was iconoclastic. Vice President Humphrey, for example, emphasized creating government programs and was not especially interested in the structural critique of government performance so central to Kennedy's views.

While I have always thought metropolitan mobility is crucial, the inner-city agenda engaged Kennedy more, perhaps because it offered more immediate results and maybe because it was more politically realistic. The inner-city speech was nothing if not ambitious. It argued that comprehensive efforts led from within the inner city and supported by outside resources could work. Some of it was manifestly impractical. Much of it reflected a false specificity — there were dozens of subproposals with little operational detail. But it was a hopeful vision. It was flawed if it meant only trying to improve the inner city without also having a way for people to move out or find work outside, but it was a vision nonetheless. Few, if any, subsequent efforts, including Kennedy's own cherished Bedford-Stuyvesant Restoration Corporation, have ever taken the vision as a literal blueprint, but thousands of community development corporations such as RFK imagined have sprung up to pursue local housing and economic goals, and a few have pursued agendas that were even more ambitious.

Bedford-Stuyvesant

KENNEDY'S PATTERN WAS that, having talked about something, he wanted to do it. Harlem was the obvious place to try out his ideas, but there were already too many players and turfs there. Bedford-Stuyvesant, a large neighborhood of Brooklyn, was more promising. It had a good housing stock now deteriorating because so many middle-class families had moved out, but a significant number of people owned their own homes and there still was a base of strong community leadership. These were ministers and judges and physicians who cared deeply about the community but whose own careers would not be threatened by such a new venture. There also seemed to be fewer "professional" poverty fighters who might see a new effort as an incursion into their turf.

People were suspicious and not particularly welcoming. Tom Johnston, the charming, smart Kentuckian who ran the Senator's New York office, began spending almost all of his time on the project, along with others in the office. Kennedy had promised that a plan would be in operation within a year. It was a tall order. Kennedy devoted a significant amount of his own time to the project, often flying up to New York for evening meetings and returning the same night or early the next morning. It was an unusual role for a United States senator.

By the end of 1966, RFK was ready to unveil the project. It had been a struggle. The leaders of the federally funded community action agency felt highly threatened and had thrown sand in the gears whenever they could. A number of authentic community leaders had emerged, but there was still residual tension when a thousand people gathered on December 10 at Public School 305 on Monroe Street to join in the announcement.

Kennedy told them there were three key pieces to the intensive effort to revitalize Bedford-Stuyvesant: cooperation with the private business community; a coordinated plan for education, employment, and community development; and a united community. He announced that there would be two new corporations, one a community-based entity that would do the local work and the other with an all-star cast of outside business leaders to help find financing and give advice. He warned that long-term financing would be there only if it was clear "that programs are soundly conceived and operated; that important positions are assigned on no grounds other than merit; [and] that there is no room here for political dealing."

The outside commitments, at least on paper, were more fully developed than the unified commitment of the community. Senator Javits had helped line up Governor Nelson Rockefeller and Mayor John Lindsay. Among the business and financial figures whom Kennedy had enlisted were Tom Watson, of IBM; Andre Meyer, of Lazard Freres; and William Paley, of CBS (whose daughter was married to Carter Burden, of Kennedy's New York office). Watson promised to locate an IBM plant in Bedford-Stuyvesant. It didn't hurt that Tom Johnston came from a very wealthy steel-company family and had his own connections in the New York business and financial community. John Doar, a Republican who had succeeded Burke Marshall as Kennedy's assistant attorney general for civil rights (and later became much more famous as counsel to the House Judiciary Committee considering the impeachment of President Nixon), was recruited to be executive director of the outside corporation. And Kennedy had succeeded in getting federal funds made available for comprehensive neighborhood development programs that just happened to be like the one designed for Bedford-Stuyvesant.

The community corporation foundered initially. Kennedy tried to get Franklin Thomas, then an assistant police commissioner in New York City and later president of the Ford Foundation, to head it, but Thomas saw too much community friction and declined. Kennedy kept after him anyway, asking him repeatedly whether he would take a different view if the feuding could be resolved. Five months after the launch, the corporation was restructured with more board members from the dissident group and renamed the Bedford-Stuyvesant Restoration Corporation. Thomas agreed to come aboard.

My own involvement in Bedford-Stuyvesant was not extensive. In December and January I spent a month going around the area with a couple of physicians, looking at what the new community corporation might do to improve the delivery of health care. Health was by now one of my issues. Nothing ever came of it, but it gave me a useful immersion in the typical reality of what happens to poor people who need medical care. New York City had a network of public hospitals that provided free care to the poor, and they would go to the emergency room for routine care. They would wait hours to be seen, and seldom see the same physician twice. Comprehensive, preventive, family-based, neighborhood-based care was mostly just a novel idea. The federal War on Poverty had put the idea into practice in its neighborhood health center program, and there were some shining examples in New York and elsewhere. But there were none in Bedford-Stuyvesant. We created a plan for a more community-based approach, but the new corporation had too much else on its plate and did not follow up.

The Restoration Corporation, as it was now called, was busy with three major projects as well as the IBM plant, which, when it got going, created three hundred jobs. One was the redevelopment of the old Sheffield Farms dairy plant in the heart of Bed-Stuy, which became the headquarters of the corporation and a hub of stores and offices. The second was the "super block" concept in which housing in a few residential blocks would be completely rehabilitated, and supportive amenities provided. These blocks were to serve as anchors for nearby development, and as models for projects elsewhere in the community. The third was to help large numbers of residents fix up the outsides of their homes, on the theory that it would discourage drug dealing and other antisocial activities, and, again, serve as a model for others.

Frank Thomas guided the Restoration Corporation into a significant program of housing rehabilitation, a mortgage loan pool of impressive bulk, and a good-sized portfolio of small-business loans. Over the years it built or renovated over two thousand units of housing, helped with energy conservation in about five thousand homes, placed thousands of people in jobs, ran recreation and cultural programs for large numbers of young people, and persuaded a number of national business chains to locate outlets in Bed-Stuy. The outside corporation gradually outlived its utility, and faded. Restoration's momentum survived for a considerable number of years after Kennedy's death and following Thomas's departure to the Ford Foundation. The corporation is less influential today, but that is perhaps not surprising. It is difficult to sustain the effectiveness of large-scale community-based efforts, especially those that rely heavily on imported leadership. Those that have stayed strong have had steady and extraordinary leadership as well as deep community involvement. This is unfortunately not routine.

The Ribicoff Hearings

WHILE THE BEDFORD-STUYVESANT planning was under way, I helped organize hearings on the urban crisis, chaired by Senator Abraham Ribicoff of Connecticut. Coming between our time with Cesar Chavez and our trip to Mississippi, the hearings continued over the better part of a year. Over a hundred witnesses testified. The hearings began in August of 1966, as another season of inner-city violence was making crystal clear their urgency.

Kennedy, in a somewhat unusual move, testified before the subcommittee even though he was a member, pointing to employment as "the only true long-term solution" and declaring that "no government program now operating" had sufficient promise. He said "the heart of the program" should be "community development corporations" which would be nongovernmental institutions that would respond "directly to the needs and wishes of" community residents.

President Johnson's people found the hearings, with their critical comments on the administration's efforts, an annoyance. Kennedy found them important and interesting, and spent a lot of time at them, probing, listening, reflecting, giving some witnesses a hard time, empathizing deeply with others. One of his many attractive paradoxes was his capacity to listen. Here was this high-energy man, this impatient man who wanted to get things done without red tape or dithering, who would also disappear frequently into his own thoughts, his own private world of post-assassination pain, who could sit silently for hours sometimes, and who could listen very intently when he thought someone had something worthwhile to say.

He was very tough on Sam Yorty, the mayor of Los Angeles, who he thought had been totally unresponsive to the people of Watts. He wasn't easy on the witnesses from the administration, or on John Lindsay, the young patrician liberal Republican mayor of New York, who certainly had good intentions but whom RFK didn't really like personally. At the conclusion of his sparring session with Mayor Yorty, who had said repeatedly that one issue or another was not under his jurisdiction, Kennedy said, "The Mayor . . . [should] stay here through all of these hearings, and I think he could safely do so, because as I understand from your testimony you have nothing to get back to."

One day Dr. Robert Coles came to testify. The two had never met. It was a late afternoon, and the sun was coming in through the windows of the hearing room in the Russell Senate Office

Building in the soft, yellowing, suffusing way that is unique to that time of day. Kennedy engaged Coles in a dialogue about what happens to black children as they go from childhood into adolescence. They found themselves in deep agreement, in effect finishing one another's sentences. Kennedy talked about the liveliness and enthusiasm of black children as compared to privileged white children being "pushed along in their prams" by their nannies. They exchanged agreement on how this changes at ages thirteen or fourteen as the black children begin to discover what awaits them in terms of racism and lack of opportunity in the wider world, how the life goes out of them, how the anger and the sullenness set in.

"Really sort of a castration begins, caused by the whole system," Kennedy said. He worried that there was "developing a whole class of people, . . . who are just going to be completely antisocial and against everything that exists in this country." Coles responded, "A usual comment . . . is, 'If only these children had more upbringing things would be better'. There is nothing more moral than the kind of punishing, Bible-quoting slum mother . . . who really tries hard to teach her children. . . . So the sense of betrayal following this extremely moral attempt to live up to the society is . . . a very horrifying thing to watch." The sensitivity, the perceptiveness, the love of children of these two men mesmerized everyone in the hearing room.

Another lifelong friendship started that day. Coles has been a gigantic one-man support system to Robert Kennedy's children ever since.

Welfare

THE WELFARE LEGISLATION we worked on in 1967 was the first shot to draw blood in what became the Thirty Years' War over welfare, culminating in the law President Clinton signed in 1996.

I was unaware of it at the time, but the welfare rolls were already perceived by some as out of control. Over the previous decade the Aid to Families with Dependent Children (AFDC) program had approximately doubled in size, from 646,000 families with 2.4 million total recipients to 1.2 million families with nearly 5 million recipients. (As of the fall of 1999 the caseload was about 2.5 million families and about 7.3 million total recipients.) The cost to the federal government in 1967 was $1.5 billion, which was projected to go up to $1.8 billion over the ensuing five years.

Organizing efforts of the National Welfare Rights Organization, the work of legal-services lawyers, more sympathetic attitudes in welfare offices due to the temper of the times, and the increasing numbers of unemployed people penned in inner cities had produced the increase. As long as local welfare offices had been able to keep people they didn't like off the rolls, and as long as the program was seen as mainly for widows with young children, it had been politically stable. Now that the clientele was increasingly perceived as black and single parent, and there was an emerging legal right to assistance, the politics were changing.

Another thing I didn't know was that the political will to help the poor probably peaked with the 89th Congress in 1965 and 1966. The Democrats lost seats in both Houses in the 1966 elections. With this change, plus the increased financial demand of the war in Vietnam, a long slide from concern to hostility began. Antipoverty legislation would be enacted through the mid-seventies and in fits and starts thereafter, but measures aimed at the confluence of the inner city, race, jobs, and welfare would be increasingly hard to pass.

Kennedy was to deliver a speech on welfare in New York City in early May of 1967. I was in New York drafting the speech, and he was in Washington. In those days, of course, there were no fax machines, no modems, no way to transmit a full draft of anything except to read it over the phone or go to the airport and put it on a plane. I called him at home and asked if he wanted to see a draft, explaining that I was mainly pasting it together out of things he had said before.

He had given a speech a year earlier to the New York State Society of Newspaper Editors in which he said that everyone who spoke to the public needed to exercise greater candor, and gave welfare as his first example. He had said that "most of us" had "deprecated and disregarded" the criticisms of welfare leveled by its opponents, that it is "degrading, both to the giver and the recipient, . . . that it destroys self-respect, that it lowers incentive, that it is contrary to American ideals." He said that in our urge to help people we had "disregarded elementary fact," that the criticisms "do have a center of truth," that "higher welfare payments . . . often lead to lifelong dependency," and that we had "ignored the real need — which was, and remains, decent, dignified jobs for all."

The earlier speech had gotten no coverage, even though it was delivered to an audience composed of most of the newspaper editors in the state. They had evidently heard the remarks about welfare only as illustrations of the general theme that money by itself does not answer the hard questions we face as a society.

Kennedy said he remembered the earlier speech and didn't need to see a draft. The next day he gave the speech and found it to be, as I had told him, mainly a restatement of things he had already said. He spoke not only about welfare but also about the shortcomings of public housing, urban renewal, public hospitals, and the public schools. Kennedy's suggested remedies went well beyond welfare, including his familiar calls for "the involvement of the community" and for "jobs with possibilities for further education and advancement."

Both of us were shocked to find the speech reported on the front page of the *New York Times*. The very language that no one had paid any attention to fourteen months earlier was now of great interest. "Kennedy Assails Welfare System," the headline read. The subhead was "Says It Is Threat to Family Life Because It Fails to Meet Basic Needs." The first paragraph of the story quoted Kennedy's description of welfare and associated aid to the poor as a "system of handouts, a second-rate set of social services, which damages and demeans its recipients."

Kennedy's critique was not received with unanimous warmth. The *Times* editorial page called it a "glib denunciation" and said its "primary effect" would be "in giving ammunition to the enemies of any form of assistance." When New York City Welfare Commissioner Mitchell Ginsberg agreed with Senator Kennedy's criticism at a Senate hearing the next day and called the welfare system "bankrupt," Kennedy's Republican colleague from New York, Jacob Javits, erupted and said, "You'd better not be in too much of a hurry to talk that way or the way Senator Kennedy did yesterday, or you may get it thrown out right now." Governor Rockefeller called Kennedy "uninformed," and added, "What are his alternatives? It's easy to criticize. . . . Why doesn't he suggest some new legislation?"

Perhaps responding to the Governor, but characteristically in any case, Kennedy wanted to follow up. One possibility, of course, would have been to redouble our effort for legislation to assure that decent and dignified jobs were genuinely available to all, but we were already doing everything we could think of about that. That, in any case, was not Kennedy's point. He had become interested in welfare itself. He wanted to connect the system to the world of work and make it a decent and effective safety net for those who couldn't find jobs or weren't in a position to work.

We invested significant time in the subject over the next nine months, because major legislation involving welfare was working its way through Congress. I started to teach myself about welfare, and discovered that President Johnson had sent Congress a bill primarily focused on the elderly but containing, almost buried, a significant welfare proposal as well.

Building on the report of a presidential commission on welfare that he had appointed, and urged on by Health, Education and Welfare Secretary John Gardner, the President offered some ideas about public assistance. These were buried, in President Johnson's message to Congress, in a section on improving old-age assistance, the then-existing cash program for the elderly whose Social Security benefits were grossly inadequate. Welfare was not a political winner even then.

President Johnson's welfare proposal was worthwhile. The way welfare worked was that each state created its own definition of family need, and then set a payment level for what it would actually provide. The "standard of need," as it was called, was intended to be aspirational, an ideal toward which each state would work. President Johnson's bill required the states to pay at the level they defined as the standard of need, and to update this standard annually.

Actual payment levels varied enormously around the country (they still do), with Mississippi at the bottom paying $55 a month for a family of four (equal to about $250 a month today). The standards of need toward which states would supposedly strive, while also widely varying, were somewhat higher. Had the proposal been enacted, it would have caused an immediate, if modest, increase in benefits in most of the states. It would have been locked in as a minimum payment level for the future, to be adjusted for inflation.

This idea was not greeted warmly in Congress. Enthusiasm for more welfare was not exactly rampant, and jurisdiction over it was in the tax-writing committees: the Ways and Means Committee in the House and the Finance Committee in the Senate. These were the most conservative committees in Congress, chaired by Wilbur Mills of Arkansas and Russell Long of Louisiana. One could be sure that any conference committee convened to resolve differences between the two chambers would come up with the least generous combination of the two versions.

Kennedy was not on the Finance Committee, so his ideas

would have to be presented in the committee by someone else, or on the Senate floor. He wanted me to proceed nonetheless.

The House was already transforming the public-assistance portions of the bill from modestly progressive toward the opposite. By the time it finished its work in August, the House had cut the heart out of Johnson's proposal, freezing the percentage of children in each state who could receive federally financed benefits. If more people applied, a state would have to use its own funds or turn people away. The House had also inserted a work requirement — recipients would have to register for work and training and accept jobs when offered (with some exceptions and protections) or lose the adult portion of the family's benefits. From today's vantage point, a properly designed work requirement seems acceptable. In 1967, far fewer wives were working outside the home; requiring low-income mothers to leave their children when well-off women were staying home seemed inconsistent to many. More troubling, even by today's standards, the proposal contained no protections regarding the pay and working conditions for the jobs to which recipients would be assigned.

There were some positive features. Day-care services were to be provided for mothers required to work, sweetened by the federal government's paying 75 percent of the cost. Instead of recipients' losing a dollar of benefits for every dollar earned, they could receive a partial benefit to supplement their income from low-wage jobs. States were to calculate wage supplements by disregarding the first thirty dollars of monthly earnings and a third of every dollar earned beyond that.

I drafted some amendments to be offered in the Senate, mainly aimed at preventing unfair application of the work requirements. As the Senate Finance Committee began its consideration, we found that virtually all of our amendments would lose at that level. The committee's Democratic majority meant nothing, power residing solidly in a coalition of Republicans and senior southern Democrats. So I organized staffers of liberal senators to join in trying to improve the bill when it came to the Senate floor. We developed a bipartisan coalition of fifteen senators (the Republicans were Jacob Javits of New York and Clifford Case of New Jersey).

At one point I convinced Kennedy that perhaps we could talk Russell Long into accepting a few pieces of our package, so Kennedy asked for a meeting with him. We went to an anteroom off the Finance Committee's main hearing room in the Dirksen Senate Office Building. Long came through another door on the other side of the room, and with him, to our surprise, was Wilbur Cohen, then under secretary of HEW. Cohen was a career government official, and as a young man had been one of the original drafters of the Social Security Act. He was widely respected for his expertise and his political survival skills. No one questioned his commitment to social justice, but everyone understood that he was also highly pragmatic, to say the least.

Long and his colleagues had been transforming the welfare portions of the administration's bill into something quite different from what the President had originally proposed, although not as nastily as their counterparts in the House. Cohen had a longstanding working relationship with Long. We surmised that Long, knowing that Kennedy had already developed considerable support for his efforts, had called Cohen for advice. And Cohen's ultimate boss was the President of the United States, who had no interest in seeing Kennedy succeed at anything. Plus, Kennedy told me that he and Cohen had never gotten along. The meeting did not go well. Long danced around, offering specious reasons why he couldn't accept the amendments. After perhaps twenty minutes, Kennedy thanked him for taking the time to meet with us, and we left. Over the following twenty-four hours, working with Long's staff, we obtained agreement that he would accept four of our more innocuous amendments, maybe because Cohen saw no harm in them after he had thought it over.

I found out many years later that neither John Gardner, the

secretary of HEW, who was Cohen's immediate superior, nor Lisle Carter, the assistant secretary who was the lead HEW policy person on welfare, knew that Cohen was in direct touch with Senator Long. Once they found out Cohen had been going behind their back, they assumed he was doing so with the blessing of the White House. Cohen wasn't completely candid with Long, either. Long was unaware that the administration's official position was in opposition to what he was doing to the bill, and when Secretary Gardner came to testify before the Finance Committee to state the administration's opposition, Long was shocked and turned beet red with anger at being blind-sided.

When debate started on the Senate floor, Senator Long's scripted summary of the welfare portion of the committee bill made it sound completely progressive. He talked about "a work incentive program . . . for the purpose of restoring members of AFDC families . . . to regular employment through counseling, placement services, and training, and arranging for all others to get paid employment in special work projects to improve the communities in which they live"; the "requirement" of day care and other social services so people could "take advantage of the work and training opportunities"; and earnings exemptions "to provide incentives for work in regular employment."

We did quite well on the floor, winning two of our key amendments, although by only three votes, and losing a third by nine votes. One of our successes, offered by Fred Harris of Oklahoma, would have made the optional program of welfare for two-parent families mandatory across the country. This was a top objective of welfare reformers, since it made no sense to require fathers to desert their families for them to get help. Harris succeeded by a vote of 39 to 36, with support from eight Republicans.

We also got passed an amendment to exempt mothers from being forced to work or go to training during times when their children under sixteen were not in school, an exception that seems generous by today's standards. The bill already excused women because of illness, incapacity, advanced age, or residence in remote locations, or if they were caring for a chronically ill or incapacitated member of their household. Senator Carl Curtis of Nebraska, a conservative Republican, had, somewhat surprisingly, amended the bill in committee to excuse mothers caring for preschool children. In the debate on the Senate floor Senator Philip Hart of Michigan said, "Maybe all of us have inherited the notion that work is holy, . . . but for a mother with a nine-year-old child, there is a higher purpose . . . to be home with the child." Senator Edmund Muskie of Maine said, "With respect to children from five to ten — I have three in that age bracket — all the recreational programs are no substitute for a mother's care during the afternoon hours."

Senator Long, noting that the bill provided additional funds for child care and required that it be available, said, "We do not want to have the mother sitting around and drinking wine all day."

The amendment succeeded by a vote of 41 to 38, with seven Republicans joining in. The biggest surprise was that we attracted Senator J. William Fulbright of Arkansas, who almost never voted with the liberals on social policy issues.

The third major amendment would have required that the minimum wage be paid to people sent to what the bill called "special work projects" for people who could not find a job on their own.

Senator Long, opposing the amendment, said that the purpose of the special work projects was "to make a job for somebody that would not exist otherwise, even if it is just picking up trash in front of one's own house, or picking up beer cans, which a person should do, anyway, if it is in front of his home. To pay a minimum wage for that kind of work, when it is not minimum-wage work, does not make sense."

Robert Kennedy spoke out strongly. He said,

> I believe the Government should never be in the position
> of subsidizing or encouraging or supporting in any re-
> spect work at substandard labor conditions. . . . In effect,
> this is slave labor. . . . One can imagine what [these
> jobs] . . . are likely to be, given the definition of those
> who will be forced into them. Sweeping out the court-
> house lavatory is one possibility. Raking leaves on the
> city hall lawn and shoveling snow off city streets are
> others. Cleaning out the drainage ditches near large
> farms and plantations is a favorite in some parts of the
> country. . . . [F]or the first time in the history of our
> country people are losing the right to choose the place
> where they will work. . . . For the first time people will
> have no conceivable right to bargain over what wage they
> will receive. . . . The compulsory labor provisions of this
> bill are bad enough. Let us not make them slave labor in
> addition.

The minimum-wage proposal, offered by Senator Edward Kennedy, lost by a vote of 40 to 31.

The conference committee dropped all our amendments, and its report came back to the Senate for approval just before Christmas. We were outraged. The Senate conferees had sold out majority votes in their own body without even a semblance of argument. In fact, the bill was now more restrictive than either the House or the Senate bill.

Spurred by liberal interest groups, the senators behind the liberalizing amendments decided to filibuster the conference report. Because the well-publicized heart of the bill was a Social Security benefit increase (Social Security had yet to be indexed for inflation), senators wanted to go home for Christmas and take credit for bringing home some bacon to their elderly constituents. Our filibuster was not received with enthusiasm even by those who had voted with us on the original amendments.

On the other hand, there was strong outside support for our

position. Trade unions, church leaders, social-welfare organizations and experts, civil rights leaders, governors, mayors, and many others spoke out publicly and sent telegrams urging senators to vote against the conference report. Senior citizens groups were supportive, too.

We started the filibuster on December 13, 1967. The next morning, Senator Joseph Tydings of Maryland was supposed to be protecting the floor from parliamentary maneuvering. He was in the back of the chamber. Long, with Majority Whip Robert Byrd of West Virginia at his side, stood up and in a whisper moved the adoption of the conference report. Our filibuster was over.

A few minutes later the majority leader, Mike Mansfield of Montana, who was the politest and kindest of men, came to the floor and said he had been unavoidably absent "when, like a flash of lightning," the conference report had been agreed to. He said he knew no rules and regulations had been broken, "but I think the way it was done raises a most serious question so far as the rights of any individual senator are concerned." Further discussion produced a unanimous-consent agreement to have a roll-call vote the next day, but the filibuster was still over. The front-page headline in the *New York Times* the next day was "Senate Liberals Caught Napping."

Kennedy was furious. He went to the floor and excoriated Byrd, whom he disliked intensely. His remarks were sufficiently salty that I went to the little editing room just off the Senate floor and cleaned up what he had said for the history books, without changing the substance. (Senators' extemporaneous remarks were taken down in shorthand by relay teams of stenographers — all male, as I recall — and transcribed for publication in the *Congressional Record*. Because there were frequent errors in transcription, staff routinely looked at the transcripts when they appeared a few minutes later to make sure they were accurate, although the substance of what had been said was frequently improved at this juncture. Had a reporter been listening in the gallery, Kennedy's actual remarks could have been reported. Apparently no one was listening.)

As the *Record* now reads, Kennedy said he wanted "to say how distressed and disturbed I am about how the [conference] report was handled this morning." He was careful to say he was not being critical of Senator Mike Mansfield, the majority leader, but then said, "I think what went on this morning is a reflection on those who participated, not just as U.S. Senators, but as individuals and as men."

Senator Byrd interrupted to say "that there was no attempt to do anything here this morning that was indecent or to do anything that would take advantage of those Senators who opposed the conference report." He said the chair had "put the question three times," that Senator Tydings had been on the floor at the time, and that Tydings "indicated afterward that it was his fault."

After a lengthy and unproductive back-and-forth with Byrd, Kennedy made a long statement about the procedural unfairness and the substantive problems. He said the House committee had never taken testimony on any of the welfare provisions, that it had written the bill behind closed doors, and that the House had adopted a closed rule so that the bill could not be amended on the floor. He said "the extent of this bill's retreat into brutality" was not made clear until it came to the Senate and that the Senate hearings were then grossly inadequate. The Senate as a body had "voted to remove most of the odious provisions of the bill," but the conferees had "abandoned every Senate vote to liberalize the bill." Now the last chance to "remedy the situation, which threatens to turn the welfare laws of this country back into the 17th century," had been, "without debate and without warning," negated by "a small band of Senators."

The speech represented Kennedy at his most passionate. Discussing the removal of any exemption for mothers with small children, he said this had been done "even though the child psychiatrists are unanimous in saying that it is absolutely critical for a mother to be with her child." He attacked the hypocrisy of the political rhetoric.

> I have heard Senators on this floor deplore the fact that our U.S. Government or the State governments have too much of a role in the lives of our individual citizens. Yet here we are agreeing to a bill which will give them more control and more direction than we have ever given the Government at any time in our history. The Government is now going to decide what mother has to go to work, what mothers are going to remain with their children, and what mothers are going to have to leave their children . . . If we think that is civilized, if we think that is anything other than a step back 200 years, I would be shocked. . . . I would like to have heard somebody stand on the floor of the U.S. Senate and defend that provision of this legislation that was passed at 9:30 this morning. . . . [This] could amount to a congressional authorization of virtual peonage. . . . If we had had a debate on this legislation, . . . and our colleagues in the Senate were aware of the facts, I do not believe the Senate would have taken the action it did. . . . I think if the measure involved no other provision than the authority of a Government bureaucrat to be able to decide to take a mother out of her house and put her to work, it would be unacceptable to all Members of the Senate.

Kennedy went into similar detail about each of the welfare provisions. The AFDC freeze evoked particularly strong sarcasm:

> It is very well for us to cut 300,000 children off the rolls. That shows a real sign of economy. . . . We have raised

the salary of everybody working for the Government. We have increased the allowances for Members of the U.S. Senate. We have done all that. We have taken care of ourselves. But we are going to save money. We are going to make sure the children do not have any money. We are going to cut them off the rolls. That is how brave we are. And we can go back and make speeches about how we are for the economy. I do not believe it is acceptable.

He said the freeze "would break" the "commitment" made to children in need by the federal government in 1935. "The experience of broken promises is all too frequent in the lives of the poor. . . . We should not delude ourselves by thinking that the poor will not realize what we have done." Kennedy warned that the time would come when "the ears of the poor will be turned to other voices, preaching alien creeds, . . . when the masses of the poor . . . will reach out for salvation in desperate ways, rather than drown in need and indignity."

Summing up, he said the public assistance provisions were "a giant step backward":

> [They] seem to punish the poor because they are there and we have not been able to do anything about them. But if this is our approach they will still be there when we are done. . . . [W]e will never succeed in restoring dignity and promise to the lives of people whose frustration exploded into violence in the cities this summer until we develop a system which provides jobs — enough jobs and good jobs. . . . This is the basic problem which we must look to. For this problem welfare is neither the cause nor the remedy. But welfare has its role: helping those in need — and the House bill will hinder it in fulfilling that role. . . . We in the Senate must go on record as opposing this almshouse approach. . . . I do think our welfare system is unsatisfactory. But every rea-

son why I think it is unsatisfactory will only be accentuated by the conference bill.

On December 15, 1967, the bill came to a final roll-call vote. The tally was 62 to 14, with RFK among the opposition. Would there have been more votes against the welfare provisions if they had not been coupled with politically attractive increases in Social Security benefits? Perhaps. The floor votes during the initial Senate debate had been encouraging, but even in the midst of the Great Society, welfare did not attract many people who run for public office. In the House there were only three votes against the conference report, the same as with the original bill.

The work requirement of the 1967 bill, known as the Work Incentive (or WIN) Program, turned out to be more porous than its adherents believed or its critics feared, leading to a continued debate. The freeze on federal funds yielded to pressure from the governors, and was lifted a year and a half later. The struggle over making the two-parent program mandatory went on, finally succeeding (as it turned out, temporarily) as part of the ill-fated Family Support Act of 1988. The modest earnings incentive, the so-called thirty and a third, stayed in the law until the Reagan onslaught of 1981.

The bill sent to President Johnson was regarded by liberals as horribly regressive. HEW Secretary John Gardner and Lisle Carter, the assistant secretary with responsibility for welfare policy, made a strong pitch to the President that he should veto it. Johnson, distracted by the Vietnam War and the gathering storm over the future of his presidency, signed it anyway, early in 1968. President Nixon's surprising proposal for a Family Assistance Plan seemed for a short while to be moving things back in a progressive direction, but the 1968 law turned out in retrospect to be the first step on the path that led to the welfare "reform" of 1996.

Kennedy Runs for President

BY LATE 1967 I had long outstayed John Douglas's admonition to remain on the Hill for no more than two years. Now my only thought of leaving was if Kennedy didn't run for president. With the escalation of the war and the crisis in the cities, his role had long since transcended that of the junior senator from New York. Hostility to President Johnson was mounting across the country, and Kennedy was being urged to run by dear friends and by people he had never met. Taught from the time he was a child not to take on battles he couldn't win, he was also deeply disturbed by the wrenching divisions in the country and he passionately opposed the direction of Johnson's policies abroad and at home.

He knew where I stood but I didn't explicitly put in my little two-cents' worth until the end of the year, when we were in California for hearings of a new special committee he had persuaded Senator Mansfield to create, to look into the education of Indian children. We had dinner with Jesse Unruh, perhaps the most powerful Democratic leader in the state, known as Big Daddy in his earlier years, when he was a hundred or so pounds heavier. Kennedy's purpose was to see if Unruh would endorse him if he ran. Unruh danced around the subject for two hours, finally committing himself only to take a poll for Kennedy to see how things stood in the state. As we walked out, Kennedy said to me, "In the old days I would have left Larry O'Brien there to keep talking. He could talk the balls off a brass monkey." (Larry O'Brien, one of JFK's key political operatives, had stayed on with Lyndon Johnson.)

I thought it was time to say something. So I said that I thought he should run for president. He said something to the effect that he knew how I felt, and then added, "You know, I don't have anyone to do for me what I did for my brother."

The first few weeks of 1968 were excruciating. At the end of

January Kennedy told a journalists' breakfast that he would not be a candidate under any foreseeable circumstances, and then walked out the door to discover that news of the Viet Cong's devastating Tet offensive had come over the wire while he had been speaking. As February wore on, Richard Goodwin, a long-time Kennedy associate and friend who had gone to work in New Hampshire for Senator Eugene McCarthy, began calling our office with reports of how well McCarthy was doing. McCarthy had become the antiwar candidate in late 1967 when Kennedy didn't jump in. The response to McCarthy confirmed the RFK staff's view that the boss had made a big mistake, and cast a pall over the office.

In early February Cesar Chavez started a hunger strike to express the depth of his concern over working conditions in the fields and the recalcitrance of the growers. His staff called me to let us know, and then, as the days passed, to say that they were worried about him and that maybe Kennedy could do something to get him to break the fast. I kept Kennedy posted, and he talked to Cesar once or twice. Cesar finally agreed that he would break the fast if Kennedy came out to be with him when he did. We figured out that Kennedy could go to California on March 10, the day after he gave a scheduled speech in Des Moines. No one mentioned anything about the obvious political aspect of what we were doing. The proposition that only Kennedy could get Chavez to break his fast and then only by showing up was a bit transparent, to say the least, but Kennedy never let on that he saw it as anything but a mission to support his friend.

The time came, and I was modestly surprised to see John Seigenthaler, Kennedy's former top aide in the Justice Department and now editor of the *Nashville Tennesseean*, show up in Des Moines to join us for the California trip, and then to see Ed Guthman, Kennedy's press secretary at Justice and now national news editor of the *Los Angeles Times,* join us in L.A. On the small charter plane to Delano, two days before the New Hampshire primary, Kennedy told us that he had decided to run for president. I was of course ecstatic, but, characteristically, the celebratory statements were brief and understated, and we immediately turned to operational matters.

Why did Kennedy decide to run? The crass answer is that the poll numbers coming out of New Hampshire showed him it was politically possible. But he knew it was not going to be easy. It was quite possible that he had waited too long. Many of the most committed people had signed on with McCarthy, and would not only refuse to switch now but would be furious with Kennedy for jumping in only after McCarthy had tested the water, and would blame Kennedy for dividing the anti-Johnson vote. He never said so to me, but he must have been painfully conscious of the consequences of his indecisiveness. Yet it is also true that he decided to run because he believed he would be the best leader for the country at an incredibly difficult time, and that he thought the hostility would dissipate once he had defeated McCarthy and demonstrated he was the strongest antiwar candidate. Yes, he ran because he decided he could win — that was part of who he was. But perhaps he also decided to run because he had finally concluded that losing in a just cause was not such a terrible thing.

The Campaign

AN AMAZING AMOUNT happened fast. Campaign headquarters had to be located, staff had to be hired, papers had to be filed for all primaries for which deadlines had not already passed, money had to be raised, and on and on. I was to be the issues director, coordinating the staff in Washington, and Walinsky would go on the plane to write speeches, along with Jeff Greenfield, who had joined us in the summer of 1967 upon graduation from Yale Law School.

We were ready on the issues. Kennedy had positions and proposals on an exceptional array of subjects. Adam and Jeff and I and a couple of others knew his thinking and, except for the rhetoric and the response to new events and attacks, could handle much of the day-to-day stuff by recycling things already in the can. That didn't mean that people wouldn't be working twenty or twenty-one hours a day, or even more sometimes.

The campaign has been fully covered by others: a dizzying series of events occurring at a pace that would be rejected by a publisher as wildly implausible if submitted as a work of fiction — Kennedy's announcement on March 16, President Johnson's withdrawal barely two weeks later, Dr. King's assassination four days after that, and Robert Kennedy's assassination a little over two months later. I began by spending the largest part of my time on the phone with Adam and Jeff at all hours of the day and night, and digging up the material they wanted for speeches. I also organized and supervised a staff, put out daily statements on issues not included in the Senator's speeches, developed a network of volunteer policy advisers around the country, and started preparing a series of policy papers that would sum up his proposals. In April, after Dr. King's death, I left my Washington perch and joined Adam and Jeff on the road, replacing myself with Bill Smith, from Senator Clark's staff.

Most of my memory of the campaign is of writing speeches and press releases in hotel rooms in Indiana, Nebraska, Oregon, and California. I came up for air mainly to see Marian. We were in Washington having dinner at the Cosmos Club with federal appeals court judge David Bazelon when Dr. King was killed. We went together to Atlanta for the funeral, where we joined the Senator in a meeting with black leaders and then walked together in the funeral procession. Marian and I went with RFK to Walter Fauntroy's church in Washington the Sunday after the funeral, as the city still smouldered. (I burned out my clutch following RFK as he walked up Ninth Street after the service.)

Marian and I were with Kennedy in the zoo in Portland, Oregon, when he was told that Eugene McCarthy had entered the zoo from the opposite side and was heading his way. Kennedy fled the zoo rather than encounter McCarthy. He had a lot of trouble coming to grips with the simple idea that if he and McCarthy were running for the same office they were competing in the same ring. He had little regard for his opponent's record as a senator, and there was some personal history. If simply greeting McCarthy civilly in the zoo was something he could not bring himself to do, it becomes more understandable, although not more excusable, that he refused to enter into direct debate with McCarthy until his loss to him in Oregon made it unavoidable.

RFK's campaign was a mission of national reconciliation — to end the war in Vietnam on honorable terms, and to reconcile the races at home. This meant, in particular, attacking racial isolation and economic disparity in America's cities. By 1967 things had worsened, with the riots in Newark, Detroit, and many other places, as well as an increasingly unsympathetic public. The Johnson administration's response had deteriorated accordingly, spurred as well by the growing fiscal constraints of the war. Kennedy had stepped up the intensity and frequency of his public speaking on the subject during the last half of 1967.

The essence of RFK's domestic prescription was jobs. "Work," he said over and over, "is, in a real sense, what this country is all about." Work and not welfare, although he strongly opposed solving the problems of welfare "by slogans — by getting tough — or cutting back, by making the system even more harsh and punitive than it now is." Nor did he propose work in isolation. "Providing a man a job" is "the most important step we can take, [but it] will not improve the schools his children attend or assure that medical care will be available even though he can't afford it. . . . [A]ction on all these matters in concert will build a community."

He talked of "resident-controlled institutions" in the inner city, but emphasized that no program to attack the problems of the inner city can be conducted in the isolation of the ghetto. . . . Jobs, education, health care, housing — all must be provided for the poor where they live or want to live.

On one occasion in late 1967 I accompanied Kennedy to a luncheon with editors and reporters from *Newsweek*. They asked him what he would do about the distress in the inner cities. He said he would call the civic leadership of each city to the White House — white and black, elected and nonelected, business and labor, clergy and lay, academic and philanthropic — and ask them to sit down there, in a room at the White House, and come up with a plan for their city. He said he would then take the plan to all the departments of government to figure out how to get the necessary funding for the part the federal government should play in each city's program. On another occasion he told Frank Mankiewicz, his press secretary, that he would persuade the television networks to show the reality of what it was like to live in the areas where the violence had occurred, and would bring business and community leaders together in each city as he had done in Bedford-Stuyvesant.

Jobs were always at the heart of Kennedy's strategic view. Once, in April, I was with RFK on his way to a speech at Purdue University. I had gone on the bus with Kennedy because I needed some direction on a welfare policy paper. We had one of our shorthand conversations just as we were about to arrive at the campus. He was already standing on the steps by the front door of the bus as we talked. I said, "Senator, we are going to say in the welfare paper that you are for a guaranteed income." He said, "I'm not for a guaranteed income. I'm for guaranteed jobs." I said, "But you're for both. You've said many times that if jobs aren't available or people can't work for one reason or another, there has to be cash help for them with a federally defined minimum level." He said, "I'm not for a guaranteed income." I began to understand. His point was one of emphasis, not of substance. He was not changing his position. He was talking about packaging the ideas so it would be clear that jobs were the paramount aim.

The position paper called it a "myth that all the problems of poverty can be solved by the ultimate extension of the welfare system to guarantee to all, regardless of their circumstances, a certain income paid for by the federal government." Later on, the paper said that "putting our primary emphasis on the guaranteed annual income would also be tremendously wasteful." Then the paper laid out a twelve-point program of welfare reform that included mandatory help for two-parent families and "federal minimum standards for welfare assistance to assure a floor of security for every citizen in need." Kennedy's point was to underscore that cash assistance should be viewed residually, to be available only when all possible efforts to get people into jobs have been made, but there as a safety net nonetheless.

His last position paper, released the Friday before the California primary, was called "A Program for the Urban Crisis," and summed up the development of Kennedy's thinking over the previous four years, with more than thirty specific policy proposals.

The program was broken down into five areas: employment, housing, education, health care, and law enforcement. Nearly everything in it was something Kennedy had proposed (or had accomplished in some form) over the previous four years. It contemplated extensive federal spending, but it also called for the participation of private business and for strong law enforcement, and was not traditionally liberal in emphasizing community resident participation in planning and carrying out initiatives.

The list of proposals began with an "emergency" proposal, which he had cosponsored in the Senate, to create 2.4 million jobs, half in public and half in private employment, in order to build and staff needed community facilities and do other needed tasks. He reiterated his proposal of tax incentives, capital loans, and technical assistance for private business activity in or near poverty areas, both urban and rural. He mentioned some adult education and training ideas from earlier speeches. He proposed assistance — from transportation subsidies to pension portability — to help people get to distant jobs, to move closer to where jobs were located, and to change jobs without risking their savings. He suggested consolidation of fragmented federal, state, and local manpower programs. And he proposed jobs for welfare recipients and other welfare reform ideas.

Kennedy's housing proposals were equally far reaching. He restated the substance of a pending bill that would provide incentives for private developers and community organizations to do low-income housing. He proposed subsidies to help public-housing and other lower-income tenants to become homeowners, steps to cut down on application delays under various federal housing programs, and support for getting minorities into construction trade unions.

The education proposals would be equally relevant today. He called for more adequate funding of Head Start and federal education programs, and then said funding was not enough. He suggested testing, research and development, and "experimental . . . competitive schools" that would encourage innovation and be "a yardstick for measuring the effectiveness of our schools." The latter idea, never fully developed although mentioned by Kennedy many times, is essentially the same as today's idea for charter schools — independent public schools given the same operating funds as a comparable public school. He also suggested that parents take classes for adults at their children's school and serve as classroom aides. He wanted to make schools into "full-time centers of community activity."

Kennedy called for neighborhood health centers and satellite clinics, new health careers, recruitment of minorities into all health fields, construction aid for hospitals and clinics, assistance

to medical schools that took steps "to expand, recruit more minority students, and involve themselves more extensively in the
community," and public-health measures "to improve the conditions which lead to poor health." Examples of these included
controlling air pollution, unsafe drivers, and unsafe cars, and reducing the number of children who start smoking.

The law enforcement section was closer to today's ideas of
community policing than the posturing that results in ever longer
sentences and more and more prisons. Kennedy said effective law
enforcement requires adequate pay and training for police; research and dissemination of knowledge about modern law enforcement techniques; better training for correctional, parole, and
probation officers; federal aid for halfway houses to help young
people charged with minor offenses readjust to the community;
new efforts against organized crime; citizen participation in law
enforcement; and improved police cooperation with communities, through integration, location of substations "in the ghetto,"
and "listening to what communities have to say."

While some of the urban-crisis paper was fiscally impractical,
and some of it skated over complex problems of changing bureaucracies and institutions, it comprised a sophisticated set of proposals that reflected Kennedy's own education in these matters.

Unfortunately, the last significant public exchange Kennedy
had on these subjects — his televised debate with Senator Eugene McCarthy on June 1, three days before the California primary — saw him politicize his position in an unattractive way.
McCarthy, smarting somewhat from the resignation of a couple
of his campaign aides after he had refused to campaign in the
black community in Milwaukee during the Wisconsin primary a
few weeks earlier, made a major pitch for residential desegregation. Kennedy, bruised from his loss to McCarthy in the Oregon
primary a few days earlier and wanting to score political points,
accused McCarthy of wanting to transport to Orange County a
large number of blacks who were unprepared to live there. He

said his own proposals for inner-city development would result in a more realistic process of desegregation, with people not moving to the suburbs until they were in an economic position to do so. There was a logic to this statement, but it was inconsistent with what he had said before, and it was framed to draw suburban votes to him as the less threatening candidate on racial issues. Kennedy's young staffers, myself included, were angry at him, and hurt.

Five days later he was dead.

The Legacy

WHAT DID ROBERT KENNEDY leave us that we could choose to live by? A passion for justice is one way to put it. A fierce commitment to make a difference is another. A genuine love for children, all children, would tie everything together.

Kennedy was an early believer in what we now call community empowerment, but he also believed that community-directed development requires outside resources. He promoted a partnership between the outside business community in New York City and the community leadership in Bedford-Stuyvesant, at the same time making sure that the actual decisions about plans were made by a community-controlled board. He knew that while the partnership could assist with know-how and expertise, it would not produce enough funding, so he asked Congress to support these neighborhood revitalization efforts.

RFK was not a promoter of devolution in the sense of block grants without accountability, but rather looked for ways to get federal money to the grassroots without its passing through the hands of governors or mayors who might play politics with it and keep it from reaching the most meritorious (if obstreperous) organizations and people on the street.

No one has ever found the perfect (or even really satisfactory) way to get federal funds to where they will do the most documentable good, but Kennedy understood better than today's politicians that federalism needs to be diverse and even kaleido- scopic. There should not be one direct route of federal to state to whomever but rather a variety of relationships, some with states, some with cities and counties, and some with nonprofit and community-based organizations, creating an atmosphere of con- structive tension. Kennedy knew the federal government didn't have all the answers, but he also knew it had deep pockets, and he believed in making federal funds available to help solve the prob- lems of poverty from the bottom up. More than anyone else, he understood the need for integrated and multiple strategies.

Some current revisionists have tried to paint Kennedy as a conservative. Ronald Steel, a respected scholar, has undertaken to "deconstruct" the RFK "myth." I don't think there is a myth to deconstruct. RFK was a man who grew every day, a man who was still developing and evolving until the day he died. Obviously he never became president. Obviously his life was incomplete. Many of us project important contributions that we think he would have made from what we know about what he did do. Doing so is not to create a myth. Our projections are grounded in experi- ence. We knew the man.

Was Robert Kennedy a "conservative"? No, but he was not afraid to stand for what some might call conservative personal values in a way that has always made some on the Left uncom- fortable. If, however, conservative means antigovernment in gen- eral or anti-national government in particular, that was not Robert Kennedy. He was a strong supporter of longstanding na- tional government responsibilities like the minimum wage, anti- trust laws, and protection of labor union organizing, as well as Medicare, civil rights laws, and prosecution of organized crime and labor racketeers. If conservative means the kind of law en- forcement that metes out justice with a nightstick, followed by ever longer prison terms, that was not Robert Kennedy. He be- lieved in law and order, not as code words with racial overtones (although he used the phrase in the Indiana primary, to the consternation of some of us on his staff) but in the sense of justice; he understood deeply and profoundly that we cannot arrest our way out of the problem of crime.

He was a work in progress. He didn't have all of the details worked out. His journey was truly unfinished, in so many ways. But he was defining anew the complex relationships among government, community, families, and individuals. He saw both the problems and the remedies with a wholeness that is extremely rare.

Would he have become president? Of course no one can say, but I think so. I believe some key Democratic leaders would have endorsed him following his victory in California, believing not so much in what he stood for but in his ability to remove the stain of Vietnam, which they feared would drag the Democrats to defeat in November.

What difference would it have made if he had been elected? For one thing, Richard Nixon would not have been elected president in 1968 and there probably would have been no Watergate. The Vietnam War would surely have been brought to an end far sooner, with far less cost in lives and resources.

How much progress would we have made on race and poverty? That is much harder to divine. Every step he took would have used up some of his political capital. Ending the Vietnam War would have been divisive, just as pursuing it was divisive. Serious work on race and poverty would have been enormously difficult and politically costly, and addressing their intersection is harder yet. But we know he would have tried. And that is what we lost when he was taken from us.

We can honor his memory by learning from him now. I have done so for over thirty years. Everything I suggest here is informed by my experience with him. Some of the details are different, and there are some things that he didn't understand as fully as he would have if he had lived longer. Some things have happened that no one foresaw, and other experiences offer lessons, too. He didn't see, for example, the importance of getting people to jobs in the suburbs even though they continue to live in the inner city, and he didn't see the need to provide income assistance to people already working. But the values are fundamentally the same, and so is the commitment.

He was both an idealist and a realist. He was tough and determined, and he had a record to show for it. But he was soft and sweet and dreamy, too, especially in his last years, and a real comfort when he saw someone's need for support.

Of course he had his faults. His intensity could be unsettling even to those close to him, and infuriating to those he decided were blocking change, including a substantial number who did not deserve the rough treatment he could mete out. He could be impatient and judgmental. His loyalty to people who had been helpful in the past, especially those who had helped elect JFK, could be excessive. His quick reactions sometimes produced hasty judgments. There are episodes in his history and things he did that were misguided or just plain wrong. But much of the debate that swirls around him is simplistic — people who say he worked for Joe McCarthy and that's all we need to know. That line of argument leaves out years of later history.

The very fact that there are people who care so much and are so determined to make things happen, even people who run for office, should be an inspiration that gives us a renewal of hope. But Robert Kennedy has left us more than that. He taught us of the power and responsibility of people to act individually and together, for themselves and their families and one another, in their communities, and through their government at all levels. But above all, he was an optimist. He believed we can make a difference. That was at the heart of his vision.

3

FROM KENNEDY TO CLINTON
The Two Americas Diverge Further

INSTEAD OF RFK, Humphrey. Instead of Humphrey, Nixon. The Vietnam War continued. Watergate happened. America took a different course.

But not just Nixon. There were huge changes in the American economy that began to emerge clearly with the first Arab oil shock, in 1973. A racially tinged offensive against the poor acquired momentum as the decades passed. The refrain is familiar by now: It's *their* fault. It's *their* behavior. *Those* people. *They* have to change. *They* have to take responsibility for themselves.

Maybe if there had been no Vietnam, or if Johnson had responded better to the urban violence, we would have had sustained progress against poverty after the sixties. Maybe we would still have had the public policy and community commitment that are needed to help people escape poverty. Maybe those purveying the idea of an innate culture of poverty and welfare dependency would have had less raw material and a less responsive audience for their arguments. Maybe we would never have had Nixon as president.

American poverty was actually quite different in 1970 from what it was in 1960. Most important, there was a lot less of it — the poverty rate was cut almost in half in the sixties. Much of the reduction came from the prosperity of the period, but the important point is that it happened. Poor communities became a lot more visible, too — to some extent because television had showed them burning to the ground, but more so because the sixties had produced new leaders who spoke up, ran for office, and often gradually joined the larger power structure (sometimes forgetting where they came from). Legal-services lawyers, added in the sixties, were important, too, bringing the case of the poor, individually and in groups, to sympathetic courts for help.

Nixon set a different tone, not uninterested in the social safety net but indifferent at best to the inner city. On his watch the politics of poverty began turning into one of blame — more specifically a politics of crime and, later on, of welfare, all racially charged and highly negative. The debate gradually shifted. Those pointing to structural problems of economics, race, gender, and schooling dwindled in number and found less receptive audiences. As the years passed, the alternative aims gelled: lock up the black men and tell the black women to go and get a job.

The transformation is nowhere more evident than in the way we respond to low-income young people, especially young men and boys of color, who are accused of crime. We do badly enough at offering schooling and community supports to children growing up in poverty, but our policies toward those who enter the labyrinthine world of the justice system, never terribly successful, have deteriorated even more.

I experienced the shifting ground firsthand when I became youth corrections commissioner in New York State, in 1975. Handed a mandate to reform the juvenile-justice system, I collided with the emerging backlash against crime, especially crimes committed by young black and Latino men. At the time, I thought the sensationalized coverage of juvenile crime in the New York City media was just a local phenomenon. I didn't fully understand that this was part of a larger reaction.

I now see how it all fits together. More effective law enforcement was certainly needed against the increased youth crime that appeared in the early seventies, but the destructive synergism between audience-hungry media and vote-hungry politicians produced policies that would give us the huge growth in prison populations we have now. Much of this could have been prevented by a big enough investment in education, prevention, and jobs.

Since 1968, our efforts to reduce poverty have basically gone downhill. The Kerner Commission, appointed by President Johnson to report on the causes of the urban unrest and what should be done about it, warned that we were moving toward being permanently divided racially into two societies. Now we have also become two societies in another way. There are the poor and the near poor, and there are the rest of us.

True, Nixon presided over innovation and expansion in benefits programs that many of today's Republicans would love to dismantle, and proposed a welfare reform plan that was in some ways positively radical even then, because it would have guaranteed an income at about three-fifths of the poverty line to all families in need. He supported and signed legislation that indexed Social Security to inflation and that enacted an important new program of income support for the elderly poor and the disabled, a huge expansion of food stamps, major help to low-income renters, grants to lower-income people to help them obtain college educations, and a job program for the poor. Medicare and Medicaid spending went up significantly. These policy gains may have been the product of leftover liberal politics of the sixties and Democratic majorities in Congress, abetted by Nixon's greater interest in foreign than in domestic policy, but they happened nonetheless.

On the other hand, Nixon tried to dismantle the War on Poverty, the individual pieces of which were saved only because Congress wanted them saved. In his aborted second term he tried to dismantle even more programs for the poor, and he walked away from his own welfare plan.

Nixon also tried to slow down the pace of school desegregation, and did nothing to attack frontally the problems of the inner cities. Although Nixon actually invented affirmative action — Secretary of Labor George Shultz's Philadelphia Plan represents another fact today's Republicans want to forget — that was something of an aberration. Daniel Patrick Moynihan, working in Nixon's White House, tried to put the most positive spin on Nixon's overall approach to race when he wrote a highly publicized memorandum counseling "benign neglect" on racial matters. White America was tired of the racial confrontations, tired of the "in your face" militancy that had overtaken the conciliatory strains of "We Shall Overcome." Moynihan counseled framing issues in nonracial terms.

Benign neglect might have been comparatively good if it had actually been the policy. At the time, I had the image of National Guard tanks ringing the ghetto with the message "Don't come out and we won't come in. You can do whatever you want to each other in there as long as you stay there." Nobody ever said that in so many words, of course, but that was what the idea of benign neglect seemed to say. And we now know that at the time the FBI and its Cointelpro program were busy infiltrating black-militant groups as well as antiwar activists and campus radicals.

Meanwhile, the national economy soured. Structural changes in the economy accelerated. The disappearance of manufacturing jobs, the energy crisis, and the seemingly endless and quite mysterious combination of simultaneous high inflation and high unemployment damaged millions. The economic squeeze created anger and resentment for demagogues to exploit, and cynicism grew about the capacity of government to do anything effective about anything. By the time 1980 rolled around, the economic vise of the seventies had squeezed out the socially progressive momentum of the sixties. Robert Kennedy or Hubert Humphrey would have tried harder to cushion the effects of these changes, but they would have had an impact regardless of who was president. Along with the Ayatollah, they helped to destroy Jimmy Carter's presidency.

President Carter presided over the end of an era. The American people may not have known that what they wanted next was Ronald Reagan, but they were happy to have him. However unfairly in retrospect, Carter seemed the exemplar of inept leadership, between the economy and the mishandling of the hostage situation in Iran. Coming on top of Vietnam and Watergate, the failings of Carter gave encouragement to the backlash against government. When Reagan said "government *is* the problem," millions of Americans nodded in agreement.

The Reagan-Bush period intensified the simplistic retreat from Washington that began with Nixon. The attack that Nixon began in his second term, and that Reagan revived and extended, was based on the premise that no government at all would be better in domestic social-welfare policy.

President Reagan did not succeed fully. He wanted deep budget cuts and a massive transformation of federal programs into block grants, but achieved only the budget cuts. His opponents found themselves mainly fighting off attacks, until the end of the decade, when the Democrats regained control of Congress. For others, the action, such as it was, was in communities, on issues of neighborhood revitalization, and at the state level debating welfare.

After the serious setbacks of the Reagan period, Congress enacted expansions of health coverage for poor children in the late eighties, a worthwhile child care initiative in 1990, and some constructive legislation during Clinton's first two years in office. The most important of these was a big increase in income assistance for working poor people, using the Earned Income Tax Credit, which had been put into place in the mid-seventies while Gerald Ford was president.

Meanwhile, the issue of concentrated poverty had become

even more pressing. When neighborhoods face a certain level of chronic joblessness, with everything that goes with it, a destructive synergism sets in. Where too many people are poor, too many people stop even trying to find work — especially men. Too many men simply disappear — and too often to prison. Too many young people, having attended inferior schools to begin with, get discouraged or succumb to the blandishments of the street, or arrive at a prospective employer's doorstep with deep hostility.

Never mind that most of these problems were on the increase in the white community as well. Never mind that unemployment and underemployment in inner cities, and among African American and Latino young people in particular, were very nearly off the charts. Never mind that changes in the economy coupled with hiring discrimination and awful inner-city schools were leaving behind huge numbers to become more isolated and disconnected as time passed. Economic and racial explanations for negative behavior lost their appeal. Blaming welfare for the problems became more and more attractive. Talking about a "culture of poverty" became more and more fashionable. Sometimes the issue was given a black face — as with Willie Horton in 1988 — and sometimes people only needed to speak in a code that everyone understood.

If economics and racism are behind the problem, the main remedies are a complex and costly mix of jobs and education and antidiscrimination measures (and steps to address the negative behavior). If too much welfare is the cause, the remedy is easy: end welfare (and deal with the rest of the mess by wholesale imprisonment). Remove all public assistance and make people take responsibility for themselves. Cold turkey. Sink or swim.

Where were the liberals while all this was occurring? They were having some success in changing particular public policies, but they never described the structural changes in the economy in terms that adequately explained why people across a wide income spectrum were losing ground at such a rapid rate. They left the field too open to those who were blaming welfare for everything.

By the time the nineties began, the simple explanation and the simple remedy were on their way to winning the public relations battle. The public debate over poverty was now cast almost totally in terms of welfare. No one could deny the bad behavior. But instead of confronting the behavior and the underlying problems with a mix of public policy, community responsibility, and an insistence on personal responsibility — as Robert Kennedy would have — too many liberals accepted the caricatures of themselves as big spenders, advocates of big government, and apologists for immoral and criminal behavior. They began inventing formulations like the Third Way that grew into abdications of public responsibility. The problem cried out for practical, nontraditional, nonideological answers. Instead, the whole debate moved to the right, with the conservatives pressing the hot buttons in the control room.

The Rise of the American Ghetto

BEGINNING AS EARLY as the fifties, urban manufacturing jobs moved to the suburbs, rural areas, and overseas, or were lost to technological change. African Americans, however, were not able to follow the jobs because of a much older problem: discrimination. Black ghettoes initially formed in cities because of discriminatory government policies. The Federal Housing Administration, the Veterans Administration, and private lending institutions were explicitly racist in their lending policies. In fact, their actions were blatantly unconstitutional. The Federal Home Loan Bank Board and the federal Home Owners' Loan Corporation worked hand in glove with local bankers and real estate brokers not only to prevent blacks from buying in white neighborhoods but also to prevent financing for building or buying even in black neighborhoods — rated "hazardous" by federal appraisers solely on the basis of their racial composition. All of this was official policy until well into the sixties.

Decisions about where to locate public housing and who could live in it were equally discriminatory. Highway and other transportation policy decisions, coupled with rules like banning home building on small suburban lots, may not have reflected discriminatory intent, but, illegal or not, nonetheless helped keep both residential areas and workplaces segregated. And job bias was as endemic as housing discrimination.

Starting in the late sixties, a new federal fair housing law, new public attitudes, and a growing black middle class allowed some African Americans to move to the suburbs, but it was never easy and still isn't. They still encounter discrimination from sellers and still have a harder time getting financing and insurance. So not everyone who could afford to and wanted to move did, and people who needed a subsidy were totally stuck.

By the mid-sixties, the inner-city ghettoes were tinder boxes. The frustration of parents continually rebuffed in both the job and housing markets began appearing as anger, even rage, in the children. The two decades since World War II had seen phenomenal increases in well-being for everyone around them. The civil rights movement and the passage of new national laws had promised change that had not reached them. The experience of their parents and older brothers and sisters was bitter. They exploded.

In the seventies, the vicious circle continued. The distance of the jobs, continuing discrimination in the job and housing markets, lack of cars, and weak public transit kept poor African Americans penned in the inner city, joined by poor Latinos as the years passed. There was also a huge wealth (and savings) gap between whites and African Americans with similar earnings.

The politicized anger of the sixties gave way in the seventies to random interpersonal violence, most often black on black, and to despair. Too many of the people left behind developed very bad patterns of behavior, involving crime, violence, gangs, drugs and alcohol, dropping out of school, nonmarital births, and too much reliance on welfare. These facts had certainly been there before in some measure, but they got worse.

President Carter had an urban strategy, but it was largely a downtown-renewal approach. The idea was that helping cities to build convention centers and associated hotels would draw other economic activity back into the central city and be of assistance to inner-city people by creating new jobs that they could get. As a part of a larger strategy, this might have been useful. As the centerpiece, it was too limited and too indirect.

The eighties were worse. President Reagan and others gave lip service to enterprise zones that would supposedly stimulate inner-city economic revival, but nothing in federal policy provided the necessary support. The shortage of low-income housing grew drastically worse. The federal government's disappearing act was mitigated by the enactment of the Low Income Housing Tax Credit in 1986, and a very modest infusion of new low-income housing vouchers in 1998 and 1999, but the shortage of affordable housing for low-income renters grew to today's nearly 5 million units.

The federal government's abdication didn't stop people from working at the local level on inner-city poverty. They responded to events by turning inward, focusing within the four corners of their neighborhoods instead of working to connect people to jobs and housing wherever they were. In retrospect one can see that this was a mistake, although an understandable one, and perhaps all that was possible at the time.

The outside world had sent the message that it was unin terested in the inner city poor. The cacophony of black power, following the civil rights movement's anthem of black and white together, implied that the inner city could be revitalized without challenging its isolation. Burned-out areas left from the violence of the sixties enticed community leaders to concentrate on building better structures to replace the ones that had gone up in flames, without pressing for jobs and housing throughout the metropolitan area. Foundations bought the rhetoric of community control and community empowerment without thinking through the dangerous racial and economic isolation that was all too likely to be perpetuated by near-exclusive focus on neighborhood revitalization.

The Kerner Commission had warned in the sixties of the futility of efforts to gild the ghetto, but the attitude of the surrounding white community and the new bravado of some in the black community pushed people into pursuing insular inner-city revitalization efforts. Even a segment of the Republican establishment joined in, although mostly at a level of enthusiastic lip service. They seemed unbothered that their espousal of black capitalism in the inner city walked hand in hand with others' black nationalism.

The black middle class was escaping as fast as it could, leaving behind a population more problem-ridden than ever. A strange alliance of black ideologues and political realists, white social engineers and idealists, and a few capitalists in both communities decided that if isolation was the condition that the outside world had imposed, the problems could be handled in isolation as well.

Inspired in part by RFK's Bedford-Stuyvesant project, inner-city, private, nonprofit community development corporations (CDCs) multiplied greatly in the seventies, growing from something like a hundred in the late sixties to well over two thousand by 1990. Most were tiny entities focused on low-income housing. A few worked on economic development as well, and a very few were genuinely multidimensional, including education, supportive services, and emphasis on creating a greater sense of community identity.

Even as this great expansion was occurring, disquiet was developing among those who began to see that these investments in and of themselves were not reducing the overall levels of poverty or the associated social disintegration. To make matters worse, cities continued to lose jobs and people. Tax bases eroded precipitously.

Three vital pieces were missing in the CDC strategy.

A person might have bought a new or rehabilitated home, but that home too often was an island in a sea of crime, drugs, and trouble of all kinds. A better strategy would have been to also tackle the surrounding environment, with public safety at the top of the list.

Also, CDCs were not doing anything about the supports needed to succeed in the workplace — child care, transit, literacy training, drug and alcohol treatment, and so on. To the extent such services existed in the community at all, they were hard to find and use.

Most important was the noninvolvement of CDCs in helping people get and keep jobs beyond the neighborhood. There were some jobs within communities in the construction and renovation of housing, and there were some jobs in new stores and expanded human-service programs, but the typical CDC did not change the basic economic equation in the neighborhood.

President Clinton took a few steps to help the inner city — Empowerment Zones, limited public-housing reform, enforcement of fair-lending laws, and loans for community development — but, especially with the net negative effects of his so-called welfare reform, there has not been much forward movement.

Welfare — The Thirty Years' War Rages

AS PUBLIC CONCERN about the inner city waned in the seventies, President Nixon's welfare plan died, and the antiwelfare rhetoric that he had adopted to sell it became unambiguously the property of the Right.

The "modern" history of welfare begins with the Social Security Act of 1935, but the concept goes back to the Bible, Roman times, the Elizabethan poor laws, and the early history of American charity. All have contributed to our present attitudes. The 1935 act created the program of Aid to Dependent Children, later changed to Aid to Families with Dependent Children, which we have come to speak of as welfare. It was AFDC that was repealed in 1996.

In the early twentieth century, as states began concluding that they should offer cash help to families considered deserving, they started enacting "mothers' pensions." By 1935 forty-six states had such programs. During the Depression, the states found it impossible to keep up with the need. Revenues declined as the number of people needing assistance rose by the day. When the omnibus legislation that gave us Social Security, unemployment insurance, and a number of other enduring programs came before Congress, the states said they also needed help with their programs for poor mothers and children. And so a federal ADC program came into being.

ADC was to be administered by the states, with benefit levels to be set entirely at the state's discretion. Its statutory language could be read to require assistance to anyone who met its definition of need, but few took that seriously in 1935. The basic sense of the provisions on welfare was that, with very little modification, the federal government was paying part of the bill for the states to continue to do whatever they wanted to do.

It was assumed that ADC would wither away as widows gradually became eligible for Social Security by virtue of their late husbands' jobs. Things didn't work out that way. After World War II many people who had come from the South to work in the war plants were left high and dry, especially African Americans pinned in inner cities by racial segregation. The transition was eased by the postwar backlog of civilian needs, but by the sixties, long-term changes in the configuration of American manufacturing were under way, with jobs leaving cities first for suburbs and other regions, and later going offshore or being displaced by technology. Welfare became the principal legal means of survival for more and more people, disproportionately those of color.

The sixties saw the battle lines over welfare drawn. While the doubling of the welfare rolls from the mid-fifties to the mid-sixties fueled the attack, there were three other factors that, though positive at first, would add to the backlash.

One was the emergence of the welfare rights movement. Inspired by the civil rights movement and community-action activism, welfare recipients organized to demand fair treatment at the welfare office, and to begin a campaign for a national guaranteed income. The long-range strategy, put forward by sociologists Richard Cloward and Frances Fox Piven, was to put so many people on the rolls that states and local governments, strapped to pay their matching share of the cost, would demand a national solution.

Second, poor people, including welfare recipients, started being represented through the legal-services program created as part of the War on Poverty, and the lawyers began to sue welfare offices to make them live up to the words of the federal law.

And third, the Supreme Court — liberalized by the addition of Arthur Goldberg and, after him, Abe Fortas — responded positively to welfare recipients in a number of landmark cases. These decisions didn't reach the key issue of whether the Constitution guaranteed people some basic level of income, but the Court's new responsiveness gave the reformers hope that it would before long.

The convergence of these forces meant that by the end of the sixties welfare had become a real statutory right instead of simply a program by which local bureaucrats could help those they liked. But the states could still set benefit levels as they pleased. Welfare reformers sought a right to an adequate income, whether found in the Constitution or declared by statute, with the only criterion for assistance being need: not marital status, not minor children at home, not capacity to work — nothing but need.

As the seventies got under way, the prospects for a radical progressive transformation of the welfare system seemed good to the activists, despite unfriendly noises in Congress. But the reformers, seeking a guaranteed income, couldn't see the forest for the trees as the economy went bad in 1973, and never dealt with the huge numbers of working people being badly hurt by the structural changes in the economy.

President Nixon astonished many by proposing a guaranteed income. Not that his proposal was perfect. In fact, it produced a split on the Left, between those who said it was a step forward and should be enacted as a first step and those who said it was hopelessly flawed.

Combined with food stamps, it would have produced an income floor at about 60 percent of the poverty line, which would have raised benefits in about twenty states. It also required participation in work or training as a condition of receiving benefits, unless there was a good reason, such as lack of child care. It would have guaranteed assistance to all families with children; fathers would no longer have to leave home so their children could get help.

President Nixon also proposed combining welfare programs for the aged, blind, and disabled, which, like AFDC, had allowed states to set benefit levels, into a single program with a national benefit floor considerably more generous than what he was proposing for needy families. This, again, had been a longstanding aim of reformers.

I started out with those who favored accepting Nixon's proposal as a foundation upon which to build, and ended with those who said it was hopelessly flawed. In retrospect, I fear I was right the first time. When the late Carl Holman, godfather to our son Jonah and a senior official at the National Urban Coalition, asked me what stand the Coalition should take, I suggested cautious support, combined with an effort to improve the legislation as it moved through the still-Democratic and largely liberal Congress. They followed this course.

George Wiley, the Ph.D. chemist turned civil rights leader turned welfare rights leader, also a friend, was at the forefront of those who said Nixon's Family Assistance Plan was hopelessly inadequate. The National Welfare Rights Organization was proposing a guaranteed income of $5,500 for a family of four, about 30 percent higher than the poverty line (and the equivalent of about $21,000 today). That was widely regarded as a fringe proposal, more for show than for action. Robert Kennedy had taught me to be practical, so I told George I favored the Urban Coalition's approach.

In the spring of 1970 I withdrew from active involvement in the issue, because my old boss, Arthur Goldberg, had decided to run for governor of New York, and needed help. Steve Smith, Robert Kennedy's brother-in-law and key New York political operative, had gotten Goldberg to run and was desperate to create a campaign organization. Steve implored me to get involved.

Goldberg lost badly and I came back to Washington. In the meantime, Nixon's welfare proposal, somewhat weakened, had passed the House, and was pending in the Senate. The Finance Committee was about to mark up a version that was even less progressive. Also in the meantime, George Wiley and his colleagues had invaded the Department of Health, Education and Welfare and taken over the offices of Secretary Robert Finch. George was pictured in the press sitting in Finch's inner office with his feet planted casually on the Secretary's desk. This was not my style; I disapproved of the action, as did a large segment of the public.

George said he needed me to get involved in defeating FAP. I reminded him that I had been in favor of enacting it and improving on it. He said he knew that but that he thought the framework and context had changed in important negative ways. He reminded me that Nixon had centered his campaigning for

Congressional candidates on a theme of getting after the dead-beats on welfare, and George thought this tone foreshadowed the final result; any bill would be a step or more backward. Neither the House bill nor the pending Senate bill was as good as Nixon's original proposal, and I knew from experience that the conservative House-Senate conference would produce the worst combination possible.

So I joined with George. We persuaded Senator Fred Harris of Oklahoma, a member of the Finance Committee, to take up our cause. A number of the most conservative Republicans on the committee, led by John Williams of Delaware (known as whispering John because he spoke so softly), already opposed the bill as too generous. Our task was to persuade the liberals (Eugene McCarthy of Minnesota, Ralph Yarborough of Texas, Vance Hartke of Indiana, Abe Ribicoff of Connecticut, Gaylord Nelson of Wisconsin, and one or two others) that the bill was fatally flawed and did not represent a foundation on which to build. Neither the conservatives nor the liberals could bottle up the bill in committee by themselves. Together, in unholy alliance, they could.

Fred Harris had succeeded the legendary Robert Kerr in representing Oklahoma, and because of that had been given a seat on the powerful Finance Committee. The occasional liberal was allowed on the Finance Committee, but only if he or she took a blood oath never to cross the chairman, such as by advocating a reduction in the oil-and-gas-depletion allowance.

Fred Harris was not thought to be a liberal, anyway. Such people didn't get elected in Oklahoma, and he looked, walked, and talked like a good ol' boy. So it was expected that he would take up where his mentor left off. He and his then-wife, La Donna, quickly became friends with Bob and Ethel Kennedy, and he began compiling a voting record as a national rather than parochial Democrat. He was a terrific politician, so he acquired a wide circle of friends and ended up after only three years as chair of the Democratic National Committee. Robert and Ethel Kennedy

(Ethel even more than the Senator, as I remember) were livid when Harris stayed in the Johnson-Humphrey camp in 1968.

Harris kept getting more liberal. By the time he ran his somewhat quixotic populist campaign for president in 1976, some thought he did so at least in part because he didn't have a prayer of getting re-elected as an Oklahoma senator and wanted to go out in style.

George Wiley and I began showing up in Fred Harris's office every afternoon at about five to drink bourbon and go over the day's events. The Senate was in a lame-duck, post-election session, and a Finance Committee vote on Nixon's welfare bill was contemplated in a week or two. George's people were writing and phoning the key senators' offices. At one point we organized a rump hearing and invited all our target Democrats to hear from grassroots people about the terrible damage that would be done if the bill were enacted. All of this had its effect, and by the time the Committee vote came, the unholy alliance of conservatives and some liberals had formed and killed the bill.

That was not the end of FAP, but it was the beginning of the end. Nixon sent up a new version in 1971, more conservative than the one we had killed, which in turn was more conservative than Nixon's original proposal. The 1971 version would have raised benefits in ten states rather than twenty. It had no requirement that the states offer a supplementary program to make sure total benefits didn't end up lower than they had been under the old program. It also had far fewer procedural protections against unfairness in compelling recipients to work.

Once again the House passed a more stringent version and the Senate considered a package even further right. Those liberals who had disagreed with us in the previous fight began to peel away from the bill. Elliot Richardson, the secretary of HEW, saw things falling apart and tried to enlist Senator Ribicoff in pushing a compromise that would hold enough liberals to pass a bill. By now, however, Bob Haldeman and John Ehrlichman, Nixon's top aides in the White House, had come to understand what was going on. No longer neophytes, they saw people within the Nixon camp pushing what was, to say the least, a rather uncharacteristic piece of legislation in their boss's name, and they told Richardson to cut it out.

So, in the end, Nixon killed his own bill, or at least administered the final blow. One important thing came out of it, though. While welfare reform died, Supplemental Security Income, or SSI, was born. It combined the aged, blind, and disabled welfare categories into a national program, which is today a fully accepted and valuable part of the limited safety net remaining. The committees pulled SSI out from the dying FAP legislation and reported it as a separate bill, which they then enacted. It was a classic "sleeper," an important proposal that had received almost no attention because it had been buried in an omnibus bill in which something else had drawn all the flak. Medicaid was enacted in the same way in 1965, buried alongside Medicare in the same measure. It's a great strategy if one could only figure how to do it deliberately instead of accidentally.

As I said, I have changed my mind about FAP, or at least the version we defeated in the fall of 1970. There is no way of knowing, of course, but I think that if we had enacted even the more conservative Senate version of that year we would have had in place a guaranteed floor for all families with children. No doubt efforts to make the system more punitive would have been made over the years, but it would have been Nixon's domestic equivalent of going to China, and the accelerating momentum to turn the whole thing into a block grant and install time limits might have been less likely to develop in the way it did.

On the other hand, the country's politics moved to the right for other reasons and in other ways, so it is impossible to know whether FAP would have survived even if it had been enacted. George Wiley took as the lesson of FAP that organizing around welfare issues was too narrow. He perceived that dealing with broader economic inequalities would engage a bigger group. He was organizing a Movement for Economic Justice when he died in a boating accident, in 1973.

While all of this was happening in 1972, Senator George McGovern surprised the Democratic Party and the country by taking the nomination away from the consensus favorite, Senator Edmund Muskie (with a little help from the Nixon dirty tricks operation). McGovern had been a good friend of Robert Kennedy. I admired him greatly, but I wanted to be practical and, with McGovern initially at 5 percent in the polls, ran as an alternate Muskie delegate in Massachusetts.

In the spring of 1972, Senator McGovern announced a proposal to provide $1,000 a year to every man, woman, and child in the United States, with a family's earnings to result in loss of a dollar of the grant for every three dollars earned. This would have meant the government would be providing $4,000 to four-person families with no other income, and would help on a declining basis until a family's earnings reached $12,000 (a little under $40,000 in current dollars).

George Wiley called. "We have to talk him out of this, Peter," he said. "He's too far out even for me." He thought that McGovern proposed to spend too much on the near poor and not enough on the poor. In any case, McGovern's proposal was definitely regarded as far out. If he hadn't gotten into such deep political trouble for so many other reasons, especially the imbroglio over his selection and deselection of Senator Thomas Eagleton of Missouri as his vice presidential candidate, his guaranteed-income proposal would have met with even more criticism than it did.

I called Frank Mankiewicz, who was managing McGovern's campaign and had been Senator Robert Kennedy's press secretary. He called me back from California, where Senator McGovern was comfortably ahead in the polls prior to the primary there. He said, "There's no urgency about this. We're doing fine. I'll talk to you when I get back east." I thought to myself, "I'm glad you think you're doing fine. I'm not so sure."

Mankiewicz invited me to join a working group that was putting flesh onto McGovern's earlier proposal. At a meeting in New York City, in an apartment in Washington Square, I argued that the proposal didn't do a thing about making jobs available. I said, vehemently, that just giving people cash was terrible public policy, that Senator McGovern should be proposing a jobs program, and that income and jobs proposals had to be carefully combined to keep the incentives straight.

It was an unpleasant meeting that included James Tobin, the Nobel Prize-winning economist from Yale, and Ed Kuh, an MIT professor who had organized Robert Kennedy's group of economic advisers. Economists are economists, even the best ones, and my ideas about jobs were far too messy for the slide-rule elegance and simplicity of their demo-grant plan. I got nowhere.

We were at the beginning of the end of liberal-style welfare reform. President Carter made a proposal that was somewhat like Nixon's FAP, but it didn't get far, and when Ronald Reagan took office, the meaning of "welfare reform" became radically different.

Meanwhile, the Supreme Court was dashing the hopes of those pressing for a judicial declaration of the right to an adequate income. In a series of cases during the early and mid-seventies, the Court said governmental decisions about income distribution were in the same category as economic regulation. They were not subject to any special scrutiny but would be upheld as long as they had a rational basis. Later decisions confirmed that states had no constitutional obligation to provide any particular level of assistance to low-income people. The high hopes that some had found in the apparent implications and tantalizing rhetoric of a series of decisions beginning in the mid-fifties were thoroughly smashed by the mid-seventies.

By the mid-seventies, welfare reform in the sense of an income guarantee was dead. The fundamental economic shifts that were occurring made matters worse. Low-wage jobs took a nose dive from which they have still not recovered. The right response would have been to shore up this end of the job market to make sure people in it were able to escape poverty. Adding to earnings from work, creating more jobs, better public education, skill development, and reducing discrimination should have been on the agenda. Instead, more and more people came to believe that welfare was the problem.

Some argue that liberals brought the backlash on themselves by not pursuing a centrist welfare reform strategy soon enough. The real problem is that liberals, collectively, have not tried hard enough to reduce income gaps. There is no monopoly on elitism, and they have never cared as much about poverty as they do about issues like the environment and civil rights. Too few people focused on the structural problems in the economy and their negative consequences for more than half the American people.

Liberal advocates in the seventies did work to strengthen the safety net, passing a long list of laws that President Nixon signed, and liberal legislators added other forms of protection and assistance whenever they could. But they never placed the same emphasis on jobs that they did on the safety net. The jobs rhetoric of the late sixties eventuated in CETA, the Comprehensive Employment and Training Act of 1973, which at its height was pumping nearly $10 billion annually into job creation. But CETA had political legs only as long as mayors could use it to rehire police and firefighters who had been laid off in local budget crunches. When President Carter succeeded in getting Congress to tighten the rules of eligibility, CETA lost its constituency. It crumbled in 1981, in the face of Reaganaut charges that its funds had been frittered away.

The expansions in programs like SSI, food stamps, and Medicaid did not encompass welfare itself. So all the while the Right was complaining about destructive welfare dependency, welfare, which was not indexed, was steadily losing ground to inflation. By the nineties, welfare payments had lost over 40 percent of their value to inflation. Even when food stamps, which are indexed, were taken into account (as they should be), the package lost over 20 percent of its real value between 1970 and 1990.

The failure of the states to raise AFDC benefits to keep pace with inflation may have been an implicit payback for the welfare activism of the sixties. The states were saying in effect that if we have to help everybody who meets the federal definition of need, we'll just help each applicant less than we did before.

Welfare went through a transitional phase in the eighties. With President Reagan in the White House and Congress more conservative than it had been for decades, the idea of an adequate income was effectively off the table, not mentioned even by Democrats. Welfare reform came to mean welfare-to-work, getting people off welfare, encouraging self-sufficiency. This was not a necessarily bad development, if it meant a genuine effort to help people get and keep jobs, and creating jobs if not enough were available. But that is not what the Reagan-style reformers meant.

The battle lines formed now not over the adequacy of cash assistance but over which policies would get more welfare recipients into the labor market. One might have expected liberals to take up Kennedy's call and argue for a genuine jobs program. Again, however, the unspoken assumption seemed to be that the private sector would produce enough jobs. The Right generally said coercion would suffice. The Left generally said the effort could not succeed without support services like child care, health coverage, and education and training. Nobody addressed the question of where the jobs would come from.

A number of states developed their own programs to move people from welfare to work. The most ambitious was Greater Avenues to Independence (GAIN) in California, which represented a grand compromise between the Democrats and Republicans. The Democrats agreed to the enactment of compulsory work requirements, and the Republicans agreed to invest substantial funds in support services.

GAIN and other state initiatives stimulated a renewed debate in Congress, and in 1988 a bipartisan compromise similar to the one that created GAIN produced the Family Support Act, which President Reagan signed into law. As Governor of Arkansas and a leader among the governors nationally, Bill Clinton was deeply involved in the passage of FSA. It was far from the kind of fundamental reform that had been debated in the seventies, but was not radical in the other direction in the way the 1996 law is. It essentially created a new set of carrots and sticks, including funding, to push recipients in the direction of work. It also embodied for the first time the idea of reciprocity, namely that recipients had responsibilities to fulfill in return for help from the state. Adherents of FSA hoped that, if fully implemented, it would reduce the rolls in a constructive way.

FSA required states to offer welfare to two-parent families but, oddly, for only six months a year. It offered transitional Medicaid and child care assistance to welfare recipients going to work. And it attempted to squeeze absent fathers further to get them to pay child support, an effort that had been going on since the midseventies, without much success.

Unfortunately, FSA went into full effect as the recession of the Bush administration was being felt. The states couldn't afford to come up with the matching funds required to claim their share of the new federal money. The welfare rolls, despite the claim that they would go down because of the new legislation, started rising. The stage was set for the series of events that ended with Bill Clinton signing the 1996 law.

Who "lost China" in the field of welfare? Did the liberals lose by failing to stress work sufficiently, or did the conservatives win for other reasons? I am of the latter persuasion. I have never given the liberals great credit for effectiveness, and I have always been more work oriented than many on the Left. But the country has become more conservative over the past twenty-five years, in large part because of people's sense of economic insecurity. This provided fertile ground for blaming those lower on the economic ladder. The Right's story is much simpler: welfare is the problem. The Left, even if it had been as consistent and vociferous, had a harder story to sell: structural problems in the economy, erosion of the wage base, export of manufacturing jobs, replacement of good jobs with lousy jobs. The simpler story has carried the day.

Not all of the poor have fared badly. The elderly are much better off, and the disabled have made strides, both thanks to positive policy changes. The income floor for the working poor — through the Earned Income Tax Credit, food stamps, and health coverage for their children — is stronger, although still more than offset by weakness in wage levels. Children, people of color, and people living in places of high poverty have been the losers.

It has been deeply troubling to watch the changes in American political culture, both generally and specifically in relation to the entrenched poor. I have been involved at least modestly in nearly every presidential campaign since 1968 and in many Democratic policy groups in between. I have experienced firsthand the political dynamics that have allowed only Democrats who were southerners to be elected President since 1960. I have worked for a presidential candidate whose handlers would not send him into the inner city at a time of day that might make the nightly network news.

And I have seen firsthand, as both participant and observer, the transformation of the politics of poverty into a politics of crime and welfare. It is a long time since we have had a president willing to say, as Lyndon Johnson did in 1967 after his poverty program had become seriously embattled, "We are not backing off from our commitment to fight poverty, nor will we so long as I have anything to say about it."

4

ENTER BILL CLINTON

Aᴀғᴛᴇʀ ᴍʏ ᴇxᴘᴇʀɪᴇɴᴄᴇ with the New York State Division for Youth, I needed to earn some money to pay for our children's college tuition, so in early 1979 I went into private law practice in Washington. Ten months later I jumped ship to run the issues staff for Senator Edward Kennedy's presidential campaign. By 1982 I was on the faculty at Georgetown University Law Center, where I've been since except for my time in the Clinton administration.

The eighties were a selfish time. President Reagan pumped up the economy artificially by running huge deficits — cutting taxes and increasing defense spending. He played covert Keynesian economics in a way that must have made Keynes turn over in his grave. He lined the pockets of defense contractors while doing nothing for average Americans so painfully pinched by continuing changes in the economy, and he injured those at the bottom by cutting deeply into the programs that helped ameliorate their problems. Paul Volcker, put in place by President Carter as chair of the Federal Reserve, was squeezing inflation out of the economy with tight monetary policies that exacerbated the injury felt by working-class and low-income people, and Reagan did nothing to cushion the hurt.

President Reagan's politics were incredibly effective, so positive and cheerfully reassuring in convincing the American people that the problem was government — a code for saying that people at the bottom were the problem. The poor continued to lose ground.

For myself, it was the first decade spent entirely on private payrolls. I stayed active, writing op eds as well as the scholarly articles necessary for academic tenure. I joined a number of nonprofit boards, cofounded a multiservice center for poor youth in Washington, and was founding chair of an organization that uses simulated job applicants to detect discrimination in hiring. I served as an expert witness in litigation challenging conditions in D.C.'s woeful juvenile-corrections system; co-edited a book on youth policy; chaired the New World Foundation and the Center for Community Change; wrote a regular column for the *Legal Times;* went on the national board of Common Cause; and became co-chair of Americans for Peace Now, the U.S. support group for the Israeli peace movement.

I had thought public service had permanently passed me by when, to my surprise, Bill Clinton surmounted steep odds and was elected president. It was a promising time. The public mood seemed to have softened since the Reagan era. The Democrats had gotten the Senate back in 1986, and the Democratic House, after flirting with Reaganism, once again reflected national party goals. It was reasonable to believe that a Democratic president and a Democratic Congress could produce progress that had been impossible for twelve years.

The historian Arthur Schlesinger Jr. wrote that twentieth-century American history ran in thirty-year cycles, with the first decade of the century, the thirties, and the sixties being the progressive periods. Many of us thought the nineties would bring a similar renascence, albeit tempered by the continuing deficits. The Democratic control of Washington seemed to prove Schlesinger right. President Reagan had taken his run at the so-called welfare state and had only limited success. Funding for most federal social programs had been largely restored later in the eighties. The Democrats were back.

I thought the welfare war was over with the bipartisan passage of the Family Support Act of 1988. While its investment in work-related issues was inadequate, it seemed that the politics of the problem had been solved. The Republicans gained recognition for compulsory work and the Democrats gained agreement that money would be appropriated for child care, job training, and other supports. I was somewhat concerned that Clinton had brought the welfare issue up again in his campaign, promising to "end welfare as we know it," but I didn't think it would result in any serious damage.

I had no such illusions about issues concerning the inner city. The deterioration had continued. I could only hope that the Democrats would make something good happen, but I had no particular optimism.

Even though money was tight, I thought, Clinton will stand for a new idealism and project it forcefully across the country. I said to myself, He is more of a centrist than I am, but whatever he believes, it is genuine. As for some of his centrist behavior as governor, it was necessary to survive in that milieu. Besides, he has enormous energy, is really smart, and is serious about governing. He cares about policy, is committed to racial equality, and has a particular concern about children. His wife, whose commitment to children is impeccable, will keep him honest in that realm if he slips. Yes, he has flirted with the revisionists of the Democratic Leadership Council, but that was a tactic to prove that he was a new kind of Democrat. Anyway, some of the DLC rhetoric emphasizing civic involvement is actually attractive.

Whatever the problems, I thought the whole prospect was pretty terrific. More important, so did millions of others. This young and appealing president, with his equally brilliant and attractive wife, had caught the fancy of people everywhere. Visions of Camelot flew through the imaginations of many. After Ronald Reagan and George Bush, the torch had passed once again to a new generation. Young people had dropped everything to work in his campaign in numbers not seen since the New Frontier. Marian and I went to Little Rock on a charter flight on election night and stood outdoors waiting for the triumphant appearance of the President-elect and his wife. We were ecstatic with the election results and carried away by the enthusiasm of the crowd. The evening and the hope of things to come were exhilarating.

I was asked to codirect the transition for the Department of Justice, with Bernie Nussbaum, my law school classmate, who had worked with Hillary on the Nixon impeachment. It took only about three days to sign up over a hundred people for the transition team, all expert in their fields. The sense of expectation was ubiquitous, and there was a bustle and enthusiasm as old friends and allies converged from across the country. Bernie and I were next door to the State Department team and separated by a partition from the education group. The whole government-to-be was within walking distance. We were on the way to a new era.

The inauguration was festive and memorable. Movie stars were everywhere. There were parties from breakfast until the wee hours. I was swamped with calls and résumés dropped on my front porch from people who thought I could get them into the new administration. Advocacy groups sought my advice on how to frame their agendas. The actor Richard Dreyfuss, with whom I had worked on Middle East peace issues, joined me at Aetna general counsel Zoe Baird's confirmation hearings to be attorney general. I introduced him to Senator Joseph Biden of Delaware, the chair of the Judiciary Committee, who whispered to me while our picture was being taken that Baird's "nanny" issue was going to stop her confirmation. Marian and I had special seats at the inauguration itself and felt a surge of hope as the young man whose rise we had witnessed and assisted took the oath and spoke to the dreams of the nation he had been chosen to lead.

I signed up with our friend Donna Shalala (who had worked for me in Justice Goldberg's 1970 gubernatorial campaign) to be her counselor at the Department of Health and Human Services. No Senate confirmation was necessary, and the job description was totally flexible. I began by lending myself to Boston entrepreneur Eli Segal, who had been Clinton's campaign chair, to help draft the legislation that became Americorps, and then gradually accumulated portfolios within HHS, becoming the lead person on drug-and-alcohol policy, youth issues, violence, the Empowerment Zones, the District of Columbia, and interagency relationships. I also sat in meetings on health reform, welfare reform, and the budget, among other things. It was a nice perch, covering many of the items in what might be called Clinton's antipoverty strategy, except that he never said he had such a strategy.

Indeed, I (and many others) had miscalculated on numerous counts. The underlying anger and cynicism of the voters were still there. People were still struggling with their family finances. They had chosen Clinton over Bush because Bush had sat by doing nothing during the recession that occurred on his watch. This didn't mean, though, that they were exactly bowled over by Clinton. If I thought a legislative deal made in Washington had quelled the anger over welfare, I was quite wrong, and if we thought that the Bush presidency meant the revival of a more moderate breed of Republican, that was wrong, too. When 1994 produced a new Republican Congress, it was a virulent group of self-proclaimed revolutionaries who turned out to be even meaner than what the country wanted, as subsequent elections have shown. There were far more true believers among them than in the Reagan years, and many of the Reagan people had been pretty far out.

Most important, I miscalculated about Clinton himself. This was only partially evident during his first two years, when he angered his DLC friends more often than people to his left. The issues about his personal behavior that had come up during the campaign were only about his past. (And I was inclined to cut him somewhat more slack, because I had known him a long time.) But once Congress went Republican, everything changed. Clinton's presidency became a tragedy: high hopes turned into the ultimate in cynicism, messages of national aspiration turned into the worst kind of politics, and expressions of values and commitments turned out to be hollow.

"Poverty" was never prevalent in Bill Clinton's public vocabulary. His use of the word in his last State of the Union Message was striking for its novelty. In the first two years of his presidency, I would sometimes say that since his proposals added up to an antipoverty strategy, the rhetoric in which they were cloaked hardly mattered. Later, I couldn't even say that.

When the Republicans took Congress at the end of 1994, whatever commitment Clinton had to the alleviation of poverty evaporated. The headline over the past six years was the so-called welfare reform, which even with the nineties boom has hurt millions of poor people, especially children. The new breed of Republicans, of course, had no interest in constructive policies, but Clinton, as it turned out, was not much better. He might have insisted on traditional Democratic values in stark contrast to the Republicans' scorched-earth approach, campaigning every day for a time when good sense would again prevail. He moved instead to the safest ground.

During his second term, Clinton appointed a distinguished commission to look into America's continuing problems with race, headed by the great historian John Hope Franklin. The commission did some good, but paid little attention to the critical intersection of race and poverty. There was almost no public consideration of the connection, and little discussion of the issue in the commission's final report. One can only infer a White House view that it would be tacky to get into the issue, given that the President had "solved" those problems when he signed the 1996 welfare law.

As his presidency was drawing to a close, President Clinton acknowledged that the rising tide had not lifted all the boats, although in his depiction very few boats were still stranded. Prompted by Andrew Cuomo, his secretary of Housing and Urban Development and a confidant of Vice President Al Gore, he did a poverty tour and other press events extolling the accomplishments of his Empowerment Zone program and selling a "new markets" program to induce more private investment in distressed areas. The image he conveyed was that the remaining problems were only in isolated areas.

But the problem was more than just pockets; we were looking at gaping holes. In every major city there were large areas where the poverty rate was over 40 percent, and in almost every state there were rural areas with similar statistics. The issue is with us still, not just in East St. Louis, Illinois, and Clarksdale, Mississippi. The President's belated acknowledgment was hardly responsive to reality.

The President's budget proposals in January 2000 were a bit better, if still belated. He proposed an important expansion of the Earned Income Tax Credit for the working poor (always more politically attractive to Clinton) as well as funding for his "new markets" idea and improvements in Empowerment Zones.

A second, even bigger "but" was Clinton's pattern of causing injury to people without power, who don't vote and who don't give big campaign bucks. This included not only poor children hit by the welfare law but immigrants hurt by extensive new restrictions and the people — disproportionately minority — subjected to the long list of new capital crimes and the highly punitive sentencing philosophy of the 1994 federal crime act.

The End of Welfare

CANDIDATE CLINTON KNEW a lot about welfare. He had played a leading role in the passage of the Family Support Act in the late eighties. He knew what to say if he wanted to push the issue toward the back burner and give the 1988 law a chance to succeed. But he did something different. His polling in New Hampshire revealed voter concern about the recent increases in the welfare rolls. He was in deep political trouble for other reasons, so, among other things, he promised to "end welfare as we know it."

This rhetoric evoked a strong response. People heard a Democrat talking tough about welfare and found it refreshing. I thought Clinton was demagoguing the issue a bit, but I felt I knew him and that he was not being destructive. His campaign book, *Putting People First,* said that "after two years" he would "*require those who can work to go to work*" (italics in original), and that he would "give the people who can't find [work] a dignified and meaningful community service job." He aired a television ad to the same effect in the fall campaign. There was ambiguity in the phrase "require those who can work to go to work," and in the television ad phrase that "those who are able must go to work, either in the private sector or in public service." Who would decide who can work? Who is "able"? Still, the basic thrust was constructive — that public jobs would be created for people who couldn't find work. And I thought the unspoken premise was that if the promised public jobs weren't created, people could continue to receive cash assistance. I wanted to see him nominated and elected, so I didn't pursue the fine points.

I still believe that at the time Clinton meant what I thought he meant. What I didn't appreciate was the power of the rhetoric, and the extent to which it contributed to new negative welfare politics. This was not evident at the beginning. Charles Murray, one of the most conservative critics of the old system and a strong advocate of doing away with it altogether, was quoted in early 1993 as saying, "There is simply no stomach for a program that would depend on the mechanism of kicking people off welfare." But after the Republican victory in 1994, Clinton's campaign formulation may have encouraged their meat-ax approach. It's possible that without his campaign rhetoric they would not have been so emboldened. It is also possible that Clinton felt more politically exposed because of what he had said and therefore more disposed to sign the welfare bill.

Some say that Bill Clinton's mistake was not to do welfare first, before health care. Their point is that if he had sent a welfare bill to Congress in 1993 instead of 1994, action on it would have been completed before the Democrats lost Congress. The problem with this theory is that, unlike welfare, health care is an issue that affects the vast majority of Americans and was clearly a matter of widespread popular concern. Health care cost increases wiped out nearly all of the increase in household income during the eighties. Clinton had a mandate to seek health care reform. It was much more important politically than welfare. The two issues are handled by the same committees in Congress, which can only deal with one complicated bill at a time. Health care had to go first.

President Clinton's 1994 welfare reform proposal was in fact not particularly earthshaking. It was built on the framework of the 1988 Family Support Act, which had made money available for welfare-to-work efforts. Clinton's proposal spoke of time limits, but underneath the rhetoric was the traditional Democratic position that if a regular job was unavailable and a publicly funded job had not been specially created, an individual could continue to receive cash assistance. This was the mainstream Republican position as well, going back to the 1988 act. Still, the rhetoric was troubling.

The reference to time limits implied the possibility of publicly financed community service jobs down the road, but they were not funded in the bill. The Clinton proposal also expanded on the 1988 act by requiring individual plans for recipients from the time they came on the rolls, and creating mechanisms to make sure welfare agencies moved people toward work. Clinton also asked for an expansion of child care spending, and proposed further changes in child-support enforcement.

To say that the Clinton bill was not earthshaking is not to be the least bit critical of Mary Jo Bane, David Ellwood, Wendell Primus, and others at HHS who worked hard to develop the best possible proposal. Politics at both ends of Pennsylvania Avenue hobbled development of a strongly progressive measure. One problem was that President Clinton and the Democrats had made an understandable and desirable commitment to deficit reduction. Leon Panetta, then budget director, and Lloyd Bentsen, the Treasury secretary, were adamant that no real money be put into welfare reform. The politics on Capitol Hill were going to be difficult, too. A substantial number of Democrats and many more Republicans favored being much tougher in pushing people into the job market rather than spending more. Too expensive a proposal would be dead on arrival.

Besides, the White House was not particularly liberal on welfare. Bruce Reed in particular pushed in a more stringent direction from the outset. Reed's title was deputy director of the Domestic Policy Council, but from the beginning he wielded power beyond his formal title. He was extremely bright, had acquired Clinton's trust during the campaign, and had an immediate boss, longtime Clinton associate Carol Rasco, who gave him great leeway.

When the interagency working group to develop the welfare proposal was finally formed in the middle of 1993, tension between Reed and the group at HHS developed quickly. Reed would sit like a sphinx in meetings and watch while everyone else came to an agreement, and then throw in a monkey wrench at the last moment. It gradually became apparent that Reed saw no reason not to consider a time limit on welfare, to apply regardless of whether a job could be found. Up to that point, the idea had not even been seriously suggested by the most far-out Republicans. Reed lost on this point. He also pressed for more severe sanctions than the HHS people wanted against recipients who failed to cooperate, including permanently cutting off the whole family. This again was an idea outside the mainstream of welfare policy. On this he achieved limited success. A recipient would have to be extremely uncooperative to be cut off irrevocably, but a major principle had nonetheless been ruptured.

Reed wanted to allow states to refuse additional benefits to mothers who have another child; HHS didn't. He won that point. He pressed for greater state flexibility to add restrictions; HHS wanted states to have flexibility mainly to assist recipients more effectively. Each side won some on this. HHS proposed procedural protections for recipients, including fair hearings and case reviews every six months. Reed opposed much of this, but HHS largely won here.

Basically, Bruce Reed wanted to spend less and be tougher on recipients. The HHS group's position was essentially to elaborate on and perfect the 1988 law. The President's proposal as sent to the Hill in the spring of 1994 looked more like what HHS wanted than what Reed wanted, but it was by no means a pure HHS product.

It is impossible to know what would have happened if the Republicans had not taken over Congress. In retrospect the Clinton bill was both politically and administratively unrealistic in its detailed prescriptions and in its rewards and punishments for state and individual behavior. The developing mood in Congress in both parties was much more devolutionary than the approach of the Clinton bill. The Republican governors were pushing hard for more flexibility. To the extent there was a mood among some in Congress for federal dictation, it reflected a moralizing impetus that produced high-profile hot-button proposals like mandatory denials of help for additional children born to families on welfare (so-called "family caps") and flat denial of assistance to teenagers who have children.

The Clinton position was itself internally inconsistent. His bill was detailed in specifying what states had to do, but he had at the same time been making it easier for states to get waivers from existing federal restrictions for their welfare-to-work experiments. Had Clinton's bill ever been seriously considered on the Hill, the states would surely have complained that it would limit the waivers the self-same Clinton administration was already giving them. Clinton himself kept his options open, giving a speech to the governors in 1994 that extolled his policy of granting waivers, calling it welfare reform by executive action.

Many at HHS were dubious about the profligate waivers, believing the law limited them to genuine experiments. They thought the White House was using waivers to allow governors to do whatever they wanted to do, including the institution of some pretty mean policies. Later, when we at HHS saw the waivers as a way to convince Clinton that he could take credit for them as welfare reform and therefore veto a bad bill, many of us regarded them in a more favorable light.

The Gingrichian ascendancy changed everything. The Republicans now said they really would end welfare as we had known it, transforming it into a block grant with near-total state autonomy, and imposing a strict lifetime limit on how long families could receive federal welfare dollars. This was genuinely radical. Whatever else was wrong with the old system, it provided that needy families who went to the welfare office looking for help had to receive help. Turning it into a block grant meant that states had no obligation to help anyone or even to have a program at all. The time limits meant that, even if the states wanted to, they could not use federal money to help a family after a certain point. Speaker Gingrich provoked an uproar by saying that if people refused to take responsibility by going out and getting a job, their children could be taken away and put in orphanages. What is wrong with orphanages, he asked — some of the most wonderful people grew up in orphanages.

The House Republicans began moving a bill that would have

cut big holes in the safety net, transforming not only welfare but Medicaid, food stamps, school lunches, and child welfare protection into block grants. They also mandated family caps and lifetime welfare ineligibility for teen mothers and for their children throughout the children's adult lives. The Republicans had always had individual members who wanted to abolish welfare, but the new majority now espoused what was even for the Republicans an unprecedented position.

The Republican position now declared the very existence of welfare an incentive to out-of-wedlock births. Enacting their proposals, they claimed, would be the route to ending "illegitimacy."

President Clinton's response, as it was to so much of the so-called Contract With America, was wimpy. This was the spring of 1995, months before the Republicans' bungling of the budget negotiations would enable Clinton to regain his political footing. It was the winter of Clinton's political life. Clinton during this period essentially assumed that the Republican revolution was already successful, and that there was broad national support for dismantling the federal government. Instead of standing up and saying that the entire Republican approach was fundamentally wrong, he picked a few details in Republican bills with which to argue. This allowed them to fix or drop the most controversial items and present him with the remainder for signature. Only the Senate, thanks to the Democrats' ability to filibuster, kept the worst of it from reaching the President's desk.

Secretary Shalala and many Democrats on the Hill repeatedly urged the President to resubmit the welfare proposal that he had sent up the previous year, so it would be clear what he favored. He did not. People who questioned his reticence were told by his staff that his continued preference for his own bill had been communicated informally. His major public expression was an attack on the orphanage issue. He said orphanages — what he meant were large institutions in rural areas — were outmoded and often destructive to the lives and prospects of children. He said Boys

Town, which Speaker Gingrich had romanticized, was no longer the Boys Town of yesteryear but a sophisticated and highly expensive combination of small residential facilities and specialized family foster care that could not possibly be replicated at the necessary scale should Speaker Gingrich's approach be adopted.

When the Republicans backed off the orphanage rhetoric, Clinton was left with no place of principle from which to make a stand. The House passed a horrible bill turning a long list of programs into block grants, and the matter moved to the Senate. During the summer of 1995 Secretary Shalala repeatedly implored the President to send a signal to the Senate that his bottom line included maintaining the entitlement to welfare, a bedrock principle since the New Deal, which provided that people meeting a federal definition of need had a right to get help. Maintaining the entitlement would mean no block grant and no arbitrary time limits, although "entitlement" had become a political no-no, so our HHS group took great pains to find a euphemism, like "conditional safety net."

The signal was not forthcoming. Instead, the President and his emissaries said little as the Senate Finance Committee considered the legislation. They continued to insist to those pushing a less punitive approach that they had communicated their preference for the 1994 bill, but there was no public sign of it. Clinton did express support for a more centrist bill drafted by most of the Democrats on the Finance Committee, led by the influential John Breaux of Louisiana and joined by Minority Leader Tom Daschle. It had a five-year time limit, but would continue aid to children after that by a voucher system. And the President criticized the pending Republican bill for leaving the states free to reduce their current contributions and for not investing enough in job training and child care.

But it was not clear what would provoke a veto. A vicious circle of mutually reinforcing uncertainty developed among the Democrats. People on the Hill, especially those up for re-election, asked why they should stick their necks out when the President was offering no support, and the White House staff asked why the President should stick his neck out when support among Democrats was so thin. Daniel Patrick Moynihan, the leading Senate expert on welfare, introduced his own bill in May, expressing his disapproval of any proposal that would leave needy families without help after a set amount of time. His was a lonely voice.

The Democrats in Congress were in disarray wholly apart from the President's lack of leadership. Many of them believed a major change had occurred in American politics, and that their survival would be in severe doubt if they did not vote for a tough welfare bill. This was especially true in the House, where traditional liberals with inner-ring suburban constituencies, like Sander Levin of Michigan and Nita Lowey of New York, were extremely nervous. Even the black and Hispanic caucuses were strangely silent, with Bob Matsui of California one of the few Democrats who stuck by his long-held principles. In the Senate John Breaux headed a group of "moderate" Democrats who counseled the President not to take a high-visibility position and later urged him to support a block grant.

In this vacuum the Senate Finance Committee completed its version of the bill, and the Senate leadership, just before the August 1995 recess began, indicated their body would take up the subject after Labor Day. David Ellwood had left in July to return to Harvard, citing Harvard's inflexible two-year maximum leave of absence. Donna Shalala had asked me to succeed him as assistant secretary for planning and evaluation. I accepted and returned from vacation at the end of August, just in time to join the effort to get the President to make clear his opposition to ending the entitlement.

Wendell Primus, Ellwood's and now my deputy, had commissioned a study of the Senate bill by the Urban Institute, using a simulation model that gauged the effects of changes in the safety net. The study concluded that the Senate bill would drive more than a million children into poverty. This was the case despite optimistic assumptions about the number of people who would find jobs under the new system and about how much of their own money states would spend. There were still large-scale effects, primarily because the cuts in food stamp benefits would drive many people below the poverty line. (Technically, changes in food stamps aren't used in poverty measurements, but the study broadened the definition.)

If anything, the study understated the projected impact of the bill. It concerned itself only with people pushed across the poverty line, without considering how many already in poverty would be pushed down further or how many just beyond poverty would lose income but not be pushed into poverty. And it made no calculation of the numbers who would be pushed into poverty as a result of hitting lifetime time limits on federally financed welfare payments.

We discussed ways to make use of this potentially powerful weapon, but meanwhile, the problem it was intended to affect had changed for the worse. Word began to emanate from HHS-friendly sources in the White House that the President was thinking of saying he would even sign a bill with block grants and time limits. His only condition would be that block grants not apply to child welfare and food stamps, as the House version had ordered.

If the President were to say this, he would place most Democrats in the Senate (and indirectly, the House) in severe jeopardy if they continued to oppose the Senate bill while their President did not. And he would be changing the future terms of the debate, since he would now be committed to signing a bill that ended the entitlement and installed a lifetime limit.

Secretary Shalala decided to hand the Urban Institute study to the President personally, which she did on a Friday in mid-September. Our sources had said that he was thinking about using his Saturday radio address to send the new signal, and perhaps her move staved that off, because his radio text was ambiguous on entitlements. The success was short-lived, however, because he sent the signal, informally, early the following week. Most of the Democrats in the Senate crumbled, and that body passed the retrograde measure 87 to 12, with one of the 12 in opposition the arch-conservative Republican Lauch Faircloth of North Carolina, who thought the bill was too kind. The eleven Democratic opponents — Moynihan and Ted Kennedy in particular — were eloquent and passionate in their opposition, but their warnings were drowned in the crush.

A couple of weeks after the Senate vote, my wife wrote the President a powerful open letter in the *Washington Post,* urging him not to sign any bill destroying the safety net for children that had been in place for six decades. This was extremely painful for her, given her longstanding relationship with the First Lady, but repeated private remonstrations to the President had fallen on deaf ears and she concluded she had no choice but to go public.

If the President thought his capitulation would produce a bill that would enable him to put the welfare issue behind him, he was wrong. As of the fall of 1995, the Republicans were not willing to let him get credit for signing a welfare bill. So, even though the President had moved far into Republican territory, that party, fully in control of the House-Senate conference committee, moved even further to the right, settling on a bill much closer to what the House had passed originally. Its combination of devolution, multiple block grants, use of aid denials to modify recipients' behavior, and budget-cutting — covering much more than welfare — went beyond what Clinton was willing to stomach. He vetoed it twice, once as a freestanding bill and once when included in an omnibus budget-reconciliation bill.

With the vetoes, the HHS group heaved a collective sigh of relief. Meanwhile the President's political fortunes began to change. Speaker Gingrich whined in November 1995 that the President had forced him to exit Air Force One by the back stairs on the return from Israel and Prime Minister Yitzhak Rabin's funeral, and followed up that gaffe by, shortly before Christmas, shutting down the government during the budget negotiations. Suddenly Clinton, who short weeks earlier had only the tiniest piece of political room in which to stand, was firmly back in the center. His repeatedly expressed determination to fight for Medicare, Medicaid, education, and the environment carried him to political high ground. Some of us were tempted to conclude that, with these changes, the President had changed his mind on welfare and would, if push ever came to shove, defend the entitlement. Rich Tarplin, the chief welfare lobbyist at HHS, pulled me back to earth regularly, telling me that the President was still ready to sign a bad bill.

In early 1996, while the governors were in town for their annual midwinter meetings, the President called a number of them aside after a black-tie White House dinner and invited them to work up a new proposal to convert welfare into a block grant. We also learned that the President had talked supportively of turning Medicaid into a block grant as well. If the latter was true, the impact would be enormous, since Medicaid was a vastly larger program than welfare. Most of the governors salivated at the idea of getting their hands on federal Medicaid dollars with no strings attached.

Medicaid, however, is primarily a program for the elderly, and in particular is the primary source of public funds for long-term care. Millions of Americans who are not poor depend on Medicaid to finance nursing home care for their elderly parents. Besides, Medicaid has support among physicians and hospitals that welfare doesn't. The various constituencies began flexing their muscles in opposition to a Medicaid block grant, and the proposal quickly lost traction.

Once it became clear that President Clinton opposed a block grant for Medicaid, the House Republicans realized that the block-granting of both welfare and Medicaid in the same bill would ensure that the President would not sign the measure. The governors accepted the President's invitation and drafted a new proposal, but the House Republicans, while ostensibly accepting their assistance, combined the welfare and Medicaid ideas in one bill and thereby assured that it would not become law.

The HHS group soldiered on, doing whatever we could to convince the White House that signing a bill was not necessary, and trying to make the legislation less onerous. We suggested that the President cite the waivers he had already granted to some forty states as proof that welfare reform was already going on. We worked with Democrats on the Hill to get alternative bills introduced that could then be cited, however unconvincingly, as the position of the administration. We worked on tactics to tie the conservatives in knots with fights over funding-allocation formulas.

The apparent stalemate continued through the spring and into June, although we kept hearing reports that White House advisers Bruce Reed and Rahm Emanuel were reminding people on the Hill of the President's interest in signing a bill. By late June, the freshman and sophomore Republicans realized that they didn't have much to show for their promises and were in jeopardy of losing control of the House. It further occurred to them that Senator Dole was a dead duck, and that there was no point in protecting his presidential candidacy at their own political expense. Over a hundred of them wrote Speaker Gingrich asking him to move a separate welfare bill without Medicaid. The President could take credit for it in his campaign, but so could they in theirs. The President — if he acquiesced in this effort, as there was every indication he would — would be assisting in the reelection of a Republican Congress as the price of saving his own skin, but that was his problem.

Things were happening at lightning speed, but not so fast as to prevent the Republicans from continuing to play clever politics. Wendell Primus had once told me that if the Republicans ever gave the President a bill he could sign, it would be a ball thrown just outside the strike zone yet close enough to tempt Clinton to swing.

Wendell was right, as he usually is. Instead of delivering a "clean" bill block-granting and time-limiting welfare, the Republicans inserted a number of other distasteful items. The most spectacular denied legal immigrants an array of federal benefits, applying even to those already in the United States when the law was passed. There were also big cuts in the food stamp program and other nutrition and feeding programs. Particularly nasty was a provision severely limiting food stamp eligibility for non-disabled childless people between the ages of eighteen and fifty. Also troubling to many was a narrowing of the definition of childhood disability. The Republicans even beat back a Democratic Senate effort to provide some assistance to children whose families had reached the welfare time limit.

Hope grew that the President would veto the bill. Civil rights, women's, immigrant, religious, and other groups began denouncing the bill, although things were moving so fast that their message was not widely noticed. The magnitude of what was looming was barely understood at the grassroots, especially in immigrant communities, which had been concentrating on high-profile anti-immigrant legislation being separately considered. A few Democrats on the Hill, especially Senator Moynihan, denounced the bill. The President, seemingly keeping his options open, said of the bill in mid-July, "You can put wings on a pig but you can't make it an eagle." Perhaps some who might have expressed opposition didn't bother, thinking the President would veto the bill and save the day.

At the end of July the President convened a dramatic morning-long meeting to hear out his advisers on what to do. I thought there was a substantial chance he would veto the bill, but in retrospect I think he had already made up his mind. His goal was re-election at all costs. Whatever his rationalizations, he was at bottom interested only in himself. His political approach was not to calculate the risks but to take no risks at all.

Arguing for a veto were Donna Shalala, Treasury Secretary Bob Rubin, Labor Secretary Bob Reich, HUD Secretary Henry Cisneros, and White House staffers Leon Panetta, Harold Ickes, and George Stephanopoulos. In favor of signing the bill were Vice President Gore and Commerce Secretary Mickey Kantor (and political adviser Dick Morris, who wasn't at the meeting).

What was most interesting about this lineup was the position of Panetta, Ickes, and Stephanopoulos. They were obviously antagonistic to the legislation on principle, but what they emphasized was that rather than being harmed by a veto Clinton would actually help himself politically. Senator Dole would attack him regularly, of course, but his stand on principle would earn him added respect among many voters.

Secretary Shalala phoned when the meeting was over and told us the President had decided to sign the bill. I was shocked. I had never really believed he would do it. It was an unspeakable blow to millions of utterly powerless people. My first inclination on the narrow point of what to do about my job was to stick it out for five more months, since I was already planning to go back to teaching at Georgetown for the second semester. Wendell had told me weeks earlier that if the President ever decided to sign a bill, he would be gone before the signing actually occurred. Since he was my deputy, I thought that perhaps my leaving would be too severe a blow to our staff's morale, and would be too tough on Secretary Shalala, who had fought the good fight. For the next day and a half I went to a number of meetings on implementation, including one with OMB and White House staff that was especially difficult. It became increasingly clear that hanging on for five more months would be extremely painful.

At the end of the next day, knowing that the Secretary was leaving town for a few days, I found myself walking to her office.

I said to her, "I just can't do it." She said, "I understand. I wish you would stay, but I understand."

Was this the sort of thing over which one should resign? I asked myself whether I was leaving my staff and my colleagues, including Secretary Shalala, in the lurch, and whether they would feel judged. I respected their decision. After all, not everyone had a choice. I had a tenured professorship to go back to. Some no doubt concluded they could do more good by staying. Many said to me I was doing it for them as well. I felt supported. And I reflected that when some of us had thought officials in the Johnson administration should have resigned over Vietnam, it had been wrong to be judgmental about those who did not.

It is also true that there is a threshold level of importance of the issue for a public resignation on principle to make sense. This met the standard. The point in disagreeing with the legislation was not retention of a flawed structure. It was that any decent nation has to provide a safety net of assistance for its children. Flawed as it was, the previous system had that safety net. Benefits varied widely, but everywhere in America a family coming to a welfare office could get help if they met the federal requirements. This had been true for sixty years. Now no state had any federally defined obligation to help needy children.

Nor could it be said that what had happened was part of the risk of joining this administration. There had been no hint that the safety net was in danger when President Clinton took office. He broke faith with America's children.

The Legacy of the Clinton Years

A BALANCED ASSESSMENT of Clinton's presidency must include several positive developments. Crime, both violent and nonviolent, is down substantially. Nonmarital teen births have declined. Poverty is down somewhat. Clinton took on Big Tobacco and pushed for stronger gun control. He contributed toward peace in the Middle East, in Northern Ireland, and in Bosnia and Kosovo. And it is true that he was distracted, practically from the beginning and long before he provided near-lethal ammunition in the form of Monica Lewinsky, by a group dedicated almost pathologically to destroying his presidency. Clinton's best claim for good marks comes from the spectacular performance of the American economy. A healthy economy has always been the strongest weapon against poverty, and Clinton does deserve credit here, even though groundwork was laid by the 1990 Bush budget agreement, which, ironically, may have contributed to Bush's loss. This agreement began the process of deficit reduction that was crucial to what followed. Clinton's deficit reduction package of 1993 was a further major step.

However, the improvement in the economy was accompanied by the glitz factor, the materialistic and amoral excess accumulating for a long time and accelerated spectacularly by the pileup of high-tech wealth. This was happening before Clinton, but he did nothing to slow it down. He worked the glitz for all it was worth, literally, as he took political fundraising to new levels of excess. He was the perfect political figure for the new Gilded Age, the Gatsby of the new world order.

Perhaps more important than Clinton's susceptibility to glitz is the fact that his penchant for elevating shadow over substance has hurt poor children — and not just poor children. He has tended generally to make things worse for the politically powerless. "The targets?" Mario Cuomo once said of Clinton's actions. "The immigrant, the prisoner, the poor, children: people who can't vote or don't vote."

After I wrote an article in the *Atlantic Monthly* about the welfare bill entitled "The Worst Thing Bill Clinton Has Done," Anthony Lewis wrote that he wasn't so sure it was the worst thing Clinton had done, not because he disagreed with me about welfare but because "there is a strong argument that what he has done to civil liberties will have even more damaging consequences for American ideals." He went on to say that Clinton "has the worst civil liberties record of any president in at least 60 years."

The list of regressive laws Clinton signed is substantial: the so-called antiterrorism bill, the 1996 immigration bill, the Prison Litigation Act, which reduced the ability of prisoners to get relief from mistreatment, and the omnibus crime bill enacted in 1994. The antiterrorism law curtailed the habeas corpus power of the federal courts to overturn state criminal convictions for violations of constitutional rights. It also lets the government deport non-citizens legally in the U.S. for alleged connections to terrorism without letting them see the evidence against them. The immigration law reduced the chances for people seeking political asylum to present their cases and slammed the door of the federal courts to many claims of lawlessness on the part of the Immigration and Naturalization Service, thereby condoning an "anything goes" approach to immigration-law enforcement.

Clinton's crime bill is also part of his record on poverty and on race. It added nearly five dozen new capital crimes and supported the wave of lock-'em-up, three-strikes-and-you're-out statutes then sweeping the country. If all we do is impose longer and longer sentences and build more and more prisons, we will reap what we sow: more and more people incarcerated, overwhelmingly poor and minority. Sentencing policies are in many ways the mirror of what we offer young people by way of education and opportunity.

The debates over welfare and crime have been linked for thirty years. The ghetto unrest of the sixties got the linkage started. I encountered the crime backlash in its early stages when I was New York youth corrections commissioner. The calls for get-tough crime laws, especially youth-crime laws, along with moves to lock up minor drug offenders for ever longer periods of time were in significant part euphemisms for more explicitly but now unacceptable racial rhetoric.

There was talk for years of an omnibus federal crime bill, but there was a deadlock through the eighties in Congress parallel to the welfare deadlock. Some smaller crime bills passed, but the big one stayed beyond reach. This changed under Clinton, and despite the fact that Democrats were in charge at both ends of Pennsylvania Avenue, it changed in a regressive direction.

There is larger damage, although it is harder to prove. The Clinton presidency began with high hopes for progress along lines that Democrats had not been able to pursue in a sustained way for nearly a quarter of a century. These hopes were encouraged by the attractiveness, energy, intelligence, and youth of the president in whom they were embodied. They were also propelled by the idea that perhaps the Democrats had found a new synthesis of individual and community responsibility, added to traditional goals. If less had been expected, the disappointments would be less severe. Cynicism can flow more from hopes dashed than from having no expectations in the first place.

Despite all the material success of recent years, I believe I am far from alone in thinking that, especially when moral and spiritual concerns are taken into account, the country was impoverished more than it was enriched by the Clinton presidency, beginning with his personal behavior in office. This was disgusting not only in itself but in the fact that he caused dozens of decent people to unknowingly perpetuate lies in order to defend him, and hundreds if not thousands more to defend him out of political necessity even after they knew what he had done. The Clinton presidency — encompassing his conduct of the nation's business, his own behavior, and the behavior of his enemies — colored the way we do our politics and the way we conduct our public life. All of that is not entirely his responsibility, but the result was a most unfortunate starting point for a new century and a new millennium.

5

LIFE AFTER WELFARE

IF THERE was ever a good time to test a cold-turkey approach to welfare, the recent years of extraordinary prosperity have been it. It had been an article of faith since the seventies that we would never again see unemployment drop below 5 percent. Yet we have been seeing it for an extended period. Many people who had been unable to find work for a long time or had stopped trying have jobs.

We hear everywhere, from President Clinton (especially President Clinton) on down, that the 1996 welfare law is a great success. The proponents of the law point to the steep drop in the welfare rolls. They tell of people who left welfare and found satisfying jobs with full benefits and possibilities for promotion. We hear about people who say they needed the push to find a job that the new law provided. We also hear of employers desperate to find workers.

All of this, though, is only part of the story. It ignores those states, freed up by block grants, that have adopted harsh policies including short time limits and extensive terminations. It doesn't mention the people who were pushed off the rolls and didn't get jobs, and barely acknowledges the people who did get jobs but are still stuck in poverty. It ignores those who found work but not steady work or full-time work, and pays no attention at all to the large number who lost jobs but were turned away when they asked for welfare. It doesn't acknowledge those who found jobs but now lack access to health care, or whose children are in unsatisfactory day care arrangements. It is silent about the precipitous drop in food stamp and Medicaid participation, far beyond what the good economy can explain. It is uninterested in the weak performance of organizations, especially profit-making companies, engaged to train people and help them find and keep jobs. It doesn't tell of the 2.5 million hard-core cases still on the rolls — people with less education, fewer skills, less work experience, and more personal problems, who haven't been reached yet — and says nothing about the imminence of the five-year lifetime limit on federally funded assistance and what will happen when a recession hits. Bad policies kept too many people on welfare for too long, but the new law invited states to make things worse, and too many accepted the invitation.

The Numbers

IN 1989 THERE were 10.8 million people — adults (mainly women) and children — on the AFDC rolls. This number was about the same percentage of the population as had been on welfare for around two decades. It was more than one would like to see in this wealthy nation, but it was not shocking. Mainly because of the recession of the early nineties, the number rose steeply over the ensuing four years, to a peak of 14.3 million in 1994. It fell by a million before the 1996 law was even enacted, and as of late summer 1999 it was 7.3 million.

The 7 million who left welfare included about 2.5 million adults, primarily women. But about 2.5 million women are still there, most of whom are supposed to have a job whenever the time limits hit them. This has already occurred for those in states with particularly short time limits, and is about to hit many more.

What happens to those who leave welfare depends on the economic health of the state and the character of its welfare policy. The devolutionary nature of the new law means that states don't have to offer any help at all to anyone they don't want to help. The ones with the biggest reductions in welfare rolls have low unemployment levels or stringent welfare policies, or both.

The percentage of former welfare recipients with jobs is about the same as under the old law. Previously, if a woman got a job and then lost it, she could get back on welfare. Now applicants are often turned away, and told to look for work. So now there is a large group of women who are neither working nor on welfare — about a million, plus their two million children. Not far down the road, the federal time limit will make matters even worse.

These 3 million people — America's "disappeared" — are not identified specifically as former welfare recipients in any statistics, but we can see them in our national poverty numbers. They are among the poorest 10 percent of single mothers, whose income actually declined 14 percent from 1996 through 1998. The overall poverty rate has gone down some recently, but the number of extremely poor — people with incomes below half the poverty line, or below about $6,750 for a family of three — has remained at around 14 million people, or about 40 percent of the poor. And they are actually poorer than they were before, because so many have lost their welfare and their food stamps and do not have jobs to make up for what they have lost.

When the new welfare law was passed, we warned that states would compete to cut benefits, to drive people out. This did not materialize, because benefits were already so low in many places and the economy so good that it would have been embarrassing to cut them further. Benefits in Mississippi, for example, were $120 a month for a family of three. But there was a race to the bottom nonetheless — a race to see who could reduce their rolls the fastest. Governors took pride in reporting steep declines in numbers of recipients, and too few people asked how it had been accomplished. It turned out that sanctions and terminations, combined with rejection of new applicants, did the trick, leaving us with 3 million "disappeared."

The Human Side

WE NEED TO understand this in human terms. We need to appreciate the real stories — the heartening ones, the sad ones, and the exasperating ones. The people involved represent every tale one can imagine. It is important not to forget that this is about real people.

Our disappeared are no longer listed as welfare recipients, and since they are not employed they do not show up in unemployment-insurance records either. Some married or moved in with a man (all too often one who is abusive to them or their children, or both), some moved in with extended families (in crowded circumstances that often lead to new upheavals), and some are homeless. They piece together an existence with casual earnings, food stamps and Medicaid (although many who are eligible are getting neither), maybe housing assistance, visits to food pantries and soup kitchens, help from family members, and, for some, selling drugs or selling their bodies. Some give up their children to foster care.

We can find them one by one. I have talked to some of them. They have names and faces, and children they love dearly. They have stories that testify to the bad effects of current policy and give flesh and texture to the statistics.

Boston

SANDY, WHOM I met at a transitional shelter called Project Hope at a former convent in the Boston neighborhood of Dorchester, was in her mid-twenties and had three children, who were five, four, and one when we met in late 1999. We talked around the kitchen table with others pulled together by Malikkah P. and Betsy S., who after being on welfare now have jobs as advocates for women like Sandy.

Sandy's baby has asthma, which is ubiquitous in the inner city. He is in and out of the hospital frequently — "like every other week," Sandy said. She worked fairly regularly until her third pregnancy, but she was sick a lot during that time and had to quit her job at Walgreen's. She never wanted to go on welfare, but did so to get income "to take care of the kids." It was never enough to live on.

Sandy had been homeless for several months and had recently gotten an apartment, thanks to a housing voucher. She said her life had become "a little raggedy." She was being treated by a psychiatrist for depression. After we talked for an hour or so, she said she was having stomach pains and needed to go home. When Malikkah came back from taking Sandy home, she said she thought Sandy might have an ulcer from all of the stress in her life.

Sandy had hit the two-year limit for welfare in Massachusetts. Her food stamps were also cut off when she hit the limit, even though that is illegal under federal law. These actions rendered her homeless. A state with a national reputation for liberalism, Massachusetts in fact has one of the toughest welfare policies in the country. Even before the 1996 federal law was enacted, Republican Governor William Weld got the Democratic legislature to enact a new system so stingy it was illegal under the old federal law. Weld had a national reputation as a "liberal" Republican because of his positions on abortion and the environment, but when it came to poor people the reality was quite different. It was a mark of the position of the poor in our political pecking order that few people noted Weld's views on welfare when judging his record.

People who hit the initial time limit can come back on the system in three years, because Massachusetts has a lifetime five-year limit, but it allows only two years at a time. Extensions are possible but very hard to come by. As of June 1999, eight thousand Massachusetts families had hit the time limit and only five hundred extensions had been granted. Sandy asked for an extension and was told she had to go into a training program to get one. She signed up, but then a required tuberculosis test came back positive. It took two more months to determine that she didn't have TB, and Sandy finally received an extension, a mixed blessing since it counted against her lifetime limit. When I met her, she was getting limited child support from the father of her baby, plus Medicaid and a housing voucher, not enough to live on.

It was hard for Sandy to see a state welfare worker personally about the food stamp cutoff, because her son was quite sick. She tried calling her assigned worker every day but the worker never called back. She finally went downtown to see the worker and was told that she couldn't see a worker without an appointment.

It was not clear what will become of Sandy, just as it is not clear what will become of all the other Sandys out there. She has family in a nearby suburb who give some help, but their resources are limited. Her depression is probably not serious enough to warrant a finding that she is legally disabled. She is a high school graduate, is literate and articulate, and wants to work. She does not want to be on welfare. But she has young children and emotional problems.

Malikkah and Betsy said they were seeing more and more women with children and no income of any sort coming into the shelters, some for the second and third time, after being evicted for nonpayment of rent. How do they survive when they are not in the shelters? "They beg, borrow, and steal," said Sister Margaret Leonard, who runs Project Hope. "People will do anything to feed their children," Malikkah added. "Before, they did prostitution to pay for drugs. Now they're doing it to feed their kids. Just the other day I saw a girl out there who I went to school with." Davena A., another former welfare recipient who joined the discussion later on, said, "There are a lot of women on the street who look so brand new. Their faces look so scared, so immature."

Dr. Deborah Frank, who sees low-income children at Boston Medical Center, told me she is seeing increasing numbers of malnourished children, because of the time limits and because Massachusetts is a "family cap" state — no welfare for children born to a mother already on welfare. (Sandy's third child is a family-cap baby.) Dr. Frank said a typical pattern is that the baby is well-enough nourished but the next child up in the birth order is malnourished, because of the mother's desperate efforts to stretch her check far enough to feed something to all of her children.

Malikkah and Betsy took turns telling me stories of women who had jobs and were laid off or had to quit because of their own or a child's health, and had either exhausted their time limit or were simply told by the welfare people to look for another job.

The one thing Sandy and a limited number of others have going for them is Project Hope. Presided over by Sister Margaret, whose caring and savvy infuse every inch of the place, Project Hope means survival for hundreds of women and their children in Dorchester. The nuns and the other wonderful women who work there convey an infectious warmth and positive spirit.

Supported by federal, state, and city grants, diverse religious groups, the United Way, local foundations, and private contributions (think of the skill required to piece all of that together every year), Project Hope has a complex mix of activities. There is transitional living space for homeless women and their children, where a fortunate few live for six months to a year while they put the pieces of their lives back together — getting work, housing, child care, and anything else needed for a decent chance of avoiding further disaster. The average residence is now eight months, up from three months a few years ago because of a huge and worsening shortage of affordable housing in the Boston area. Massachusetts actually has an extra two thousand housing vouchers under a special federal program, but they do not help as much as they should, because there is so little housing available.

Project Hope has a licensed and nationally accredited (a rarity) child care center for twenty-six children age zero through six, unusual both in its provision of infant care (there are hardly any infant slots available around the country, even though many states require women to work when their children are three months old) and in its willingness to take a few children whose mothers have no voucher from the state to pay for the care. There is an adult learning program that serves twenty to thirty women a year, many of them immigrants, and sends many of its graduates on to higher education. There is a community organizing unit that reaches out to build civic awareness and political participation in the neighborhood, which helped to triple local voter turnout in 1998 and elect a dynamic young Haitian American lawyer to the state legislature. There is a food pantry open three days a week for neighborhood families. As is typical throughout the country, demand for its assistance has increased substantially over the last few years. And there is a transition-to-work collaborative, where Malikkah and Betsy work, involving a number of local homeless shelters.

Project Hope is unusual in that Sister Margaret and her colleagues are also effective policy advocates, bringing an authentic message to decision makers who know and respect (but don't necessarily heed) them. Project Hope residents and staff are frequent witnesses at state legislative hearings.

The Dorchester neighborhood has more services than most, but the large numbers of people hurt by current welfare policy swamp its ability to cope. When we think about the even larger numbers — block by block and neighborhood by neighborhood — affected in places like New York, Chicago, Los Angeles, Detroit, and Philadelphia, we can begin to appreciate the magnitude of the crisis. There are marvelous helping organizations and advocates in all these places, but their efforts are dwarfed by the numbers needing help.

Malikkah, herself a success story of the old system, said she was not sure what would have happened to her if she had hit the time limit earlier. In her late twenties when we met, with four children, she was on public assistance for eight years, but she always had a part-time job, and sometimes two. For her, welfare was always a small supplement, never her only source of income. While on it, Malikkah got her high school equivalency and graduated from Bunker Hill Community College, and now was pursuing a B.A. at the University of Massachusetts College of Public and Community Service (which I helped to found as vice president of the University of Massachusetts). Her children are doing well. Her twelve-year-old, she said proudly, had been on the honor roll since fourth grade.

Welfare was an important help, but there were other factors. Malikkah's parents, her grandmother, and her whole family always pushed her to finish her education, in contrast to many families she knows "that give women a hard time for going to college." And, she said, "I was lucky. I met Sister Margaret."

Not that welfare was any bed of roses for Malikkah. The welfare people tried to push her out of community college, and refused to pay for full-time child care while she was there. Because benefit amounts were based on her previous month's earnings, the welfare check didn't reflect her current earnings, and it was hard to manage. Nonetheless, she had the extra funds to help keep things together. Under the new system, welfare payments to supplement low wages, if offered at all, are subject to time limits unless a state uses its own money to fund them. The federal Earned Income Tax Credit helps, but not enough. Malikkah, who now has a job, a car, and child support, would very possibly not have been able to finish college if she had hit a time limit. Besides, Massachusetts has been in the forefront of states that force women on welfare to drop out of college and go to work or participate in a work program.

Betsy, who when we met had three years of credit toward her degree at the University of Massachusetts in Boston, said she "would still be in retail" if she had been subject to a two-year time limit. She was no longer receiving cash assistance but was still getting child care help. Like everything else in the world of public help for the poor and near poor, this is intensely bureaucratic business. Betsy had to turn in her pay stubs regularly to prove that she was still qualified for the child care help. She lost a pay stub once and was cut off. "When you lose the slot," she pointed out, "you go to the back of the waiting list, and it can be two years before you get back on. You have to go to the child care office in person to fight them, because they don't return phone calls. So you have to have a sympathetic boss. A retail store wouldn't let someone do that."

Another bureaucratic absurdity in Massachusetts and many other states is that child care help is not available while a woman looks for a job. Even worse, in some states vouchers are not provided until the woman produces her first pay stub. This can mean that a woman obtains a job, can't get child care before she is to start work, and then loses the job before she starts because she has no child care. One of the four women profiled in a Connecticut public-television documentary for which I was interviewed had exactly this experience. As Malikkah said in our conversation, "If your child care isn't right, nothing's right."

The whole welfare-to-work structure in Massachusetts is unsatisfactory, according to Malikkah and Betsy. Malikkah reported "awful experience with all of the welfare-to-work programs. Only one or two out of three hundred women we've sent have completed the programs and found jobs." Women find jobs, but not because of help from the system.

Betsy was receiving child support from the father of one of her three children (she is married to the father of the other two) — but in fact the state was getting the money and keeping all but fifty dollars a month to offset the benefits it gave her in earlier years. (Many men pay more than fifty dollars directly to the mother, because it is less than what a court would order. Mothers strong-arm this money out of them by threatening to report them to the welfare authorities.) Betsy said that when she started getting the fifty dollars, the state took away seventy-five dollars of her food stamp allotment. When I protested that you're only supposed to lose thirty cents of food stamps for every dollar of additional income, Malikkah interrupted and said, "We're not talking about the law, we're talking about the practice."

Publicly funded support has always been meted out grudgingly, with crackdowns running in cycles. If you go back to before the sixties and the advent of legal-services lawyers, sympathetic courts, and welfare rights organizers, there was broad local discretion to decide who deserved to get help. The 1996 law took us back to that time in many ways. With a federal entitlement (at whatever meager level) repealed, many states have chosen to turn away as many applicants as possible and to terminate people when they fail to show up for an appointment or are late for a workfare job. These people can typically apply for reinstatement in a month or two but they may not be approved, and by then they may be homeless.

Malikkah said many of the women she knows have left welfare for "administrative reasons," as the classification jargon puts it. They are told that they missed an appointment or didn't file a required form, often when they didn't know they had an appointment or actually did turn in the form. Malikkah continued, "You have to hunt your worker down. They have often moved to another office. It's always the client's fault. People finally say, 'Okay, I give up.' The only light we have through the tunnel of welfare is Greater Boston Legal Services. They can get things done. But their caseload is outrageous."

Front-line workers are sometimes explicitly told to be extremely stingy with food stamps and Medicaid, even though these benefits are still federally guaranteed. More often the antiwelfare message confuses both workers and computers, resulting in erroneous terminations or denials of food stamps and Medicaid, or failure to tell people they are immediately eligible for food stamps and Medicaid. Further, applicants often don't know the rules. For such reasons, food stamp and Medicaid rolls are down by far more than one can attribute to economic conditions. This is one of the reasons why food-pantry and soup-kitchen business is on the rise in so many places.

Debbie G. and Davena A. joined the conversation. Debbie, who was in her forties, moved back to Boston from Atlanta with her five children in the early nineties to get away from a violent relationship. She went into a battered-women's shelter and was there for eleven months because, even though she had a housing voucher, she got the runaround looking for housing outside the inner city. I asked if she thought it had been for racial reasons. She looked at me patiently and said it could have been the fact of her race, the fact that she had five children, the fact that she was renting with a housing voucher, the fact that she was a single parent, or all of the above. She finally found a place in Dorchester.

With three years of college and after going through a training program at Roxbury Community College, Debbie was able to get a job as a family advocate. But one of her children had mental-health problems stemming from the domestic violence, and when Debbie started missing work to deal with her child's situation, her employer started docking her pay. Debbie decided to quit the job and finish college. She went on welfare, but the welfare people wouldn't let her go to college. What saved her was Americorps, which placed her for two years at a place called Connecting the Dots for Boston Tots, paid for child care, and enabled her to get her B.A. In late 1999 she was working to help other women develop their skills. "I'm giving back," she said proudly.

She was still struggling with depression, but was proud of what she had accomplished.

Debbie said the significance of her experience is that "community support can help women who are transitioning. It helped me as an older woman. They say everybody can do it," she continued. "That's not true. The ones with high school diplomas or GEDs [high school equivalencies] and work experience, okay. But the ones with a third grade education, the ones with language problems, the ones who don't say anything, they get terminated. Emotional problems? The welfare people don't take those into account."

Davena was in her late twenties, and lived at Project Hope for six months in the early nineties. She and her daughter (she had two daughters when we met) had been living with her mother and sisters and brother, but she felt overwhelmed and constantly undermined by others in the household. She was a high school graduate who had worked in convenience stores and at a yogurt shop, and she "was going to prove to my mother that I was not going to be someone on welfare," but she fell apart with the stress of working, parenting, and going to a computer-learning center. She ended up on welfare and at Project Hope.

A social worker named Nina began working with Davena, who ignored her at first. Nina would push notes under her door, and finally they connected. Davena was given a job as a resource coordinator at Project Hope, and then went to Bunker Hill Community College when Nina pushed her to apply for a scholarship. She remembers Nina's support when she got a C-plus on her first paper, which came back all marked up with a red pen. She was the first in her family to get an A.A. degree, and when I met her was going to UMass Boston while working at a settlement house to "help clients who need extra help" with family reunification, getting drug treatment, or finding housing. She said, "School is my second love. They can't stop me now. And my mother is proud of me now." She believes Nina "made all the difference."

Many of the mothers who end up homeless are not that different from those who don't. When a two-bedroom apartment costs almost all of a minimum-wage paycheck, it is not that hard for things to fall apart. More and more women who could make it with a low-paying job if they received some extra cash help beyond their wages are showing up in crisis. And women with particular problems and limitations are even more likely to hit the wall.

While women in crisis have the most dramatic stories, the workers emphasized to me that, as Malikkah said, "There is a second layer — the people who get jobs but can't support their families, especially the ones with four or five kids. It's a treadmill, like the hamster. They have to get a second job, they never see the kids, and the kids start acting out." Betsy said, "Once you're on the right track you start losing all the various kinds of help you were getting. But you're still not out of the woods." Davena said, "I still owe money." "So do I," said Debbie, "from three years ago. I couldn't pay all the bills while I was on welfare."

Chicago

MY VISITS IN Chicago were to the far southwest and the far southeast parts of the city — miles of neighborhoods that house masses of low-income people and offer few supportive services. The southeast side was once working class, with nearby steel and other heavy manufacturing jobs, but the jobs are long gone.

Compared with Massachusetts, Illinois is not exceptionally punitive, although policies vary around the state and their application varies from worker to worker. Illinois uses the federal five-year time limit and, on paper at least, has made a good investment in child care.

The places I visited in Chicago were transitional shelters for women with children, run under Catholic auspices. One was in a former convent and the other in a former rectory. Both were

cheerful and projected a sense of warmth and welcoming. Neither seemed to be as directly involved in policy and advocacy as
Project Hope, although both were affiliated with the visible and
effective Chicago Coalition for the Homeless.

The seven women with whom I talked were some of those
having a tough time making it under the new rules. All but one
talked freely, although I am sure they omitted facts they preferred
not to share with a stranger, and gave altered accounts of others.
Only one engaged more in a political diatribe about the racism of
the system than in a conversation about her life. I'm not going to
use real names here, because I learned some facts about some of
the women that they didn't tell me themselves.

Each of the seven had a different story, a different combination
of problems, and different needs. The seven ranged in age from
the early twenties to the mid-forties and had from two to nine
children. (The average number of children per welfare family is
slightly more than two.) At least three and probably four were
coping with problems of depression (one to the point where she
is legally disabled and receives Supplemental Security Income), at
least two were learning disabled, two were abused as children,
one told me she had used cocaine, and one had serious alcohol
problems and severe asthma as well and had an SSI application
pending. Two had siblings who were college graduates and other
siblings who had steady employment. They were the only ones in
their families who ended up on welfare. One woman's parents
and brother had been murdered (in three separate occurrences),
and she had been sexually abused by her stepfather. Two of the
seven were homeless because of fires, and most of the rest had
been kicked out by a boyfriend or a relative who couldn't continue to house them or whose husband or partner didn't want
them around. Three of the seven were high school graduates, two
had GEDs, and two were working on their GEDs. I'll tell five of
the women's stories in more detail.

Mary was thirty-one and had seven children, ranging from

two to twelve, with a number of different fathers. She had been on and off public aid, as welfare is called in Illinois, since the first child was born. She had a couple of jobs along the way but couldn't keep them because of a lack of child care. She dropped out of high school and told me she had recently scored at the second and third grade level on tests given her at the start of a GED program. She said her math was especially bad but her reading was good.

Mary's mother was a drug addict, which Mary didn't realize until she was twenty and the mother had a stroke. The mother kept her "sheltered" in the house throughout her childhood. "She beat me all the time and ordered me around. Sometimes she would tell me to stay in one spot and not move, and I would sit there, for hours." The mother put her out of the house at nineteen when she was pregnant with her first child. She "didn't know anything," not even what welfare was. Her godmother took care of her at first, then she moved from place to place, working at part-time jobs to get extra cash, and having more babies with different fathers.

The new welfare law precipitated the crisis that caused Mary to end up in the shelter. In late 1998 she was cut off for three months for a failure to cooperate or show up for an appointment — she is not sure exactly why it happened. Her gas and heat were cut off and she went into a "real bad" depression. "It was Thanksgiving and there was no gas and no heat and I had seven children looking at me." Children and Family Services (the child-protection agency in Illinois) came and took all the children for four days. Mary was able to move in with an aunt, and she got the children back. (Her godmother works for Children and Family Services as a foster parent, which may have helped.) The aunt put them out on Christmas Eve and the godmother took them back in. In early June, the godmother's husband said they had to leave, and they ended up in the shelter where I found them five months later.

Mary's experience of not knowing why she lost welfare is typical. Illinois aggressively terminates for "noncooperation," and has poor notification practices. It is easy to get back on, but a couple thousand people every month fail to reapply, including those who don't understand what happened and what to do about it.

Mary said the staff at the shelter had arranged for her to move into subsidized housing in early 2000, into a place for large families. When I spoke with her she had been going for two months to a GED and job-readiness program that she had found on her own. She hadn't started a job search as yet, and didn't know what kind of job she would look for, but, she said, "I've come a long way in a little bit of time. It took over ten years. Now I want to go to school. I don't drink. I don't do drugs. I'm too scared to do any of those things, because of the way my mother hid me from the outside world. I was twenty-nine the first time I went into a lounge [bar]. I've come so far. I couldn't get out of the rut for nothing. I couldn't do anything. I would get so depressed about all the stuff that was happening." She said she would have her godmother to babysit for her now, which wasn't possible before. In her mind this was critical. "I worry about my kids all the time. How are they going to get back and forth to school? When will they eat? Is the caregiver going to beat the children?"

Mary projected optimism and a determination to succeed. Her math and her reading skills suggest a problem, as does her mental health history (although who wouldn't be depressed by her situation?). And I probably heard only part of her story. If she actually had the subsidized housing that she claimed, and is able to keep it, that is a big plus, especially for someone with seven children. Housing vouchers (and housing itself) are hard to come by in Chicago, as elsewhere. One woman told me she had been on a housing-voucher waiting list since 1981, and another told me the typical wait in the city was fifteen years, although it was much shorter in the suburbs. (The relative availability of housing vouchers in Massachusetts is unusual.)

Another big plus — and unusual outside of Illinois — is that if Mary gets a low-wage job for thirty or more hours a week, it can be supplemented not only by the federal Earned Income Tax Credit and a reduced food stamp allotment but also by a partial welfare check, provided by Illinois, that is not subject to time limits. (Illinois is putting its own money into this.) Also, Mary's godmother can get paid by the state for babysitting — $9.50 per child per day if she is not licensed and more if she gets licensed. Illinois has one of the best child care programs in the country on paper, but if the babysitting falls through and Mary has to ask the welfare bureaucracy for child care help, she may encounter a sixty- to ninety-day delay in getting money for the caregiver.

Latasha was probably the brightest of the seven, an articulate high school graduate with considerable work experience. She was twenty-six and had five children, aged from ten to one. Her father, a gang leader, was murdered, her mother was beaten to death by her stepfather in her presence, and a brother was shot in the back on his way to the bus stop, an apparent victim of mistaken identity. Latasha told me about the brother, and the nun who runs the shelter told me about the other two. The nun also said that Latasha was sexually abused by her stepfather from a young age, and that her mother was an addict. Latasha had had a lot of counseling along the way and was "a very compassionate mother."

Latasha told her story as though she had things under control. She described herself as "a determined person," who was going to see to it that all her children went to college. She has worked since she was sixteen, in customer service and as a secretary, and has been on public aid on and off between jobs, but "only when I really need it." She had come to the shelter in 1997 after her living situation fell apart, left to get married, and then returned in August 1999 when the husband began to show signs of becoming abusive. Latasha said to me she had started beautician school the previous Monday, and that she was starting a job the following

Monday with a marketing company on the near North Side with flexible hours that would allow her to pursue her schooling. She also said she was to get a housing voucher in about a month that she would use to move to the suburbs, where she wouldn't have to worry about the kids getting shot.

The nun in charge said the story was not exactly accurate. Latasha "is always about to begin something. She has had two jobs during her two stays at the shelter. Neither lasted more than two weeks. I doubt she's starting a job on Monday." On the other hand, Sister Catherine (not her real name) said she probably did have the housing voucher. With Latasha you "never really know. I love her a lot. She is a good mother, very kind, and very bright, but she is also very slippery. And her reactions to things that happen are very strong."

There is no question of Latasha's brightness. It is clear from a conversation in which she described the welfare system and all of its complex rules with total clarity, and discussed her own life articulately, if with less than total candor. Her take on the welfare policy changes was somewhat ambivalent. She said, "They have gone to the extreme in a negative way, but some of the policies are good policies. I don't necessarily agree with the five years. I can live with it but some can't. But it does push you to get going." She was opposed to the policy of cutting off public aid to people who go to school full time. "They say you don't have to go to school. Work is what you have to do." (She apparently did not know that Illinois recently had changed its policy to allow welfare recipients to stay in college if they maintain a grade average between a B and a C, although it is still hard to get a caseworker to approve college in the first place.)

Latasha described and evaluated in impressive detail the various bureaucracies she dealt with. "Until the middle of ninety-nine you could get a check even if you missed an appointment. Now they cut you off and it takes thirty-five to forty-five days to get back on. They change your caseworker all the time, every couple of months. You have to go down there to get your medical card. They won't send it out. Child care is a completely different subagency. Housing is another place, and you have to get information from public aid to give them. The employment agency is very bureaucratic and not helpful, especially because they have no jobs at all with flexible hours."

One thing Latasha was absolutely clear about. The shelter "is a lifesaver." She went into a church shelter on the West Side and stayed two and a half months, and finally talked her way into the transitional shelter. She was grateful for it.

Is she right that she will be able to live with the five-year limit? No one knows. (Five months later Latasha still did not have a job and was not in school, but she and her husband had "done some good work on their relationship," according to Sister Catherine, who reiterated that Latasha "has a lot of potential and is not discouraged.")

Chamique was the youngest and most immature of the seven women. When I walked into the shelter on a nippy fall morning, the mothers, their children, and the staff were having a cinnamon roll treat to celebrate her receiving a certificate for two weeks of perfect attendance at a job-readiness program. Chamique was twenty-one and had two children. She dropped out of high school when she was pregnant with her first child and got a GED by mail in August 1999. She told me she didn't get along with her mother's boyfriend and hadn't been in her mother's house since she was fifteen or sixteen. She went to a temporary shelter while she was pregnant with her second child and had been at this transitional shelter since he was born, thirteen months prior to my visit. She had been working at a fast-food restaurant but, because they kept cutting back her hours, decided she would be better off if she quit and looked for another job, although she also wanted to go to college, she told me. She was on public aid, but previously had been cut off for three months for some infraction. Her check and food stamps had been cut in half ($586 a month total down to $255) when she took the job at the restaurant. Because she quit, rather than being laid off, the full check and food stamp allotment had not yet been restored. Her baby, like Sandy's in Boston, is a "family cap" baby, born while Chamique was on public aid and therefore ineligible for welfare. Chamique said she was in touch with the father of the second child, who was in a Job Corps program in another city, and hoped to "get together" with him.

Sister Catherine told me a somewhat different story. Chamique is "very limited," and has a serious learning disability. Her friends probably helped her with the mail-in GED. She "doesn't know how to make good decisions." Her mother was "more committed to her boyfriend than to her," and "gave all of the children [Chamique has three siblings] up to foster care until they were teenagers." Sister Catherine also told me that Chamique was having affairs with two young men at the same time, both related to another resident at the shelter.

Chamique's future seemed precarious, with one exception. Her siblings seemed to be doing all right. She told me two brothers were in college, and one was working for UPS as well. Her sister was a senior in high school. The contrast was not unusual. Linda, another of the seven I met in Chicago, had a sister with a B.A. degree, a brother with an A.A. degree who worked at UPS, and another sister studying radiology therapy. Many welfare recipients are learning disabled, as Chamique is, or clinically depressed, as Linda is (she was on SSI), but have siblings who are doing well. It was not clear what would happen if Chamique's siblings were not going to help her. She might not be disabled enough to qualify for SSI, in which case she would be likely to fall through the cracks when she hit her welfare time limit.

Five months later I had surprising good news from Sister Catherine about Chamique. She had successfully completed the job-readiness program that she had just begun when I visited. She had not gotten a job, but had faithfully pursued many interviews to which she had been sent by the welfare bureaucracy. The problem, Sister Catherine said, was that "her limitations are a real block in the workplace." (Of course if Chamique had an advocate she might have gotten some consideration for her impairment instead of being sent by the bureaucracy on wild-goose job chases.) The best news was that she had married the father of the second child, who had found God while in the Job Corps and abandoned his former gang life in Chicago. He had a job lined up doing housing rehabilitation work in Indianapolis when he finished Job Corps, and Sister Catherine said she believed "they have a solid chance to make it."

Jeanne was learning disabled, too, and had nine children besides, ranging in age from two to nineteen. She was burned out in a fire that was set by the father of her last four children, who had just recently been released from jail. She had been the caretaker of the building, for a hundred-dollar reduction in her rent, but that was gone now. She was on public aid from 1979, when her first child was born, until 1981; off until 1986; and then back on since, except for numerous times when she was erroneously terminated. She said one of the cutoffs was correct — once she actually did miss an appointment. She told me she was a good cook, loved to do it, was cooking at the shelter every day, and hoped to get a job cooking there, although what she really yearned for was to own a restaurant someday. "All things are possible," she said.

She has known about her learning disability since she was twelve. She has serious trouble reading. It seemed that things had gotten worse for Jeanne in the past few years. She was married to the father of the first five children, and as of 1999 he had a job at Marriott, where he had been for ten years. She said she was "working on" getting child support from him. The father of the last four (ages six, five, three, and two) is an electrician who "knows how to build things," but just couldn't stay out of trouble. She told me that after breaking up with her husband she just "gave up on" herself, and started using cocaine in 1995. She said she did cocaine only once a month and never "messed up" or "had to go through rehab," never traded sex for it, and never free-based, only snorted. But she was clearly ashamed, and said she had been clean for two and a half years.

Jeanne was "sad a little bit now, kind of depressed. The time is almost up here. Like, where am I going? I am praying for an extension." She was working hard on getting housing. Jeanne was the one who had a housing-voucher application pending since 1981. "You got to know somebody" to get a housing voucher, she said. She said she wouldn't lie on a lease application about how many kids she has, and she didn't want to move into a public housing project. She did not want her children exposed to gangbangers. "I'm the gangster in my house," she suddenly said fiercely.

Her strong supervision of her children was apparent during our conversation. The two oldest were not with her in the shelter, and her fifteen-year-old son took the brunt of frequent instructions from her to keep the others in line so she could concentrate on her conversation with me. Her oldest daughter was in college studying to be a mortician, and her oldest son had graduated from high school and was working for UPS. The fifteen-year-old was a junior, and she said he was doing well.

"I'm putting it in God's hands," she said as we said goodbye.

Frances, the recovering alcoholic who is seriously asthmatic, told me that she was working in Elgin, Illinois, as a security company dispatcher until she lost her job because her asthma was flaring up too often. In Elgin proof was required that a person had applied unsuccessfully for forty jobs before they would make cash assistance available. And in Chicago's Cook County, where you can be required to take a work assignment, Jeanne told me of being assigned to Reggio's Factory, a pizza place, to work off her check. The company was supposed to — and did — hire some of the welfare recipients as workers after a three-month trial. But,

Jeanne said, they don't really have to, and in any case it was a good deal for them, because they were able to open up a second shift without any added labor cost, and could look forward to an unlimited supply of free workers.

Even though Illinois is not unusually punitive, what is written on paper is not necessarily how workers interpret it, especially when they are under pressure from their superiors to push people to work regardless of individual situations. And these women's experiences showed how troubling even a five-year time limit can be when applied to human reality.

New York City

WHICH BRINGS US to New York City, the capital of workfare. Mayor Rudy Giuliani's pledge was not to end welfare as we know it but to end welfare altogether — the mother of all bumper stickers, if you will. He turned political attacks on the poor into an art form — by, for example, proposing to throw homeless mothers and children out of shelters for various forms of noncooperation and mild malfeasance, sending them to God-only-knows-where. Yet almost everything Giuliani is doing or wants to do is perfectly legal under the law Bill Clinton signed in 1996.

My visits in New York City were arranged by Community Voices Heard, a feisty little group that organizes welfare recipients to take on Giuliani wherever and however they can, brings the voice of welfare recipients to the state legislature and the city council, and provides effective assistance to individual recipients as they try to navigate the perils of the bureaucracy and the complexities of the job market. It also helped to get a $12 million state appropriation for a modest transitional job program for welfare recipients unable to find work — of whom there are many, contrary to popular belief.

Among the women I talked with was Jacqueline Marte. She had two children. Andrew, the older, was born when she was eighteen. Jackie said that before welfare turned nasty, it was "the glue" that enabled her to survive. She hid her first pregnancy for seven months, but when her father learned about it he threw her out of the house. Her odyssey is typical of so many young women who are trying to juggle working at low-paying jobs, going to school, making sure their children are safe, and just plain surviving. She had a job as a "reservationist" at the Discovery Zone but lost it when she refused to work overtime because of Andrew. Another job, at Au Bon Pain in kitchen preparation, became untenable when her hours were reduced to twenty a week, less than she needed to survive.

Jackie met Andrew's father when they were both living in the Dominican Republic. He has no communication with her or her son, and sends no help. She started LaGuardia Community College in 1994 but dropped out when her mother passed away from cancer. She was "devastated" by her mother's death, and besides, her mother had helped out with Andrew. Her father remarried, sold the family home, and moved to New Jersey with his new wife. Jacqueline moved in with a friend. That proved unworkable, and she ended up living with her boyfriend and becoming pregnant with her second child, Silvia.

Jackie went back to school to study word processing and office management after Silvia was born, in 1996. Silvia's father had verbally and physically abused her throughout her pregnancy, hurting her badly enough after the baby was born that she went to the emergency room. She stayed with him two more years before she was able to break away. When I saw Jackie she needed one more semester of credit to graduate, but had been stalled for over a year because of the demands of working, the welfare bureaucracy, and caring for her children.

When Jackie left Silvia's father, she was fortunate enough to get help from a special New York State housing program called "Jiggetts." New York State's constitution promises a right to shelter. Some years ago, legal-services lawyers in New York City won a state court decision, with Jiggetts as the plaintiff, that this language means more than a bed in a homeless shelter. Further maneuvering finally produced a fund from the state to pay for housing for people at risk of being evicted, from which Jackie obtained $650 a month.

When Jackie was one semester away from graduating, Mayor Giuliani's workfare program entered her life. The theory of workfare is that working thirty-five hours a week in return for a welfare check will lead to a paying job. In practice the work experience is typically not useful, job-finding help is not provided, and the workfare job leaves little time to look for work on one's own.

Recently, Jackie had been "fired" from a workfare assignment because she had called in sick. This turned out to be a good thing, because it gave her time to look for a job while the welfare bureaucracy was deciding what to do with her next. Community Voices Heard, in which she had become active in 1995 (she is now a board member), helped connect her to a private community service program called Public Allies, which in turn resulted in two assignments, supported by federal Americorps funds. One was at the Community Food Resource Center in lower Manhattan, where she helped people having problems with food stamps. At the other, a project to measure and publicize the impact of the welfare changes on poor people, her task was to interview people about their welfare experiences. The job paid fifteen hundred dollars a month, plus health and child care coverage, and was to last until June 2000, when Jackie was to graduate to a longer-term position. She was working four days a week at CFRC and the welfare-monitoring project. The fifth day was for training and helping junior high school students in upper Manhattan organize a community health fair. Jackie was getting support and encouragement from a variety of sources, in stark contrast to the normal experience with workfare.

Jackie glowed when she talked about her children. "It's really my kids that I live for," she said. "I call them my little crew. I tell them, 'I'm your father and your mother both.' " They, however, have problems. Andrew, seven years old in 1999, had attention-deficit syndrome and was in a special class with fifteen mainstream children and ten special-needs children. Silvia, who was three, was late in starting to talk, and was in an early-intervention program for preschoolers.

Still, Jackie was one of the lucky ones, like Malikkah and Betsy in Boston. The numbers of women for whom there is no Community Voices Heard or Project Hope or Chicago Coalition for the Homeless are staggering. Many are making it without much extra help, of course, but many others, though reasonably resourceful, nonetheless fall through the cracks or cannot deal with the bureaucracy.

Kimara Nicholas was twenty-four in late 1999, had a five-year-old son (in the "smartest class," she said proudly), and had just started working at CVH as its office manager after volunteering for a while. Kimara has lived in the heart of Harlem almost all of her life. Her son goes to her old elementary school. Kimara graduated from high school when she was eighteen. She was in the "talented-and-gifted" class from the first grade on. In high school she interned at two law firms and with the city's corporation counsel and also had a job at a union local. In school she was in a dance company, was on the yearbook staff, and worked every year with disabled children in the local Special Olympics. She was accepted to John Jay College but didn't go, because her mother became ill and she needed to help with her little brother and sister.

It was about then that Kimara became pregnant, and things changed. The relationship with the young man had been serious — including talk of marriage — but it ended before either of them knew she was pregnant. The idea of abortion never crossed her mind. She was depressed, came close to losing the baby, cried all the time, and didn't eat. She started going to church, where a deaconess told her that God does not make mistakes. That encounter helped her face her situation. When we met she was praying and reading the Bible every day, and reading passages in it to her son every night when she wasn't too tired. She told me, "I talk to God. That really helps."

During the first five years of her son Jabari's life (Jabari is "Swahili for brave," Kimara told me), Kimara was on welfare. She worked on and off, but also spent a lot of time with Jabari. It had become easier to leave him once he started school, and she was proud of the fact that both she and her mother were attending the College of New Rochelle, which has a campus in Harlem. She told of frequent struggles with the welfare bureaucracy. She was cut off numerous times. They said she missed appointments when she had in fact shown up. They sent checks to the wrong address and used an incorrect middle name, which added to the confusion. Once, at a hearing about one of the cutoffs, the hearing officer asked the welfare worker why Kimara had been cut off. The worker was unable to give a reason and finally admitted it was a mistake. She had been off the rolls for six months at the time.

After workfare came in, Kimara was summoned to the office and told to bring her son. She was there from nine to six, and then was told she would have to come back again because she had brought the wrong child care form. When she asked about her assignment, a worker told her it would be sanitation or transit. Kimara said she had a bad back and could bring a letter from her doctor. Then she noticed a list on the wall that included clerical child care positions. She asked about it and the woman said, "That's an old list." (Stories about people being pushed around by the workfare bureaucracy are legion. Kimara said people who had no high school diploma or who didn't speak English were sent to sanitation immediately. Assessments of skills and aptitudes were haphazard at best.)

Kimara was no longer on public assistance and seemed to be in a good place. I asked her whether, given the prosperity in the economy, people in her neighborhood were having an easier time finding jobs. She laughed at me. Her friends are all high school graduates and some have college degrees. She said there "are no office jobs," and the men could get only construction work and maybe security ("and that's a maybe," she added). She said one male friend who had graduated from Alabama State in the top 20 percent of his class couldn't find a job doing anything except construction. "They think every black man has a gun on his hip and belongs to a gang, and every black woman has ten kids and has been on public assistance since she got out of the womb."

The third woman I met was Brenda Banks. A thirty-eight-year-old mother of fifteen-year-old and thirteen-year-old daughters, Brenda had been working hard looking for a job. She brought with her a meticulously organized notebook containing versions of her résumé tailored to different types of jobs, a personalized fax form, and a record of all her job applications and interviews. Like Jackie, her best recent experience with the welfare bureaucracy was when they got confused and left her alone for a while. They couldn't decide whether they wanted her to be at a workfare assignment five days a week, or only three days a week with the other two days to be spent at job club. The issue was sent to what Brenda calls "conciliation," which she said gave her uninterrupted time to look for a job. (Job club, she said, is a place that "nine times out of ten is overcrowded, where two hundred women spend the day with one computer, the Yellow Pages, and several telephones" trying to arrange for job interviews.)

Brenda had nothing good to say about workfare. "They don't really want you to look for a job," she said. "What they want is the free labor." She described one assignment she had at an office in the city Department for the Aging. "We [the seven workfare people] ran the office," she said. "The employees took two-hour lunches. They gave us the work of an employee but not the respect." She said the attitude of the welfare bureaucracy now was, " 'This is temporary. You're going to get off on your own or we're going to hound you until you do.' I can understand temporary, but I think it's unfair to push people off. Sometimes they don't have the education, and there are many people who have other good reasons. It's easier to look if your kids are older. They are pulling mothers who have three-month-old babies. That's not right."

I was troubled about Brenda. She was presentable, articulate, and trying hard. To me, the reason she couldn't get a job was spelled r-a-c-e. The next day, after I spoke to a group of insurance executives interested in public-interest issues, a woman told me she had a federally funded Americorps slot at her project on promoting microenterprise lending and wondered if I had any leads on how she might find someone. I said, you want Brenda Banks. She got the job and is doing well, but what about the other Brendas?

Getting Beyond the Myths

AS MY INTERVIEWS illustrated, the overwhelming message of the new welfare law is that one size fits all. The fact that people are individuals with specific situations and stories is shoved under the rug. Even when state policy is somewhat individualized, front-line workers are overwhelmed, undertrained, and under pressure to get caseloads down.

The arbitrary numbers in the law are bad policy: rigid time limits, ceilings on the number of exceptions to the time limits, minimum percentages of the caseload that have to be in work activities. Frustrated that previous directives to get people into the workforce had been flouted by welfare bureaucrats, the legislators resorted to group punishment. Unable to find and punish the guilty, they decided to punish the innocent as well, to make sure of getting the malefactors.

The 1996 law expires in 2002. A debate will begin in Congress in 2001 over how to change it. There are three stories to which that discussion should respond.

One is the story of people who have gotten jobs but do not earn enough to support their families or even escape poverty, do not have health coverage, and cannot find affordable child care. They need more support to retain their jobs and advance. Many of them may need cash help again, or may need a partial check because their pay is so low. For them, a five-year limit will be insufficient, even though they have done everything we asked.

This first story is also about what has happened to the American economy over the past generation; it is a symptom of the widening gap between the top and the bottom. It has been exploited by divide-and-conquer politicians who have appealed to lower-wage workers by blaming their economic problems on those at the bottom, when both groups suffer from the weakness in the economy and the failure of government to respond.

The second story is of people who could function in a job but have special problems. These are the "hard to serve" — reachable but not easily — and they include victims of domestic violence, the learning disabled, the chronically depressed, the barely literate, the geographically isolated, and people with problems of drug and alcohol abuse. They need not only extra attention but, in many cases, some kind of supported work if they are going to succeed in doing something outside the home.

We really are two Americas. During the summer of 1999, when unemployment was at a thirty-year low, I would read about college students having their pick of five jobs, or fast-food places bidding up wages to get people, and I would wonder: What am I missing here? Where is the boom for the 2.5 million women still expected to get jobs or end up in the street, or the men, not mentioned and not counted, who are so discouraged they are out of the labor market altogether? When Federal Reserve Chairman Alan Greenspan warned of impending inflation because of labor shortages, I could only conclude that he, like most of the rest of America, had closed his eyes to the bifurcation: a hot economy in which museums are receiving visitors in record numbers and actually operating in the black, and a much smaller America where the recession never ends, where the monsters that children dream about are real.

There is a third story, which is about "the disappeared" — the ones for whom things are already worse. These are the people who present the most dramatic case for the resurrection of a safety net. This group is the one for which there is perhaps the least public understanding and sympathy and which in many ways presents the strongest test of our compassion as the wealthiest nation on earth. This group includes the considerable number of people caring for chronically ill children or infirm relatives — real and hard work in itself. Among them are a surprising number of grandmothers caring for grandchildren because the children's mother is on crack or methamphetamines or in jail or otherwise out of the picture. If the grandmother is poor and wants to be included in the calculation of benefits for the family, then she is subject to the work requirements and the time limits just as her daughter would be.

What we should ideally do in response to these three stories is scrap the 1996 law and start over, defining a baseline of decency below which states cannot go — assuring a safety net for children, preventing the most punitive policies, providing stronger encouragement for states to be genuinely helpful in promoting work, and addressing the income shortfall of all low-wage workers. We should be asking whether we really believe raising children constitutes a contribution to society and, if so, what that means for welfare policy. We should have a serious debate about what it actually costs to support a family, and what public policies — not just cash supplements but health coverage, child care, and housing assistance — are needed. We should ask hard questions about how profit-making contractors have performed.

We need to approach the reauthorization debate with a special sense of fairness. Welfare-to-work policies have presented too many perverse situations in which people quickly lose all or part of their health coverage and child care when they go to work. This is "equitable" in the sense that those recently on welfare and those never on welfare are shafted equally, but it is not fair. A better policy would not only continue health and child care for as long as a person cannot afford them on her own but extend the benefits to everyone in similar need.

If the welfare block grant and time limits are to remain, federal law should reflect more clearly what is needed for people to get and keep jobs and get out of poverty, and what happens when people are unable to find a job or are not in a position to work.

If there is going to be a clock, it does not have to tick for all cash assistance. It can be stopped for help extended to people already working, for help in times of high unemployment, for people taking care of small or chronically ill children or infirm relatives, for grandparents taking care of grandchildren, for people pursuing job training or higher education, and for situations involving domestic violence. Exceptions to work requirements can be extended similarly.

We can reward states that reduce poverty. Funds can be directed more specifically to child care, transit, literacy and training, drug and alcohol treatment, mental health services, remediation of learning disabilities, help for victims of domestic violence, and all of the other assistance people need to be able to get and keep a job. And we can treat legal immigrants more fairly.

Perhaps the health of the economy will allow our anger at the poor to recede and we will be more realistic in judging people's needs and capacities. Maybe we can genuinely value families instead of just mouthing family values. Perhaps we can dispel the welfare mythology that obscures the truth of how lives are being destroyed by policies at odds with human reality.

6

REKINDLING THE COMMITMENT

Politics and Poverty in the New Century

CAN WE RESUME Robert Kennedy's journey? Can we rekindle the commitment to achieve a better life for those on the margins? Can we build from the rubble of the welfare debates policies and action based on enduring values but with a fresh view of solutions? It will be difficult, to be honest. The people at the lower end are now so marginalized. And there is so much money devoted to electing people whose only real impulse is to do what their major campaign contributors want.

We need three things. One is ideas and proposals — models of success. Without substance, a movement has no direction. Second, we need organizing. There has to be a constituency for change. Without organizing, a movement has no fuel. Third, we need to use the organizing to do the politics, both electoral and civic. Without politics, a movement has no vehicle to get from here to there. All of these are necessary. None can succeed without the others.

Doing the politics is crucial. We need to have the solutions, but they will not be put in place unless we do the politics. This means persuading elected officials to behave differently and electing different people to public office, and it means persuading all of us to vote, participate in political life between elections, and act differently in our daily lives.

I believe the politics of economics can be changed. But more of us have to start thinking politically if that is going to happen. Too many of us have given up on politics. Too many who run agencies serving low-income people act as if the inadequacy of their resources were unrelated to politics. Tax-exempt status chills political activity far beyond what is actually demanded by the Internal Revenue Code. Some in the foundation world seem to believe that initiatives begun with their funding will survive purely by virtue of their evident quality. Basic change does not come without political action, and political action does not come without organizing.

Of course not all things that would change the politics are good. A depression would shake things up. So would a big war. Nobody wants either of those. We could wait for a principled national leader to come along. We can't bank on that. Recessions do occur and tend to produce, however temporarily, better policies. Decent leaders do appear, but the current political equation keeps them from getting enough done. Even money is not uniformly a bad influence.

What doesn't work is the politics we have now. The debate is sterile. "The best government is no government" versus "the best government is a little government." "The answer is entirely in the private sector" versus "the answer is mainly in the private sector." "The answer is let them eat cake" versus "the answer is throw them a few crumbs." People who talk about the poor as "those people" versus people who talk about them as little as possible.

So what is the theme, the message, the framework?

There are many apt concepts: fairness, justice, opportunity, equality, compassion, morality, self-interest, children, family, race. All are powerful and pertinent, but they won't produce an effective politics if "poverty" is the only word that connects them.

About six out of seven Americans are not poor, and the ones who are don't vote much.

Stressing moral imperatives won't put us over the top, although it is important. Nor will the worthy argument that it is in our self-interest to reduce poverty, although that, too, will help. There are too many voters who aren't poor for arguments directed solely at poverty to be politically salient.

But we also know that many people who aren't classified as poor are having a tough time making it and aren't getting a fair share of the country's steadily increasing income and wealth. People don't understand that the gap has widened so greatly in the past twenty years.

Who doesn't make enough money to live at a decent level? Not just the poor. Who is terrified of being one paycheck away from having no health coverage, or has a job but no health coverage right now? Not just the poor. Who is deeply concerned that the public schools are not doing an adequate job of educating their children? Not just the poor. Who has trouble affording decent child care or finding child care at all? Not just the poor. Who has trouble finding affordable housing? Not just the poor. Who has trouble paying for a college education for which they or their children are otherwise completely qualified? Not just the poor.

So here are some ingredients: a politics based on a fair shake for everybody, with a special emphasis on children and families — an approach that includes millions who are not poor and is strengthened by the fact that there are promising solutions already being demonstrated in various locales.

The heart of the idea is a politics based more on what people have in common than on what differentiates them from each other. It would be unifying, a refreshing change from the identity politics of the past three decades.

There is one more ingredient — getting beyond labels. The current political discourse spans a range from A to B rather than

A to Z — from the hard right to the soft center. The traditional liberal position has been marginalized. If we are going to revive the Left, those of us on the progressive side have a responsibility to redefine our stance. We need to speak for fairness, and for children and families. We need an inclusive politics that invites everyone's involvement in pursuing better public policy and in helping people directly.

This new progressivism insists on an important role for both government and community. So many Americans today live atomized lives, working hard but not really connected to anyone beyond their families; even that connection is only a maybe with people scattered hundreds and thousands of miles away from parents and siblings. Active efforts to build a sense of community, based on faith or professional affiliation as well as geography, are part of my new progressivism.

Community is especially important when we consider the lives of poor and lower-income people. Decent jobs reduce income disparities, but destructive behavior has to be addressed, too. The increase in concentrations of poverty over the past thirty years brought a disintegration of community cohesion along with more violence, drugs, unmarried teen births, and all the rest. Strengthening the role of parents and building stronger families in better-knit and safer neighborhoods is vital to addressing these problems. It will be an arduous process, but it must be undertaken. It will require, among other things, a commitment from the broader community to help connect people to jobs throughout the region, improve the public schools, and nurture the children and youth of the neighborhood.

The word "community" was not central in traditional liberal politics. The word "poverty" has not been common in the vocabulary of those who have been promoting ideas of the civil society and communitarianism. The new progressivism would apply the idea of civic renewal to the issue of poverty.

And poverty — in fact, fairness to all of those at the lower end — is the issue, not welfare. Welfare should be merely the safety net — important, but the last thing we do when everything else fails to produce self-sufficiency. I learned that from Robert Kennedy thirty years ago. It is just as true today.

There are some good signs. The so-called welfare reform is in some places, almost accidentally, connecting the idea of civic renewal to the question of poverty. The need to implement the new law has energized business and professional, religious and secular, and low-income community leaders who see the need for a conscious effort to help welfare recipients get from here to there. There is a stirring in the world of labor unions, and an awakening of interest in low-income people in churches and synagogues and mosques. There is a mounting wave of voluntary involvement in helping others, especially among young people. All these things move in the right direction.

One thing the traditional liberal position had going for it was its optimism. Liberals believed their proposals, if implemented, would solve the problems. Americans were responsive. We believed the New Deal had helped get us through the Depression. The government had mobilized us to win the war. We grew up on Roosevelt, Truman, Eisenhower, JFK, and the Johnson of civil rights. We had a good run for over thirty years. Government was a good thing. Public service was a good thing. People who ran for office were respected.

We have lost that confidence. People have been bombarded by incessant propaganda, especially during campaign seasons. There is enormous cynicism about the efficacy of politics and public policy. From Vietnam to Watergate to Reagan to Clinton, we have had a run of national disappointment.

It will be an uphill battle to restore a shared sense that we can make a difference. It involves getting enough people to see that they have the same concerns and that there are practical steps that would make a difference. If this exercise takes hold, a larger number of able and decent people will begin to run for office and other able and decent people will see the worth of involving themselves in their communities. More people will decide it is worthwhile to vote and to try to influence government decisions on a regular basis.

Those of us on the progressive side need to mobilize people. Money and star power will help, and the courts are valuable sometimes, but our base is not money power. It is people power.

The civil rights legislation of the sixties did not get enacted because the elites planned it behind closed doors. It was helped by *Brown v. Board of Education*, but it came primarily from a movement of incredibly courageous people and an ensuing national revulsion to the brutal responses of Bull Connor, Sheriff Jim Clark, the Ku Klux Klan, and the mobs, all brought before the rest of the nation by the then-new magic of television. The environmental movement and the women's movement did not have their successes because the wealthy and powerful made things happen, although some certainly helped substantially. The war in Vietnam did not end because Richard Nixon and Henry Kissinger woke up one day and decided we had done enough.

I have no easy recipe to offer for a movement or a better politics for economic and social and racial justice. Better national leadership that appears accidentally or because of a recession will help. Changing fashions in popular culture may make a difference. Some event or series of events may catalyze action for a time. A wave of media attention may take hold. Progressive foundations and wealthy individuals may hit on a way of popularizing relevant ideas.

But the only truly reliable source of action is the people — demands for action from the bottom up. That means as many people as possible have to plant seeds, everywhere they can. The challenge for readers of this book is to ask, What can I do, how can I help, how can I make a difference?

Tackling the Connection Between Place
and Poverty: The Case of Sandtown

A MOVEMENT TO reduce poverty and increase economic fairness would attack both structural and individual problems. It would address current jobs and income needs, and invest in the future. And it would pay special attention to a major issue: what to do about places in which too many poor people live side by side.

Only a minority of the poor live in the inner city and isolated rural areas, but these are the places where poverty persists most stubbornly from generation to generation. The number of poor people living in inner-city, concentrated poverty doubled between 1970 and 1990, a direct effect of the failure of antipoverty policy during this period. Life is worse and escaping poverty is harder for people who live in places with too many other poor people. For these reasons antipoverty strategies must focus on place.

There are three critical points here.

First, poor neighborhoods, for all of their problems, have assets, both human and physical, on which to build. In even the highest-poverty neighborhoods (real neighborhoods, not the disastrous high-rise public housing projects that we built in a fit of temporary insanity), most people have always had work. In an important book, *Poverty and Place,* Paul Jargowsky points out that 72 percent of the income coming into neighborhoods of concentrated (over 40 percent) poverty in 1990 was from earnings. There is community leadership in those neighborhoods. There are young people graduating from high school and going to college. There are churches and nonprofits and other community institutions functioning and contributing to the life of the neighborhood.

Second, given what has happened to cities, there is no way that everyone in such neighborhoods will ever find a job in or adjacent to their community. Strategies for the inner city must help both men and women, and especially young people just entering the job market, to get and keep jobs wherever they are to be found in the region. In the sixties, we talked of residential mobility, and we talked of neighborhood revitalization, but we somehow missed the need to connect people to jobs wherever they are located. That is perhaps the biggest poverty lesson of the past three decades.

Michael Porter, of the Harvard Business School, is only the most recent observer to note that inner cities possess unexploited competitive advantages, but that is different from saying that inner cities can become self-sufficient in employment. No one thinks a middle-class or wealthy neighborhood should be self-sufficient within its own borders. Yet some persist in believing that this is a reasonable goal for low-income neighborhoods.

Third, these neighborhoods cannot lift themselves by their own bootstraps. Not only are the bulk of the jobs going to be located elsewhere, but much of what needs fixing within the neighborhood is controlled from outside. Public housing, schools, health care, public safety, and services of all kinds are run from downtown. Those who would change a neighborhood have to press for change in the behavior of the outside actors who have so much say in the lives of the residents.

Neighborhood revitalization is extremely important. A neighborhood needs safety, successful schools, health services, and child care. Housing must be habitable. Senior citizens need to feel protected and supported. People need to feel a sense of connection to one another. There must be visible progress, especially on public safety and education, to entice people to stay and to attract people back.

Some inner-city community development offers promise. The vast majority of the two-thousand-plus community development corporations are still small low-income housing developers, but there is a growing number of more comprehensive efforts.

One such effort is in the Sandtown-Winchester neighborhood

of Baltimore, a direct descendant of Robert Kennedy's work in Bedford-Stuyvesant.

Cab Calloway grew up in Sandtown and Thurgood Marshall went to school there, but this area of ten thousand people, just west of downtown Baltimore and nearly all African American, had fallen on the hardest of hard times by the late 1980s. Unemployment was officially 25 percent, but it was more likely 50 percent when one counted those who had stopped trying to get work and those working part-time or sporadically. Seventy percent of the households were headed by a single parent. Infant mortality was four times the national rate. Three-quarters of the people lived in substandard housing, and nearly a fourth of the housing was vacant. Family incomes were astonishingly low: half below eleven thousand dollars, a quarter below five thousand. Everything else followed: violent crime, drug dealing practically everywhere, dropping out of school, teen pregnancy, HIV-AIDS, large numbers of men in jail or with criminal records, epidemic lead poisoning among the children, you name it.

Behind the Sandtown effort were the then-new and first elected African American mayor of Baltimore, Kurt Schmoke, and the late James Rouse, the highly respected developer and urbanist. Mr. Rouse, as everyone called him, had already been talking to the new mayor about working to transform a poor neighborhood when the Mayor went to Sandtown to announce two large-scale housing programs. Community residents told the Mayor that the improved housing would do no good if the other problems of the neighborhood weren't addressed. When Schmoke and Rouse heard that, they knew they had their site.

A decade or so later, much has happened. The city and Mr. Rouse's Enterprise Foundation — a nationally respected developer of low-income housing — have been partners from the beginning. Mayor Schmoke created a special staff to deal with Sandtown, and provided extra funds from federal block grants and other sources. Enterprise provided senior people, technical assistance, and start-up funding, and played a crucial role in selling the project to foundations, corporations, and government agencies. It also recruited assistance from outside professionals — architects, planners, developers, educators, and so on.

There have been major gains — in housing, health care, public safety, education, employment, community activities, and neighborhood appearance. It is easy to find people who have been helped. They don't talk in abstract terms about a newly wonderful "community." In fact, many people say that some community problems, like drug dealing, have gotten worse. What they talk about is what has happened in their own lives.

Three young people I talked with — Andre, Josh, and Shaquetta — told me they were pretty sure they would still be dealing and doing drugs or maybe in jail if it hadn't been for Sandtown's local YouthBuild program. (YouthBuild is a national program, with outlets in over a hundred communities.) Andre said he wanted to be a "bank project officer," Josh said he wanted to work for Habitat for Humanity (which built a home for his mother in the neighborhood), and Shaquetta said she wanted to be a preschool teacher (she has a five-year-old child). They are all articulate and frank about where they were going wrong before. They emphasized that they were not just learning skills at YouthBuild. Josh, the youngest at sixteen, started building pigeon coops as a child, and said he was "learning how to get used to talking to people." All three stressed that they were learning about respect and relationships, to value people of the opposite sex for reasons other than sex, and to be responsible with money. Andre talked about the "hype" on television, the advertising for cars and beer and other products. "It's all sex, it's everywhere," he said. I asked them what high school was like. All three talked about the peer pressure not to go to class. "Somebody's always jumping somebody," Josh said, contrasting the "good peer pressure" in YouthBuild. "Teachers in high school never ask, 'Why aren't you learning?' " Andre said. "The teachers at YouthBuild want to know about *you.*"

James Underwood (not his real name), now in his thirties, told me he spent five years in prison, having been a gangster, a hit man, and a drug dealer. He said proudly that he now runs four companies that do landscaping, janitorial work, and odd jobs like boarding up vacant houses. He said the "programs" have helped people like Andre, Josh, Shaquetta, and many others to see that "there is another way" without traveling "the long painful road" that he traveled. He said he told everyone in the neighborhood to come to "the Center" — the converted school that is head-quarters for the Sandtown program. He said the problem in East Baltimore, where he lived until 1995, was that they didn't have anything like the Center. They "need an anchor," he said.

Three women with whom I talked at the Kelson elementary school — Mrs. Burns, Mrs. Carroll, and Mrs. Nelson — got involved in the neighborhood transformation by going to work at the school. After being at home with their children or working outside Sandtown, they were now working with the children of the neighborhood. Mrs. Burns ran the computer room at the school, a job she worked up to after she decided to stop being a "home mom" and took a computer course. Mrs. Carroll and Mrs. Nelson were teacher aides in the school. Mrs. Burns and Mrs. Carroll had children in the school, and Mrs. Nelson was a grandmother, retired from years of service at the Social Security Administration and at Citibank. The pride they took in the school and in their contribution to it was enormous.

On the other hand, questions about the long-term commitment of both the city and Enterprise were beginning to arise at the end of 1999. A new mayor was about to take office, and, with Mr. Rouse having passed away, senior Enterprise officials were beginning to wonder out loud about whether enough progress had been made to justify their continuing immersion. A second turnover in senior staff was occurring, and the community still felt it wasn't a full partner. By the summer of 2000 the city and Enterprise had suggested that the neighborhood develop a new, totally community-driven organization to run things. They pledged continuing support, but people close to the situation sensed a coming change in Sandtown's decade-long special status.

The two years of planning at the beginning were resident-driven, but it was hard to get around the ministers, heads of agencies, and chairs of associations to the rank and file, and even harder to reach the unemployed, the addicted, the convicted, and the otherwise hurting. It was hard, too, to get people to think beyond the drug dealers, the gun violence, and the garbage in the streets, and to focus instead on getting children ready for school and graduating competent young adults.

One positive point was the human and institutional assets. There were neighborhood leaders, working people, consumers, churchgoers, and a stock of physical assets. Sandtown was also fortunate in having the unstinting support of its city council (Sandtown is in the home district of the city council president) and state legislative representatives. People with tiny and not so tiny pieces of power can feel as threatened by the prospect of good as by the prospect of harm, if they are not going to control or get credit for it, and that was less of a problem in Sandtown than it has been elsewhere.

Sandtown also illustrates that community revitalization requires outside resources. Among the early federally assisted activities were two housing projects, a neighborhood health clinic specializing in infant care, and the renovation of a school building as a community center and administrative offices. By 1996 outside funding reached more than a hundred grants from more than eighty different public and private funding sources, causing complaints that Sandtown was too dependent on outside money and would never be economically self-sustaining.

This, however, is the wrong way to look at it. The neighborhood was heavily subsidized to begin with. Anything that reduces the costs of welfare, extra policing, and so on, is a plus. The wealthy suburbs get back more than they pay in taxes and nobody complains. They use their political clout to get an outsized share of transit- and capital-development money. The Sandtown leaders believe a combination of residents getting jobs, new businesses moving in or starting up, and self-sufficient new residents coming in will produce economic stability or at least a great improvement over present conditions. But it does take time, and the investment required is significant and has to come largely from the outside. By 1999 about $80 million in new outside funding had come into the neighborhood over a nearly ten-year period.

By 1999 1,600 of the neighborhood's 4,000 housing units were new or renovated, or on their way, with sixteen different developers involved. Most of the 600 vacant units that the Mayor had pledged to rehabilitate were finished, and the neighborhood had been designated by HUD as a Home Ownership Zone, which meant construction of 322 more new units. In contrast, only 15 units of housing had been built in the neighborhood between 1988 and 1992. On the other hand, more housing fell vacant between 1993 and 1999, increasing the number of havens for drug dealers and users.

Six outside health providers are providing primary health care, backed by a $2 million grant from the Kellogg Foundation to get residents enrolled in the programs. By 1999 the health consortium had greatly expanded drug treatment. There was a brand-new nursing home. Three school-based health clinics had opened. Infant mortality was down, birth weights were up, and virtually 100 percent of the children entering elementary school were immunized.

Violent crime in Sandtown dropped by over 20 percent during the nineties, and homicides went way down. Through police-community cooperation, more than a hundred block captains were organized, and fifteen crack houses were closed. With support from the Annenberg Foundation, the school system, in consultation with the community, instituted in two of Sandtown's three elementary schools a model curriculum that already had proven results elsewhere, and trained parents as well as teachers to use it. An intensive preschool readiness program was started, to go along with the new curriculum. In 1999 Annenberg, impressed with the progress in the schools, renewed its $1 million grant for another three years, which was an unusual step for them.

The municipal market in the area was given over to management by a nonprofit organization, which hired community residents and attracted new business nearby. More than seven hundred residents had been referred for drug treatment, a needle-exchange program for heroin addicts had been introduced, and the rate of HIV infection was down. There were community gardens all over the place, a new community newspaper, a calendar of community events, Pop Warner football and Little League baseball, a pumpkin festival, an annual recognition dinner, food baskets at holidays, and seventeen hundred new registered voters. (After Parris Glendening was elected governor by six thousand votes in 1994, his opponent, Ellen Sauerbrey, charged that the election was stolen from her in Sandtown. She couldn't believe that many inner-city residents would vote.)

When I first visited in 1994, I was troubled by the lack of progress with jobs. Only about three hundred previously unemployed residents had gotten jobs, and four hundred more had gone through job training. The record did not match other accomplishments. The gap was particularly evident with young people. This was especially disappointing to me, because I had pressed the White House for a national youth-development policy, and had been speaking around the country urging what I called clear pathways for young people, beginning no later than their early teens. Sandtown-Winchester seemed to have missed the boat.

This is not simple stuff, of course. People with criminal records, addiction problems, and deficient basic skills are not attractive to employers, especially those with racial prejudices. Younger people have less baggage, but if they have gone to schools that taught them little and had peers who scorned academic achievement, they are likely to be unprepared for community college or a full-time job.

A jobs strategy, regional in scope, is key to neighborhood transformation. It needs three basic elements: a job, wherever it is located, the support that will enable the individual to keep the job, and preparation for the job. The economics of the neighborhood must also change, but this will not happen unless the broader community assists in pursuing the three basic elements.

By late 1999 there was noticeable improvement. About a thousand residents had been helped to obtain jobs both outside and inside the community, most after participating in training or a job-readiness activity run by a neighborhood organization. Sandtown's YouthBuild program was teaching construction skills to young people who had dropped out of school, and attempting to build self-esteem. It was taking in about twenty-five young people a year, most of whom were finding jobs. Many were obtaining their high school equivalency, and some were going on to college.

There was an impressive array of new institutions in Sandtown employing residents, many of them ex-convicts, recovering addicts, former welfare recipients, or school dropouts. There was Community Building in Partnership (CBP, the organization created to drive the rehabilitation process), the health clinic, the nursing home, Habitat for Humanity, the Sandtown-Winchester High Blood Pressure Program, the Lafayette Market, and the health consortium. The job training and placement programs were doing a reasonably good job. Sandtown Works, started by CBP, was teaching "soft" skills and providing employer-linked training. EDEN Jobs was run by New Song Church, which had a long record of neighborhood service and ran the local Habitat for Humanity program as well as an independent school.

Accumulated trash was another problem that CBP tackled. Much of it was dumped by people from other places who believed that Sandtown wouldn't care. CBP created an Americorps-funded team of fifteen people, nearly all neighborhood residents, to start a cleanup. By the fall of 1999 an incredible 2 million pounds of trash had been hauled away, and the community was visibly cleaner. CBP leaders believed the cleanup also helped to reduce crime and violence. It disrupted drug dealers, who were using the trash piles as places to stash their goods. Children were now playing in the streets more freely because the safety hazards presented by the trash were gone.

Among the many Sandtown success stories, the story of Sylvia Peters and the elementary schools may be the best of all. A former Chicago high school principal who made her mark turning around a couple of tough schools in that city, she was hired by Enterprise in 1995 to coordinate a community effort to improve the neighborhood's three elementary schools.

Things were jumping the day I first met Sylvia Peters, in the fall of 1998. The schools had just enjoyed a strikingly successful summer program in which three hundred children had achieved an average gain of a year in their reading. Twelve master teachers, all from the community's own schools, had worked with novice teachers, students, and parents in the classrooms, so there was a seven-to-one student-teacher ratio. The teachers received performance-based bonuses, and the whole program cost only seventy-eight thousand dollars. Peters said it was "dynamite," a "well-oiled machine."

Peters and her colleagues had also finally succeeded the previous spring in removing the recalcitrant principal of the third elementary school, Gilmor. She had steadily refused to participate in the model curriculum despite the exciting results at Kelson and Pinderhughes. The day I was visiting, every child at Gilmor was being tested before undertaking the new curriculum. Teachers were complaining that Peters was moving too fast. Peters was outraged at the percentage of students who could not read. At Kelson and Pinderhughes, students now enter first grade performing a month ahead of national norms. Despite the palpable damage being done to the children, getting the principal at Gilmor out had been a big political fight. Many parents fought the move, because they liked the principal personally. Peters said, "People think being a principal is a social position." Her goal is to have all of the children in all three schools at grade level by the fall of 2001.

Computers are especially important in all this. Kelson's computer center was being used by the children as part of their education and was offering computer courses to parents before and after school. It charged a small fee to the parents, which helped maintain the program and leverage other funding. There was great enthusiasm about the computer center, with about eight hundred community residents having made use of it during the three years it had been in existence. It gave hope that some adults, and even more children, would develop skills that would enable them to be full participants in the twenty-first century economy.

Sylvia Peters said repeatedly that she was sixty years old, but she projected the energy of a twenty-year-old. She took some of the teachers from Kelson and Pinderhughes to visit a school in Houston that was using the same direct-instruction curriculum as the Sandtown schools, and she said they all saw children "blowing the lid off the Stanford Achievement Test." She said "there is a difference between being certified and being qualified," and that at Kelson and Pinderhughes, "*everybody* is now teaching," and "people are starting to admit what they don't know." She was proud to have created an atmosphere in which no one was hitting children or yelling at them. Seventeen other schools in Baltimore had adopted the direct-instruction curriculum as of 1999.

"School change is arduous," Peters concluded. "Superintendents and administrators send shock waves through the system every time they come and go. People in schools say this too will pass and figure they can just wait it out. . . . In Sandtown now parents respect education. That's been missing from the schools for the past twenty-five years."

Sylvia Peters was still in great form when I went back in late 1999. We walked into Kelson at about ten on a Wednesday morning, through hallways so quiet one would have thought school was not in session. "You see how quiet it is," Peters said. "Three years ago these halls were c-h-a-o-t-i-c," her voice elongating the word. "College begins in this room," said a computer-generated sign on a second grade classroom door. In every classroom teachers were speaking so quietly that I had to step well inside the door to hear. Peters pointed out how gentle the teachers were in dealing with their small charges. "We're doing private education in a public setting," she said.

The classes were small, all between twenty and twenty-five students. In several of the classrooms some of the children were working independently — diligently and quietly — while the teacher worked with a smaller group. The younger children also had teacher aides. I could not tell who was the teacher and who the aide on seeing two instructional clusters at work in a classroom. Peters whispered to me that the strongest factor in the changes at the school had been the involvement of parents, especially the nonprofessionals working there. I thought she downplayed what she and Joyce Hughes, the principal since 1996, and the teachers had done.

There were male teachers, too, providing role models seldom seen in elementary school. Peters pointed proudly at a young woman teaching first grade, telling me that she was extremely gifted and on her way to a master's degree. She had grown up poor in the neighborhood, had a child at fourteen, and found her way to college. Peters and Joyce Hughes had taken her under their wing, helping her develop her skills and ambitions.

The girls wore maroon plaid jumpers with yellow blouses, the boys maroon pants with yellow shirts. A few children didn't have the uniforms, because they were in the wash or because of family finances, although the school usually found a way to help those who were unable to afford uniforms on their own. Joyce Hughes said the uniforms had made a great difference in the atmosphere at the school, which was spotless, with precise time schedules posted on every door. Even when the children changed rooms at the end of their reading and language instruction, there was very little noise.

In a fifth grade classroom, the children read to me, beautifully, from *The Wizard of Oz,* and answered questions clearly and correctly about why the Cowardly Lion was cowardly and what the Scarecrow lacked. Peters told me that the curriculum exposed children to what they will need to survive ("kids need to learn what the middle-class game is") and to their African American heritage at the same time. "They think Julius Caesar is soooo cool," she said over lunch. "You should have seen how they acted out the parts in the Boston Tea Party." Peters said it takes four years to teach reading properly. The teaching was broken down into units beginning at the simplest level and becoming more complicated as the grades go up. I saw first graders reading out loud individually (and impressively) to their teacher while an aide worked with the rest of the class and some of the children worked independently. The first graders also kept impressive journals about what was going on in their lives.

Peters's quest to get a toehold in the third school, Gilmor, was cut short in the spring of 2000. The state, citing the school's dismal record, took it over along with two other failing schools in the city, and turned it over to the Edison Project, a for-profit company. Edison was given substantial funding for air conditioning and new lighting and free rein to reconstitute the school. The move may be positive, but one can only wonder what Sylvia Peters could have done with the same power and infusion of resources.

After the state acted, it turned out that Peters's belatedly accomplished intervention in Gilmor was paying dividends. New test scores showed spectacular increases, from dismal single digits up to the mid-twenties on national norms. It was too late to reverse the takeover, though. Peters, meanwhile, finally broke into Harlem Park, the middle school into which the three Sandtown elementary schools feed, and is training thirty-four teachers there in the direct-instruction method. Equally important, Annenberg drafted Peters to apply her talents, with a generous dollop of new funding, in two low-performing inner-city elementary schools in Los Angeles and Atlanta, in both cases as part of a broader strategy of neighborhood revitalization and mixed-income housing construction to attract middle-income families to the neighborhood.

This work takes a long time. It is never finished as long as new children come to life every year. Newark's New Community Corporation — a pioneer — has existed for over thirty years and has an annual budget of more than $100 million and more than fourteen hundred employees, and still has plenty to do. The Sandtown effort had been going for about a decade when I last visited, and had already gone through a number of transitions. The impressive new leadership team that had been in place for about three years was about to move on. There was a slight sense of uncertainty about the future despite the tangible improvements.

A continuing problem is that the neighborhood has never had a full share in the ownership of the effort. Community Building in Partnership has essentially been run by people sent in by the Mayor and by Enterprise. Manny Price, who directed CBP from 1997 on, came from Mayor Schmoke's office. He understood the neighborhood, having grown up in poverty in East Baltimore, but he was not from Sandtown and was not hired by the people of Sandtown. The CBP board was chaired by the Mayor's housing commissioner. Joan Thompson, Sandtown's main representative to the outside world in the late nineties, worked for Enterprise. This meant that Sandtown was well served by the city and Enterprise, and received vital outside resources. But there has never been any comparable leadership from the community. "Every community needs a person like me," Manny Price told me during one of my visits, taking evident pride in what he had contributed. "But they have to be *from* the community. They can't be part of the actual government entity." CBP has added new board members from the community and worked to bring along younger community leaders, but there is still more to do.

The news in the summer of 2000 that the city and Enterprise were preparing to turn over total control to the neighborhood was directly responsive to Price's point, but the move also heightened the sense of uncertainty about the future. Sandtown is still a poor neighborhood. Many of its adult residents are at a point where positive change is hard for them. There are still too many influences, both at home and on the street, that pull children in the wrong direction. Drug use seems to have actually increased. Nonmarital births are still four times the national rate. Two of the elementary schools have improved phenomenally, but it is not yet even near the truth to say that the school system is consistently turning out job-ready graduates from Sandtown. Too many employers still do not have open minds about people from places like Sandtown. The job situation is a little better, but people from all over the city are vying for jobs, and one wonders what will happen when the next recession comes.

The Sandtown leaders are deeply concerned about the new approach to welfare. So many who are expected to go to work have drug and alcohol problems, have criminal records, are HIV-positive, or have other difficulties. The looming time limits and the likelihood of a recession sometime present a troubling prospect.

If employers outside Sandtown are not especially welcoming, some in the neighborhood are not pulling their weight, either. With a few exceptions, the churches are not deeply involved in the revitalization. The police have not been sufficiently responsive, either. A large police district headquarters is half a block from the CBP offices, but the interaction is slight. The situation is a natural for community policing, but little has happened.

Mayor Schmoke, who took a lot of heat for favoring Sandtown, is no longer mayor, and Mr. Rouse is dead.

Still, the community is being rewoven. What is going on in the two schools is remarkable, and many other good things have happened. There are still questions about neighborhood leadership. But the civic and political commitment and the tangible accomplishments it has produced present a model to build on.

The Inner Cities and the Outer Metropolis

THERE ARE OTHER examples, of course. The New Community Corporation has made a big difference in Newark, New Jersey. The South Bronx, once infamous as America's version of a bombed-out city, looks quite different today, because of the work of community development corporations and especially because of the work of something called the Comprehensive Community Revitalization Program, a go-between that has helped the CDCs find resources and build connections in the outside world. From Boston to Chicago to Los Angeles and elsewhere, there are examples that address the total quality of life in neighborhoods.

Important new entrants are on the scene, too. Classic community organizers have gotten into concrete community development. Since much organizing is faith-based, in the current fashionable terminology, this means more religious institutions are doing neighborhood revitalization. Perhaps the most celebrated example is Project Nehemiah, an effort by two dozen churches in the East New York section of Brooklyn that has produced about twenty-two hundred single-family homes in a tough part of the city.

As in Sandtown, other neighborhood revitalizers are paying attention to education and to youth issues generally. Multi-city organizations like the Industrial Areas Foundation, which embodies the legacy of the legendary organizer Saul Alinsky, and ACORN, as well as numerous local groups, are improving schools, running child care and after-school programs, and starting charter and other kinds of alternative schools.

The federal government has taken a modest new interest in neighborhood revitalization by way of the Empowerment Zone (EZ) program. It is still too early to say what will come from this, but it has stimulated activity in a number of places. The contributions are varied: the high-visibility Harlem USA commercial development in New York City, the recommitment of Chrysler and GM to the inner city in Detroit, technical assistance to neighborhood small businesses, training and job-finding help for neighborhood residents, and a variety of services and activities to make neighborhoods safer, families stronger, and local culture more vibrant.

The EZ experience also illustrates the uneasy tensions between big-city mayors and the neighborhoods of their poorest residents. A mayor's aim is to make the city hum again: to attract middle-class residents and businesses back, to develop cultural and recreational amenities, to improve the schools, and so on. The best thing to do for people who consume more public revenue than they contribute would be to turn them into taxpayers, but that is hard to do, so it is tempting to push them out of the city or at least keep them isolated and make sure they do not bother anybody else. Some mayors have taken a positive approach. A few have clearly not. Most are in between, talking the talk but not consistently walking the walk: embracing new federal programs but using them more for patronage than real revitalization, tearing down the worst high-rise public housing but not paying close enough attention to the relocation of the residents, and talking school reform but concentrating on magnets and charters that attract the middle class.

The EZ experience shows that it is hard for neighborhood revitalizers to do their jobs without a good relationship with city hall. So much of what affects the quality of life in the inner city comes from downtown. Strong community-based leaders can be an effective force in keeping mayors and school superintendents and public housing authorities honest, especially if they find other partners to join in their politics, but sophisticated neighborhood revitalizers have also discovered the limits posed by an unresponsive or ineffective city hall.

One major remaining question is how to connect residents of high-poverty areas to jobs in the bigger world. The best answer would be full residential mobility, but, at the least, people should be able to connect to jobs wherever they are located.

There is a framework in place, but it is operating badly. We need to enlist employers and get applicants to them, and assure that applicants receive training that fits the employers' needs. We have to take on the transit issues, be sure there is child care and health coverage, tackle addictions and afflictions, and confront discrimination. Not simple, but possible. Jobs, supplemented by public income support, are critical to reducing poverty and promoting fairness. Full employment requires local effort as well as national policy.

Much of this is connected to race. Discrimination in hiring is still there, and not just for African Americans. Latinos, Hmong, Filipinos, disabled people — among others — experience it.

Nor is hiring the only area where race is a factor. Why do some people live so far from jobs? Why don't they have networks of family and friends who know about available jobs? Why is their education so deficient? Race is part of the answer to every one of those questions.

There is a proven way to identify discrimination — testing. It has been used for years to detect discrimination in selling and renting housing. It is used to detect discrimination in hiring, too. You send in matched pairs of applicants, with the minority person or the disabled person having a slightly better résumé. You send the minority or disabled person first and the white or Anglo or nondisabled person half an hour or an hour later. If there's nothing available to the first person and something there for the second one, bingo. In Washington, D.C., testers from an organization I helped to start found overt discrimination — i.e., the employer was open and obvious about it — one time in five. Even worse, private referral agencies, which funnel people to all manner of jobs, discriminated two times out of three. Antidiscrimination enforcement is clearly part of the answer.

Strategies to get jobs into or near the neighborhood are also important. There are substantial job possibilities associated with helping other people go to work — child care and van companies to transport people to the jobs are obvious ones — but the big task is getting people jobs outside the neighborhood.

What do we do if there aren't enough jobs out there? And what do we do for people who need a year or so of work support before they can make it on their own?

The ultimate aim should be unsubsidized employment for everyone. But we need transitional jobs programs to help people move on. Such efforts are in employers' interests, too. Offering a stream of better-prepared workers will even out the labor supply and reduce the temptation to automate or to flee offshore or to rural areas when the supply of labor gets tight.

We are as close as we ever come to full employment. Much of the remaining unemployment is structural. People are too far from jobs (rural as well as urban, remember), underskilled or not as able, or suffer discrimination. Some without jobs are taking care of chronically ill children or older relatives. Some have mental illness, or are victims of domestic violence. And some, to be honest, are in fact criminals, addicted, or just plain lazy.

We hear it said that anyone who can't find a job now is someone we shouldn't bother to care about. My view is that we should offer treatment to the addicted and the mentally ill, and that we have to protect the children. And the even bigger point is that we have to take responsibility for the structural failures of the economy and not blame its victims.

This is essential. We are talking about people who have been involuntarily isolated from the rest of society. Yes, they have to take responsibility for themselves. We all do. But the job market that is "natural" to the rest of us cannot help those who do not use it because of lack of skills, education, or physical or mental shortfalls. We must get people to where they can take responsibility for themselves.

The broadest current effort to connect isolated people to jobs is the Casey Foundation's strategy to promote "better connections between disadvantaged job seekers and good jobs in the regional economy," to quote the first report on the project. The foundation chose six cities — Denver, Milwaukee, New Orleans, Philadelphia, St. Louis, and Seattle — with inner-city target areas of fifty thousand to one hundred thousand people each. The regional economies range from "extremely robust to stagnant," and the target populations range from predominantly African American to significantly Latino to one that is widely diverse.

The Philadelphia Jobs Initiative is indicative of the potential. Involved are two mostly African American neighborhoods on the northwest edge of the city.

The heart of the strategy is to reform the job market by reforming the practice of neighborhood revitalization — that is, for a community development corporation, in this case a group called the Ogontz Avenue Revitalization Corporation, to connect neighborhood workers to suburban jobs. Working for nearly a year and a half with some thirty organizations representing employers, public agencies, nonprofits, and foundations, Ogontz and its partner, the Delaware Valley Community Reinvestment Fund, came up with a two-hundred-page plan analyzing the skills and needs of the hundred thousand people in the target area. It proposed three sectors — manufacturing, health care, and back-office data processing — as priority areas for training and placement.

Ogontz is responsible for recruiting, assessing, training, and connecting neighborhood residents. The shortest training is a three-week readiness program that in its first year placed about two-thirds of its participants in service, retail, and light-manufacturing jobs throughout the region paying an average of eight dollars an hour. Another short-term program is a fourteen-week course for home health aides, with temporary assignments that evolve into permanent jobs. Still another is a sixty-one-week program that responds to a critical local shortage of machinists. Ogontz also has a small-business loan fund, which will make capital available to promising ventures based on their commitment to hire disadvantaged workers.

Then there is the Jobs Policy Network, which Delaware Valley sponsors with a civic group, the 21st Century League. The network — now comprising over a hundred employers, advocates, service providers, policymakers, foundations, churches, and community organizations — is developing a regional-workforce strategy.

Emphasis on residential mobility is in order, too. There has been considerable success in breaking down discrimination by sellers, banks, and insurance companies, but there is a long way to go even there. Subsidy for those who can't afford decent housing is even more difficult. So-called Section 8 federal low-income housing vouchers can theoretically be used anywhere in a metropolitan area. But housing for which vouchers can be used doesn't exist everywhere, and the supply of housing is in general so tight that obtaining a Section 8 voucher doesn't mean it can be used. Getting more funds for the Section 8 program, which finally began to happen to a modest extent in the last couple of years, is a high priority, and new ways to increase the supply of affordable housing need to be found, too.

This is a time of renewed possibility for central cities, with associated possibilities and perils for the least well off. The reduced density of central cities is going to produce development possibilities that have tremendous implications for inner-city residents. The enormous development that is set to occur in Boston in the old port area is a good example. A thousand acres are up for grabs for a mix of housing and commercial activity. Handled well, with proper transit connections, it will be a boon to city residents. Handled badly, it will produce economic activity that is physically inaccessible and otherwise irrelevant to most city residents, and high-end housing that is similarly elitist. A number of skyscraper-housing and -office proposals have already surfaced and been defeated, but the big battles have yet to be fought. There will be similar, if less extensive, opportunities and hazards in other cities.

Central cities have improved political possibilities, too. Because inner-ring suburbs have changed so much and are attracting poorer populations more like the cities next door, alliances with them in state legislatures and elsewhere are an emerging possibility for cities.

One important target for such alliances is the metropolitan bodies that distribute federal transportation funds, currently controlled lock, stock, and barrel by the outer-ring suburbs. Huge sums of money are involved. When the federal transportation-funding law was reenacted in 1998, and Congressman Bud Shuster of Pennsylvania and his allies set aside well over $200 billion to pave over what seems like every piece of gravel in America, a coalition of grassroots organizations succeeded quietly in inserting some important items in the bill. They obtained a five-year authorization of $150 million a year for reverse commuting systems to help inner-city people get to jobs in the suburbs. Potentially even more important, they took some steps toward public scrutiny of the decision making by metropolitan bodies that carve up the federal money. This enhances the opportunity for central cities and inner-ring suburbs to work together on transportation funding.

No less important are the possibilities for righting imbalances in state legislatures. Disparities in spending and tax policies that favor the outer-ring suburbs are obvious targets, as are rules for land-use planning and runaway growth, including regulation of exclusionary zoning and the placement of affordable housing.

Cities have to think actively about their potential place in the new economy, and what they need from the federal and state governments to get them there, culminating in smart growth policies that begin to knit urban places back together in more coherent form.

If cities take advantage of their lower population densities to make once teeming neighborhoods greener and more friendly, if they try to reverse the forces that penned too many people of color deep in the city, the fortunes of the past three decades can change, leading to a twenty-first century that is better for the inner-city poor and the central city than the last third of the twentieth century turned out to be.

The work that goes on in the Sandtown-Winchesters of this world is necessary but not sufficient. The danger is that a new generation of mayors will try to lure successful people and businesses back without attending to the inner-city poor except to push them out. Every city needs organizers and activists, as well as far-seeing civic leaders, who will join together to convince enough others that the city of the future, to be most successful, must attend to the quality of life of all of its people.

7

BREAKING THE CYCLE

Children and Youth

ROBERT KENNEDY'S special commitment was to children and young people. It was a passion central to his being, reflected in the large family that he and Ethel nurtured so lovingly. Publicly, it came out as a concern for children denied the same chance to succeed that his own children had, especially children of color. His visits, speeches, and ideas, and the conversations he had with children and young people, returned over and over to the need to do better at giving all children a chance. He understood profoundly that reducing poverty for the long term meant doing much more to help poor children escape the circumstances of their birth.

Well over half the poor are families with children. Children are a lens through which we can judge most of what we do to reduce poverty and promote fairness. The working situation of parents — whether they have jobs, whether they earn living wages, whether their workplaces are family friendly, whether they have decent child care — has a big effect on how children will turn out. Our approaches to health care, housing, enforcement of laws against discrimination, and how we run our criminal-justice system all affect the futures of children. The way we deal with violence both in the street and in the home, sexual intercourse and childbearing at unduly early ages, and drug and alcohol abuse and treatment has a particular effect on poor children. The strength of the community — whether it is safe, helps parents do the hard work of rearing children, supports marriage and fatherhood without denigrating mothers struggling to raise children on their own, and truly stands against the negative messages bombarding children every day — makes a big difference.

No institution is more important to help children acquire the tools they need to escape poverty and do their best in life than the public schools. If jobs are one leg of a serious antipoverty strategy, education is the other. If all children's capacities were nourished in our schools, far fewer would grow up into continuing poverty.

At the same time, children of any background need more than good schools: role models, help with learning, enrichment, organized activities, chances to help others, exposure to the world of opportunity — an extra shoulder to lean on, an extra leg up, an extra source of strength and protection to fend off the appeal of destructive behavior.

What America now does for poor children needs enormous improvement, but exponentially worse is our approach to those we call "youth." At least babies and small children are cute. Nearly every one exudes the potential that new life brings. But our interest wanes as they get older. Adolescents — even our own — are hard to get along with. If they didn't learn to read and do arithmetic when they should have, they are harder to teach. If they were abused or ignored at home, they have wounds that may never heal. Some begin making trouble in the community or have a child at much too early an age. Too many of us think, Forget that one, maybe we'll succeed with the next. If they make enough trouble we send them away, increasingly to a criminal-justice system that punishes them as if they were adults.

Adolescents of color, in particular, figure out what the larger world has in store for them, and get downright angry. Our reaction to teenagers from poor families, especially those of color, too often is to cross the street, literally and figuratively.

Too many adults in poor neighborhoods who could help don't. Parents and family. Next door and down the corridor or down the block. In the church on the corner. In the elementary school nearby, and in the high school a little farther away. Too many outside the neighborhood don't help either. In the mayor's office, in businesses, in labor union offices, in colleges and universities, in foundations, everywhere.

There are exceptions, of course: an inner-city high school that sends a phenomenal number of its students to college, a youth project that shapes up the toughest kids, scholarship programs like I Have a Dream, individual teachers and coaches and scout leaders and clergy and probation officers and mentors of all kinds who make a fantastic difference in the lives of countless children.

But they are exceptions. For low-income young people the rule is huge high schools that don't seem to care whether students show up, neighborhoods where there is little to do but hang out and get into trouble, unfriendly job markets, juvenile- and criminal-justice systems that criminalize youth at younger and younger ages, and welfare offices that mostly admonish young mothers to go out and get a job.

The risks begin at the moment of conception, but they multiply as children begin to be aware of a larger world that doesn't welcome them — as they see people graduate but find no steady work, watch their older brothers or others going to jail or dealing drugs or hustling, or observe their older sisters or brothers or others having babies at far too young an age.

The issue is becoming more urgent. For most of the past decade the number of youths turning eighteen each year was on the decline, which eased the pressure on the labor market to absorb them. But in 1996 the number of eighteen-year-olds began to rise again, and by 2005 the number of eighteen-to-twenty-four-year-olds will have increased from 24.7 million to 29.1 million.

We need to create safe passages to adulthood for all young people. Millions of caring adults already make it their business to help, but we have no systemic approach, especially for those isolated by poverty or ethnicity.

A safe passage includes a destination. It will not work to tell young people to stay in school if there are no jobs, no careers, no futures. There has to be opportunity that welcomes them on the same terms as everyone else: the same chance to go to college and to get jobs, the same chance for those who finish high school, and so on.

A safe passage also includes the journey itself. It means acquiring the preparation needed at the destination. It means help from the community to clear obstacles from the path. It means taking personal responsibility to steer clear of obstacles remaining along the way. For some who have strayed, it will mean finding the way back to the path, perhaps with help from others.

Schools that teach what one needs to know are critically important, but especially for young people growing up with parents who have problems of their own and in neighborhoods where risks of all kinds abound, the hours when school is out are also critical. The community must take responsibility for every young person. It must give the young a chance to help others, and to learn about the workplace. It must take on the attitudes of the street that devalue learning and achievement. This is far more than an "after-school program." The task is to do everything possible to help parents and children win what the ethnographer Elijah Anderson calls "the war between the decent and the street."

A powerful series in the *Washington Post* in November 1998, by Leon Dash and Susan Sheehan, chronicled how two brothers in a poor, violent, drug-infested neighborhood in northeast Washington grew up to be killers. No, "grew up" is wrong — Tyrone and

Russell Wallace became killers when they were sixteen and eighteen years old. I am not arrogant or foolish enough to assert that I know specifically what would have kept those two particular young men from killing, but I do think I know what we can do to reduce the number of such boys who grow up to be killers, as well as the number who become drug dealers and muggers and dope addicts and alcoholics and what Robert Kennedy once referred to as men who "drift about the city, separated from their families, as if they were of no greater concern to their fellows than so many sparrows or spent matches." We need to do everything I have talked about in this book, but most especially we need communities that take responsibility for every young person.

This means involving them fully, not just in sports and academic enrichment and computers and ballet, but in helping others, and in learning to think well of themselves and in coming to believe in their own future. Helping others builds resilience and a sense of self-worth, as does being challenged to think about ethics and values and personal responsibility. Healthy communities pull their weight in the war between the decent and the street, directly taking on the forces that pull young people toward fast money and casual violence and trivialized sexual relationships.

Making the Public Schools Work

EVER SINCE, IN the wake of World War II, we theoretically committed ourselves to educate all children through high school, we have been talking school reform and getting little done. We actually lost ground for a variety of reasons. Talented women found newly open and better-paying opportunities in fields other than education. Unions, protecting their declining turf, got in the way of change. Self-interested bureaucracies smothered initiative and courage. White flight and increased use of private and parochial schools by people of all races transformed urban public schools into near-monolithic populations of low-income children of color. Tax bases crumbled. Buildings were not maintained. Many of the best teachers fled to the suburbs or out of the profession altogether.

For Robert Kennedy and others of his time, the goals included federal aid for the education of disadvantaged children, and helping parents gain a greater voice in decisions about their children's education. In retrospect these aims were worthwhile, but inadequate. Civil rights advocates focused mainly on implementation of *Brown v. Board of Education,* trying to increase the numbers of black and white children attending school together. Newer black leaders argued that the issue was not integration but who controls the schools. Educational results and the quality of teaching were effectively pushed to the back burner until the landmark report *A Nation at Risk* catapulted to national attention in 1983.

Since then a generation of school reformers have tackled the question of systems change. Sometimes because of their efforts and sometimes not, specific schools have sparkled and outstanding teachers have been liberated to be fully productive. But until recently, no urban school system as a whole showed signs of systemic change. In the nineties, the Chicago school system underwent a broad effort at reform. It still faces big problems, but enough has happened to make this experiment worth examining.

Chicago is no longer unique. Serious attempts at systemic change are under way in a number of states and cities. State standards are not enough; city school systems must steer their own course toward reform. But few cities have attempted reform with the aim of reaching all of their children.

Here, briefly, are some of the steps school districts should take, backed by adequate funding from states and Washington.

Any city that wants to educate all of its children has to make sure they are ready for school at the start, and are reading by the time they hit third grade. Computer literacy for all is vital. Every high school should offer all of the core subjects needed to function in today's economy. Reducing the immense, impersonal high schools of our cities to a human scale is important.

Two million new teachers will be needed over the next decade. Schools with the highest number of low-income and minority students will have the hardest time filling vacancies. We need a national commitment to teaching, with better pay, improved status, steps to attract midcareer people, and bonuses and education-loan forgiveness for those willing to teach in geographic or topical areas of special need. And we need sustained professional-development programs, reduced class size, and professional working conditions — everything necessary to enable a teaching corps to do its best.

Schools will do a better job if they are closely connected to the surrounding community. This means a more welcoming stance toward parents and more partnerships with community organizations to enrich children's education, with particular emphasis in high schools on partnerships that prepare students for careers.

Finally, the physical infrastructure of urban school systems is crumbling, with current population trends adding an extra urgency to the need for investment in bricks and mortar.

Competing with such legitimate strategies are magic bullets and simplistic solutions that are given exaggerated importance, are actually useless, or are even destructive.

Choice and charter schools, for example, are good ideas that are not panaceas. The ability of parents to choose within public school systems, which in a number of places is statewide, is a good idea, although not without pitfalls. The issue becomes more complicated when public schools are given over to profit-making companies. Some of these operators inveigle desperate parents with unfounded claims of success. Nonetheless, if coupled with careful attention to quality and encouragement for schools that emphasize needed specialties, choice is a plus.

Charter schools can be a plus, too, although they are subject to even greater risks thanks to overreaching entrepreneurs and inexperienced people who get charters through sheer enthusiasm and, sometimes, political connections. Charter schools are independent public schools that receive charters from the state or the local school board. They typically receive the same operational funding per child as other public schools, but without capital funds for acquisition and renovation of buildings. They are generally required to admit children on a nonselective basis. Their numbers have increased by leaps and bounds, with over a thousand operating now nationwide. Some of them are truly at the cutting edge of innovation. Others are awful.

With proper supervision to weed out the fly-by-nights and incompetents, charter schools could become a system within a system that incubates new ideas and visions. Some could focus on new strategies to reach students who have not responded well to traditional settings. Some could receive extra funding to experiment with larger-scale change. Some could be professional-development centers working in concert with struggling public schools. They could be partners in community-building and -organizing strategies, too. When the North Star Academy Charter School was getting started in Newark, New Jersey, it was desperate for financing to buy and renovate a building. The New Community Corporation came to the rescue. Given all the vacant buildings in America's cities, this kind of partnership could be replicated a thousand times over.

Choice and charter schools necessarily leave the vast majority of children behind. Children in low-income neighborhoods typically will be the ones with the least aggressive and most overburdened parents. The funding siphoned off will drain resources from the rest of the local schools, and the remaining population will have a higher percentage of students needing extra attention. The more charters there are in a city, the more problems for those left behind.

Market theory says that in a competitive environment, most schools will improve in order to hold on to students and the rest don't deserve to survive. But while some schools will no doubt be driven to improve, many others will inevitably deteriorate further unless systemwide strategies are pursued. Choice and charter schools can be part of the answer, but only if they are embedded in a serious effort to change the whole system.

Vouchers for private and perhaps parochial schools are a different matter. Vouchers could drain away unacceptably large amounts of funding from the public schools and leave behind many more children than those hurt by choice and charter schools. One cause of urban school failure is inadequate funding, and vouchers may accelerate the problem.

Still, there is not a bright line here. We have long had public high schools with selective admissions policies. Magnets have been around for some time, too. Now we have charters and choice. Each one takes some cream off the top and represents a tradeoff.

Some of the strongest supporters of charter schools and vouchers are African American parents and community leaders who are terminally disgusted with the public schools and are willing to try anything that might deliver better education. Where vouchers are being tried, parents are reported to be pleased with the schools their children now attend. Some parents have indicated that too many teachers in the public schools project negative attitudes about race, and that their children's new schools are free of this feeling.

Still, for me, vouchers are on balance undesirable. If I could be sure that their funding would always be in addition to adequate funding of the public schools, I would be less inclined to oppose them, even though they would still drain away many of the most enterprising parents who would otherwise use their talents to improve the public system. In the real world, I fear vouchers will take too much of everything — money, energetic parents, better students — out of the public schools. The public schools are crucial to building a shared national view of what we stand for. The challenge is to fix them, not destroy them.

Vouchers are not an issue in Scarsdale and Winnetka and Menlo Park. The people in those places will fight to keep their public schools as they are. When we talk about problems in our public institutions, the word "public" is often a euphemism for institutions that serve black and Latino poor. Public schools, public welfare, public hospitals, and public housing are all in egregiously worse shape when their clients are people of color, and the remedies that are fashionable today tend to put a wrecking ball to the institution rather than pursuing the more complicated task of setting things right.

The debate over vouchers is part of a longstanding and continuing tension between uniformity and flexibility in public education. We have to preserve public schools as a fundamental communal institution in order to build citizenship, shared values among people of differing backgrounds, and civic commitment. We must not allow policies that are destructive of the very idea of the common school. But we also need to prevent overreaching and indoctrination, and leave room for people to choose alternative ways of educating their children. Finding the right balance is the challenge.

Standards and tests have also been turned by some into a magic bullet. A thoughtful policy on standards and tests, adopted after broad consultation and not punitive toward underperforming students, is essential. But what we find in the name of "ending social promotion" is often a new form of blaming the victim. It is proposed to test children who have not been taught competently and then push them out of school when they fail.

We should spell out standards for what students are expected to know *after* being taught the material, and we should hold teachers and schools accountable for delivering the material. And we have to invest in help for students and teachers to do what is expected of them.

A number of states are attempting not just to develop thoughtful standards but to accompany them with accurate and fair measures of student performance. A growing number allow the state to take over local school systems or individual schools that do not meet bare-minimum performance norms.

In too few cities, however, is there hard, detailed work being done to improve instruction school by school, so all students have a fair chance to meet the standards by virtue of the quality of teaching they receive from the minute they start kindergarten. In short, both urban school reform and adequate funding are essential.

Chicago: A Model for the Future?

SOME GOOD THINGS are happening in Chicago. Over four-fifths of the more than four hundred elementary schools in the city (in Chicago "elementary" means kindergarten through eighth grade) improved the reading scores of their children between 1990 and 1999. About half of the improvements are substantial. Improving schools can be found all over the city, including some in the poorest, most racially isolated neighborhoods. (The schools that are not improving are disproportionately located in the poorest, predominantly African American neighborhoods.)

Even though test scores are not by themselves an adequate measure of educational results, this is significant good news in a system of 430,000 students, and it cannot be an accident.

There are two explanations: the 1988 reform and the 1995 reform. The proponents of each minimize the relevance of the other, but both are really involved. The 1988 reform was one of decentralization, creating elected local school councils for every school in the city, with power to hire and fire principals and to decide how to spend substantial discretionary funds from the state. The 1995 reform was one of recentralization, giving great power to the mayor, and significantly weakening the ability of the unions to throw sand in the gears of change.

The two stories merge into one because the recentralization didn't wipe out the local school councils or change their powers significantly. Decentralization and the recentralization exist side by side, uneasily but also constructively. The 1988 reform expanded participation in governance at the school level; the 1995 reform cleaned up policy at the central level and made the local school councils more accountable.

To read the national press you wouldn't know there are local school councils that might have had something to do with the improvements in achievement. Everything is about Mayor Richard M. Daley and especially about Paul Vallas, the CEO of the schools, who personifies the reform both nationally and to most Chicagoans as well. But despite Vallas's public stance that he inherited a mess, the test scores began going up long before he came along. Vallas has repeatedly attacked the local school councils and the reformers who back them, seeking to diminish their powers and undermine their authority.

On the other hand, the most ardent proponents of the 1988 reform and the local school councils, though leveling many criticisms at Vallas, give credit to the 1995 reform and to him for bringing financial stability and a measure of accountability to the system.

In governance, the Chicago approach is a combination of shared power at the school level with strong central oversight. In educational policy, the essence is twofold: to improve the poorest schools and reach underperforming students by combining standards with large-scale remediation, and to attract the middle class back, particularly by creating a series of magnet schools integrated with the Mayor's housing and community development strategy.

The national headline is that Vallas has ended social promotion — the practice, long decried by liberals and conservatives alike, of moving children from grade to grade regardless of whether they had learned anything. The real story is much more complicated.

On the positive side, large numbers of children are performing better. There is labor peace. The finances of the system are stable. The schools open on time every year. A multi-billion-dollar capital improvement plan has produced construction, physical improvements, and repairs. Schools have new roofs, new windows, and needed additions. Janitorial services, privatized in many schools, are better. The schools are in effect a department of city government now, so coordination between the schools and other city services, notably the police and parks departments, has improved. Universities, businesses, museums, and other partners are extensively involved in the schools. Parents and people from the neighborhoods are heavily involved, too, in particular through the local school councils.

On the negative side, the large summer school effort at remediation and the retention in grade of those who fail are leaving many children behind. Dropout rates are going up as the ending of social promotion has created a brutal sorting process. Student achievement gains are spotty thus far in the high schools. As in many places, the suburbs have vastly more funds, typically about two thousand dollars more per pupil at the high school level, or around sixty thousand dollars per classroom.

Virtually all other school reform efforts have been top down, emanating from a governor, mayor, or school superintendent who made education a top priority. The Chicago reform started with a bottom-up upheaval, feeling for a while like a latter-day civil rights movement, although with the added involvement of elites from the business and philanthropic communities. Paul

Vallas gives little credit to this, but the momentum that still exists from the upheaval is key to many of the good things going on in the schools.

Things coalesced in the fall of 1987, when the ninth teachers' strike since 1970 occurred. It was then that U.S. Secretary of Education William Bennett called Chicago's schools "the worst in the nation." People all over the city — parents, especially — reacted to the strike. Alternative schools popped up. New organizations arose to urge reform, and existing community organizations turned their attention to the schools as never before.

The strike was settled after nineteen days, but the genie was out of the bottle. The spontaneity, intensity, and breadth of the activism added up to one of those rare times when a genuine movement for change occurs. Mayor Harold Washington, who had previously been wary of the racial tensions connected with school reform, jumped into it with both feet. A week after the strike was over, he called a public meeting to discuss school reform. Five hundred people received invitations, and more than a thousand came.

Harold Washington died suddenly on November 25, 1987. Much of what happened in the following year was a memorial to him, and might well not have occurred if he hadn't passed away — much as the enactment of the Civil Rights Act of 1964 stemmed in no small part from the death of President Kennedy.

Neighborhood meetings were held all over the city. Intense work went on among business leaders, parents, and others. They finally agreed on building-by-building local school councils with some central monitoring and some assurance of an equitable distribution of resources.

In 1988 the plan went to the state legislature. CEOs came to Springfield on their corporate jets. Busloads of parents and other neighborhood people came in waves, financed in big part by the business community. Legislators from all over the state were impressed by the parents' obvious deep concern for their children.

The final legislation represented radical change in some ways and no change in others. It altered governance fundamentally, creating local school councils with real power, but offered no direction for educational policy beyond whatever would happen in individual buildings as a result of the governance changes. There was no citywide set of standards and no new system to assess outcomes.

The redistribution of power was significant. The new local school councils (LSCs) were to be composed of six parents, two teachers, two community representatives, and the principal, plus, in the high schools, a student member. The councils could hire principals and renew their contracts and make decisions about how to spend state aid for disadvantaged students, which averaged $470,000 per school. They were also to draw up three-year school improvement plans, in consultation with committees of teachers in each school. Principals' lifetime tenure was replaced by four-year performance contracts. In return, they received new power to choose teachers and remove nonperforming ones and new authority over engineers and food-service staff. The new central school board would be chosen by the mayor from lists generated by the local school councils.

The new mayor, Richard M. Daley, appointed an impressive interim school board. They quickly revised the budget drawn up by the old board, cutting $40 million from central and district offices, reducing class sizes, and restoring music and art classes jettisoned years earlier. They negotiated a new teachers' union contract, organized the first local school council elections, restructured special education to avoid losing federal dollars, and hired a new superintendent.

The local school council elections at first drew little interest, but extensive organizing efforts by the new school board, the corporate community, and community organizations produced more than 17,000 candidates for the 5,400 parent, community, and teacher seats on the new councils. The election, held in October 1989, drew about 250,000 voters. Tensions surfaced immediately, but so did an outpouring of civic commitment, often supported by grants from local foundations: lawyers offered to mediate conflicts and to help in drafting guidelines for evaluating principals; accountants volunteered to assist in budget analysis; several groups offered training in how to run meetings and how to search for and interview principal candidates; educators and arts professionals submitted advice on curriculum and professional development; community organizers put forward leadership development training for parents.

These partnerships came into being easily because the councils did not need to get central bureaucratic approval and because so many volunteers offered their time. They remain today and there is a clear correlation between the wise use of volunteers and the schools with notable educational gains.

The LSCs developed unevenly. Some, especially where principals were cooperative and open, began to move to a new learning atmosphere, succeeded in getting repairs to school buildings, and made wise acquisitions of new materials and equipment. Others experienced racial and ethnic conflict, were manipulated by overreaching principals (even if not always to bad ends), or were unable to get entrenched teachers to change their ways. Some observers think the major impetus for change was not the school councils but the ability of the good principals to break the shackles of the central bureaucracy and institute reforms.

The next four years were relatively quiet. Reading scores started upward in 1992, although the data did not become visible to the public right away. There was no significant improvement in the high schools. Every year in the early nineties featured a fiscal crisis, so the LSCs usually did not get their discretionary funds until well after the school year had started, making it hard to plan ahead. Many believe the central office's annual delays with these funds were attempts to sabotage the reform.

By the fall of 1994 there was a projected three-year school

deficit of $1.3 billion. Then, with the Gingrich revolution, both houses of the Illinois legislature went Republican and Mayor Daley, a Democrat, saw an opportunity to gain control of the school system. Elite businesses were willing to help him, because they had not seen enough improvement. Both the Mayor and the new majority saw it as advantageous to weaken the teachers' union. The Republicans saw it as a fair trade to give Daley the power without giving him any new money, some probably believing the Mayor would fail.

This time things were done behind closed doors. The school board and the position of superintendent were abolished, replaced by a five-member mayorally appointed board of trustees and a CEO. The board was given broad authority to intervene in nonperforming schools. The union was forbidden to strike for eighteen months, and collective bargaining was thenceforth to be over wages only and not over working conditions. The new CEO was given authority to privatize a number of support functions, such as building repairs.

The recentralization was neither monolithic nor unsophisticated. The authority of the LSCs was not disturbed. They were now required to receive training, but this was to strengthen them, not weaken them. Principals were given more authority over teacher selection and removal, over building engineers, and over spending. On the other hand, the amount of state discretionary funds going to the school level was frozen.

Daley appointed Paul Vallas, who had been his budget chief, to be the CEO of the schools, and Gery Chico, his former chief of staff, to be the board president. The three of them have effectively controlled things since (although they don't always agree, and by the summer of 1999 some of their friction was seeping out publicly).

The heart of the push to end social promotion is an extensive summer school, coupled with substantial new extended-day programs. The summer school targets children who have done poorly in third, sixth, and eighth grades. Those who cannot cut the mustard by the end of the summer are held back. After the summer of 1997, some sixteen thousand students citywide were held back. In 1999, Mayor Daley ordered that half the first, second, and third graders go to summer school in the year 2000.

The summer school program has been a success for a substantial number of children. It has better teachers, more spending on books and other instructional resources, and reduced class size. Many children are getting back on track and staying there.

But then there are the students who keep failing. Many of those retained in grade have been reclassified as special-education students. For some this is a judgment that should have been made earlier, but for others it is simply an admission of defeat. Even more troubling, in the fall of 1998 a thousand children citywide began the third grade for the third time, and two thousand in all had been held back twice. Many educators fear this is a recipe for disaster, affecting the system for years to come.

The consequences are already visible. Students who fail to pass eighth grade are sent to transition centers, from which they theoretically go on to high school when they are ready. In practice, these centers are holding pens rather than places offering real help. Meanwhile, high school enrollments are dropping as large numbers of students fall by the wayside. Bill Ayers, a University of Illinois at Chicago professor and a leading force in the small-schools movement, says these children are "leaving in droves," and that this is "the great untold story" of the Chicago school reform. Martin Luther King Jr. High School, for example, lost about half of its students from 1995 to 1998.

Mayor Daley's order that half the first through third graders go to summer school is a step in the right direction, but the better answer is schools that do their job in the first place. Earhart Options for Knowledge School, which is 85 percent low-income and

99 percent African American, went from 33 percent of its students at or above national norms in 1990 to 75 percent in 1997. It had one child in jeopardy of being held back in 1998. Oriole Park, which is 63 percent low-income and has a diverse mix of white, Latino, African American, and Asian American students, raised its reading scores by 37 percentage points. It had no children in danger of being held back in 1998. At the very least, a better strategy would be to move low-achieving children along with extra help rather than pursue the zealous retention policy currently in vogue.

There is no citywide policy to help all schools be like Earhart and Oriole Park. That would require systemwide staff development, which still does not exist. It would entail more meaningful standards for teachers and weeding out teachers who don't meet them. It is perhaps understandable that the city does not wish to pick another fight with the unions, but it is a barrier to improving schools.

In late 1999 Vallas launched a Professional Development Academy, which is to be a model school of twelve hundred students staffed by ninety master teachers. But no planning preceded the announcement, and observers were pessimistic about its prospects. The only somewhat systematic staff development comes from partnerships created by individual schools and groups of schools. Every university in the city now has a center that works with the schools. The forty-four networks of three to five schools supported by the Chicago Annenberg Challenge, involving various nonprofits, university centers, and community organizations, include staff development in their work. This reaches some teachers in a third to a half of the schools. The funding, however, is explicitly time-limited.

A particularly important challenge is to develop a citywide vision for what should go on in the classroom. From the beginning the Chicago reform has been one of form, process, and bricks and mortar more than one of classroom and curriculum. The theory of the 1988 reform was that the LSCs and the empowering of the principals would take care of this. Vallas has offered no new educational strategy. Observers say that while he has shaped up the business side of the system, he lags on the educational side, because he himself is not an educator and the educational people around him are not of the same caliber as the people he has brought in on the business side.

I don't want to be unfair to Vallas here. He has tried to tackle the worst schools. In the fall of 1996 he and the new board put 109 poorly performing schools (71 elementary schools and 38 of the 77 high schools) on probation. He formed contracts with outside partners, mainly schools of education, to work with many of them. Mike Klonsky, Bill Ayers' colleague at UIC, says this is the first time in fifty years that there has been any kind of serious intervention in failing schools. The interventions have produced positive results, although more at the elementary level than in the high schools.

The high schools are still a serious problem. In 1997 seven of the high schools were completely "reconstituted." This did not work well. It was controversial, and too drastic, trying to do too much too fast, with little leadership from the central board and administration.

By mid-1999 Vallas had replaced "reconstitution" with the milder "re-engineering." At that time it was still true that only one in ten of the city's high schools had a majority of students reading at or above national norms, and only one in eight had more than half surpassing national norms in math. There is still a 50 percent dropout rate, and youth who drop out say no one cares whether they stay.

High schools are hard to change. The die is already cast for many students by the time they get to high school, the departmental structure of high schools is a barrier to change, and parents take a bigger interest in the schools when their children are in the lower grades and do not object to their involvement.

Nonetheless, Ayers says energy for change in the high schools is developing. Mayor Daley continues to cheerlead, and a number of foundations have begun to invest in the high schools on a scale they never did during the first wave of the reform. Some high schools have begun to turn around, but in general they are all much too big to relate individually to their students.

The most promising development in the high schools is a growing small-schools movement. Developing since the early 1990s, it acquired more momentum when Mayor Daley declared in 1995 that no public high school should be larger than five hundred students. The central board has encouraged small schools — both freestanding and schools within schools.

One outstanding example is Robeson High School, which in 1995 had an 85 percent dropout rate, student achievement levels in the sub-basement, and incidents of violence on an almost daily basis. It was one of the schools that Vallas had put on probation. It has been broken up into six small schools, and things have changed phenomenally. Between 1998 and 1999 reading and math scores doubled, and arrests in the building for crimes like assault and weapons possession, previously a routine occurrence, dropped to almost zero. The Robeson story illustrates the limitations of LSCs. Mike Klonsky says there was a great local school council at Robeson, but the dropout rate was still horrible after nine years. Then again, smallness alone isn't the whole answer. Resources are necessary, too. In 1999 Robeson still had no science lab, no hot and cold running water for science students, and no Bunsen burners.

Another good small-school example is Chicago Vocational School, the initials of which, it used to be said, stood for Crime, Violence, and Sex. No more. The U.S. Department of Labor named it as one of the five most impressive new school-to-work projects in the country in 1999. Ayers and Klonsky are working with a total of 130 small schools at both the high school and elementary level, located in 77 buildings around the city.

One other improvement is providing core academic subjects, including real math and science courses, in every high school. Done right, this will be a major step forward, enabling low-income young people to go to college and to be better prepared for the job market. Other high school improvements include new reading specialists, and paying teachers extra to take on individual advising responsibilities.

Probably the closest thing to a citywide educational strategy has been the introduction of scripted instruction. Vallas's office has sent out lesson plans, one for every day of the year. This is an insult to good teachers, although it may be the only practicable step in the absence of an extensive staff-development effort. Still, it raises serious questions of whether Vallas is creating a system dominated by robotic teaching with no room for creativity or individual initiative.

The second part of Vallas's overall strategy is to attract students from middle-income families. He has reconfigured the magnet schools to cover smaller regions within the city and set aside more seats in them for children from the neighborhoods where they are located. Since they tend to be located in gentrified or gentrifying neighborhoods, this will make them more accessible to wealthier students. Location decisions for new magnets and small schools are being made on this basis, too.

Some observers believe that the middle-class agenda is the true heart of Chicago's strategy. Big-city mayors such as Mayor Daley have come to realize that the quality of their schools is a major impediment to attracting business and middle income families. That mayors are taking responsibility for their cities' schools means that they are tying their own political fortunes to school improvement, which creates an opportunity for those who want to help poor children. The critics' concern is that new money will be invested disproportionately in schools targeted at the middle class. The equity issues, by the way, are not racial. Many of those attracted back to the city will be people of color. The challenge is to get a fair share of the money for the children of the poor. (The meaner side of the problem is the desire of some big-city mayors to push out as many of their most costly poor people as they can, by demolishing high-rise public housing and not replacing it, and in some cities, like New York, by pushing people off the welfare rolls.)

Making things more difficult is the precarious condition of the Catholic schools in Chicago. With a relatively low tuition that does not cover operating costs, and serving a population that is substantially non-Catholic, the Church finds them difficult to justify, and has closed a significant number. It's not yet clear how this affects things. For example, it may push some good students with energetic parents back toward the public schools, but it is, in any case, an important factor.

Vallas has played the politics well. He feeds the media so much good news that they are seldom tempted to look underneath the surface. He has given his home telephone number to the education reporters and is always accessible to the press. He was in office less than a month when his new management team discovered, to major media attention, a warehouse filled with furniture, classroom supplies, and toilet paper that should have been issued to schools. He has doled out resources to a variety of constituencies, helping to mute their criticism. The principals' association has received funding for training, the teachers have received generous contracts, and local colleges and universities have received contracts to work in the schools. The only fight he has picked with people who should be his allies is with some of the advocates of local school councils. Otherwise, almost everyone who could make trouble is happy.

One can only hope the ice water now being thrown at Chicago's low-income children, which is largely the result of schools that have failed to teach, will startle decision makers into intensifying efforts to improve school performance. If things continue on their current course, Chicago, for all of its positives, could turn out to be a case study in what happens when standards are imposed without a strong enough commitment to improve education itself. Even large-scale remediation cannot undo the damage of poor teaching.

Tony Bryk, one of the pre-eminent education researchers in Chicago, is still optimistic. He believes broad agreement on strategy is developing, and that there has been great progress. He says the schools are far better than they were ten years ago or even four years ago. Skill, understanding, and support are building within businesses, foundations, community-based organizations, and among leading teachers and principals. The real payoff will come perhaps five to ten years down the road, Bryk thinks. Mike Klonsky adds that not only has progress been made that five years ago was impossible but there is more potential for change than ever — more openness, more focus, and more research.

With all of its mixed bag of accomplishments and shortcomings, Chicago deserves careful study as a place where change is going on and results can be judged.

Safe Passages for Young People

EVEN WHEN THE public schools do their job, and more urgently when they don't, it is imperative to pay attention to the needs of children and young people during the hours when they are not in school. There are many who do: parents themselves, other family members, neighbors, and those who work with the young for pay and as volunteers. But we clearly need to do more.

I have met welfare moms all over the country who had gotten jobs but told me they didn't know what they were going to do come summer because they didn't want their teen-age and pre-teen sons out in the street without supervision. And the problem is not just during the summer. Whether we call this school-age child care or after-school activities or settlement houses or community centers or Boys and Girls Clubs, it is vital.

One key model is New York City's Beacons, which are schools that have been turned into community centers in the non-school hours. Working with nonprofit organizations, they are open into the evening, on weekends, and during the summer. The Beacons model has been picked up in a number of places. It is only one of many approaches that have been tried, dating back to the venerable settlement house of a century ago.

Richard Murphy was Mayor David Dinkins's youth commissioner in 1990 when a young tourist from Utah was murdered in a Manhattan subway station in front of his horrified family. The Mayor's staff proposed more police, but Dinkins also wanted to do something about prevention. Murphy was asked to propose $20 million in new annual spending. He dusted off an idea he had sent to Dinkins's transition team advocating use of school buildings after hours, and suggested $40 million to implement it. He was stunned when the Mayor decided to recommend it in full.

Murphy had been a long-distance runner for young people. He was a young city welfare caseworker when, in 1968, he met a ten-year-old truant named Tony in a Woolworth's store in the Bronx. Helping Tony, who had multiple problems, convinced him that special attention must be paid to truants, and he founded what he called the Rheedlen Foundation to do that. It took three years to get his first funding, but by the time he joined the Dinkins administration, Rheedlen had a budget of $3 million and was running after-school programs at multiple sites, for kids who weren't in any trouble as well as some who were.

The name Beacons came about following an argument Murphy had with his staff about whether there should be a hyphen in the phrase "school-based centers," the term they were going to use in their proposal to Mayor Dinkins. They finally realized what they really needed was a better name that would convey a symbolic message about the program.

The state legislature passed the necessary legislation on Valentine's Day in 1991, although with less funding than the Mayor had requested. Murphy was given $10 million to open centers in ten schools. A later budget crunch pared him back to $5 million, with which he still opened ten centers. The core city-funded budget of each Beacon is still about $500,000.

Murphy added ten more Beacons the second year and seventeen more the third, for a total of thirty-seven by the time he and Dinkins left office. That meant there was a Beacon in a majority of the City Council districts. Perhaps for that reason, Mayor Giuliani has been supportive, and there are now over eighty Beacons altogether.

Murphy is proud that the idea originated inside the government. People say that government won't do anything unless it is pushed from the outside, or that the only authentic proposals come from the grassroots. This program was designed by the Mayor and his staff and voted into being by the city council, with funding by the state legislature. The city's budget office people, career as well as political, liked it because using the schools after hours is efficient. When government does something right, it can do it at a scale unachievable by private organizations operating alone. The Beacons enjoy the largest state or local commitment of public funds to this type of program. Equally important, the program is an effective partnership with the nonprofit world.

The Beacons are not just a program, but really a system of neighborhood revitalization. They are part of the struggle of neighborhood residents to maintain and build community life. Many of them have extended their work into the surrounding neighborhoods, working with local police precincts toward creating drug-free and violence-free zones.

Perhaps the most highly publicized Beacon is run by Rheedlen, where Murphy's successor, Geoff Canada, has become a national figure so identified with Beacons that they are often seen as "his" program. Canada's life and work are a model and an inspiration. His first book, *Fist, Stick, Knife, Gun,* is a must read for anyone who wants to understand the escalation of violence on inner-city streets, and is a deeply moving story of his own odyssey from poverty. If Murphy's story is a rare example of a white man functioning successfully in Harlem, Canada's is the less-rare but all-too-unusual story of an African American young man who grew up poor, achieved brilliantly at an elite white college, *and* came back to the inner city to devote his professional life to its children.

The roster of nonprofits involved in the Beacons includes many well-known youth-serving organizations like the Police Athletic League, the YMCA, and a number of New York's historic settlement houses. Other Beacons are run by local heroes and heroines, like the Center for Family Life and Sister Mary Paul and the late Sister Geraldine in Brooklyn, Good Shepherd Services and Sister Paulette, also in Brooklyn, and Alianza Dominicana and Moises Perez in upper Manhattan.

The Alianza Beacon is perhaps the most youth driven. If you come to the building on a Saturday, you find five young people in charge. Like most of the Beacons, it is genuinely a community center and not just a youth center. You could come to the building on a rainy Monday night and see three hundred people there for citizenship and English classes. At the Rheedlen Beacon, Alcoholics Anonymous and Narcotics Anonymous groups meet every night of the year. Rheedlen also runs what Geoff Canada calls a "baby college" for young parents.

Creating and operating the Beacons was and is not easy. Even the strongest of them still feel they are walking on eggshells in the school buildings. Getting custodians to cooperate is not easy, and principals and teachers are understandably nervous about having others in the building when they are not there.

Beacons and their sisters and brothers and cousins help make safe journeys for young people. If people like Geoff Canada or Moises Perez or Luis Garden Acosta of El Puente in Brooklyn and organizations like theirs had been present in the neighborhood where Tyrone and Russell Wallace grew up, it is just possible things would have been different and the decent might have triumphed over the street.

People with the charisma of Geoff Canada, Moises Perez, and Luis Garden Acosta are scarce, to be sure, but there are many who would get involved or would do more if the money and public approval were there to help. Volunteers are important, but people who do this for a living are crucial, to provide continuity, to coordinate volunteer involvement, and especially to work one-on-one with the young people most at risk of getting into trouble. Public policy and public funds have to be part of the solution.

While the Beacons are mainly for school-age children, Youth-Build represents the next stage. Thanks in part to federal support, it has grown in a little over a decade to 130 locations in around three dozen states. It teaches young people solid skills in the construction business, builds character and self-esteem at the same time, and graduates close to five thousand participants annually.

YouthBuild serves sixteen-to-twenty-four-year-old men and women, who spend about fourteen months learning construction skills by building and rehabilitating housing, mostly in their inner-city communities. They also pursue their high school equivalency certificates, develop leadership, and learn to connect to the larger world. Workshops teach decision making, negotiation, and public speaking. YouthBuild equips its graduates to compete against the culture of the street. Respect — how one earns it and who deserves it — is a key concept at YouthBuild. Responsibility is another.

The YouthBuild population is heavily African American, Latino, and Native American. Three-quarters are young men, over half are parents, three-fourths lack a high school diploma, and two-fifths are on welfare when they start. Significant numbers are sent by the courts. The clientele are not cream-puffs. About

70 percent make it through the whole program, and 95 percent of those get jobs starting at around seven dollars an hour, get into union apprenticeships, or go to college.

The program's gifted founder, Dorothy Stoneman, began her work in Harlem during the civil rights movement of the sixties. Over a twenty-five-year period she went from community organizing to running a parent-controlled community school where she had started as a nursery school teacher. In the seventies she worked with Bank Street College of Education and Goddard College to train parents to become certified teachers, helping to give continuity to her own school.

YouthBuild is based on a vision of love, responsibility, and what is good for everyone. Stoneman believes, as Dr. King and Gandhi did, that everyone is your potential ally if you can just persuade them, and thinks that the confrontational approach of some during the early community action days of the War on Poverty "proves that when you activate people to attack everything you lose everything." She is critical of organizing based on getting people to act out of self-interest, and says that love can sustain longer than anger, especially with young people who are already angry. They contain a polarization within themselves, which can go one way or the other. The question is how you liberate their positive energy and intelligence.

The seed for YouthBuild was sown in 1978. A group of young people in East Harlem, advised by Stoneman, decided to restore a rundown tenement in that area. She helped them raise money and find professional builders to train them and supervise the renovation. The activity gradually spread citywide, and by 1988 she felt that the program could be replicated nationally.

Stoneman decided that Congress should create a program called YouthBuild, with funds to be awarded on a competitive basis by some federal agency. Getting your own program through Congress if you're not a big-time lobbyist backed by corporate dollars is not simple, but she pulled it off, attracting Senator John

Kerry of Massachusetts and Housing and Urban Development Secretary Jack Kemp, along with key staffers who offered quiet advice and helped orchestrate things behind the scenes. Youth-Build is living proof of the necessity of public funds to support community building.

Ten years ago Dorothy Stoneman was dreaming about how to get a hundred locations. Now she is talking about a thousand. Don't bet against it.

The Ten Point Coalition represents what religious congregations can do. It is a group of churches in Boston that have gotten out into the street, committed to ending youth violence and building youth strength. Working in conjunction with the Boston Police Department, they have had remarkable success in reducing gun violence in that city.

Nowhere is the contribution of the faith community more important than in reaching young people who are at such risk of irrevocably ruining their life possibilities. The catalytic event for the founding of the Ten Point Coalition was a chase, stabbing, and shootout inside the Morning Star Baptist Church, in Boston's Dorchester neighborhood, at a 1992 funeral for a twenty-year-old killed in the crossfire of a drive-by shooting. Gang violence was endemic in the neighborhood, but the Morning Star shooting represented a new low.

What developed was an unusual (but replicable) partnership between African American ministers in Dorchester and Boston law enforcement officials — the police department, probation and parole officers, and prosecutors. The strategy boils down to a combination of law enforcement and prevention: prompt action to get bad guys off the street and positive alternatives for those on the edge of serious trouble. This involves shoe leather — high energy, hard work, late hours, physical presence on the street, visits to schools and homes. The underlying faith is always there but not necessarily worn on the sleeve.

Ten Point is now well heeled enough to have an executive

director and a growing budget of more than three hundred thousand dollars. It has sixty-two member churches, although not all are equally active.

Reverend Eugene Rivers is the outside man, the one who made the cover of *Newsweek*, met with President Clinton and then-Speaker Gingrich, called the mainstream African American churches "the major crime families," and to the Right came to embody the virtuosity of those who are antigovernment. Rivers loves the limelight, but lives by the streetlight. Since he moved to Dorchester in 1988, he has been connected to kids all the time. He reached out to drug dealers and gang members, looking for ways to touch the toughest customers with his ministry. One can fault him for showboating and allowing himself to be used by politicians, but there is no faulting his commitment, genuineness, and effectiveness with some tough young people.

But Ten Point would not be what it is without Gene Rivers's less well known partner, the Reverend Ray Hammond, who is the chair of the board. Hammond, who is pastor of Bethel AME Church in Dorchester, was out in the street from the earliest days, but not especially interested in being noticed. He is a physician who turned to the ministry in midcareer, and is the glue that holds things together. If you want to work with Ten Point you go to Ray Hammond and the staff. If you want to broadcast its message, you go to Gene Rivers.

Ten Point would also not be what it is without its relationship with Boston law enforcement. Together they have produced stunning reductions in violence, aided by the Boston Police Department's success in implementing community policing.

Homicides in the city decreased from 152 to 36 between 1990 and 1997, and there were *no* youth homicides between July 1995 and January 1997. Shootings are back up a bit now, although nothing like before. These are problems that don't stay fixed without continuing effort. A new generation of youth shows up on the streets virtually every year.

When Gene Rivers started, he was operating as an individual, not only on the streets but in relation to the rest of the city. He was constantly critical of the police and the law enforcement establishment, and Curtis Wilkie wrote in the *Boston Globe* that "he dismisses elected officials as 'pathetic' and he mocks mainstream ministers as caricatures of the pious, fried-chicken-eating clergymen with fancy Cadillacs and a reputation for servicing women in their flock."

At about the same time as Rivers arrived, the police stopped denying that there was any special violence problem and announced that they would fully prosecute all gang-connected arrestees. Their strategy was to be aggressive, attacking gang- and drug-related violence by "kicking butt and cracking heads," as one police captain put it, making race a cause for suspicion and engaging in indiscriminate stop-and-frisk tactics. The initial community satisfaction was shortly replaced by outrage at the number of innocent young men being routinely harassed.

In the wake of the Morning Star church incident, several primarily African American congregations came together and adopted a "Ten Point Proposal for Citywide Church Mobilization to Combat the Material and Spiritual Sources of Black-on-Black Violence." Cardinal Bernard Law endorsed the plan, which opened doors within the predominantly Irish Catholic police department.

Meanwhile, Bill Bratton became police commissioner, and implemented big changes, which have been extended by his successor, Paul Evans. The previous antigang unit was replaced by a multi-agency Youth Violence Strike Force. A new Operation Scrap Iron focused on shutting down illegal gun trafficking. Area arrest sweeps were instituted to pick up people with outstanding warrants. In Operation Night Light, probation officers rode with police officers at night and picked up people in the street in violation of their probation.

All of this led to Operation Cease Fire, the collaboration between the police and the Coalition. The partnership changed the behavior of both. By now Hammond and Rivers and their colleagues had credibility with youth on the street. They did not lose respect when the police arrested a person who had committed a violent crime — what Rivers calls a "bad player." It was understood that the ministers would retrieve from police custody or prevent the arrest of "kids that are borderline and wannabes." This intersection between the community and the law enforcement system is missing in most communities, with the result that young people slide and slide, without intervention or support, until they get into trouble so serious that prison or a juvenile correctional institution is the next stop.

The presence of street patrols of ministers and lay people is critical but not enough. It does not substitute for substantive programs. Young people are looking for help with real problems, not just talk. The church members of Ten Point offer mentoring, fatherhood programs, after-school activities, music camps, computer camps, and sports leagues.

This is more than youth development. It is also violence prevention. When the shooting began to recur in 1997, and the word on the street was that the Crips and the Bloods were forming groups in Boston (and interracial groups, at that), Ten Point's judicial coordinator went with police to fifty-five schools to bring a message that a new generation hadn't heard: "We don't want to have to bury you. We don't want your mothers grieving. We in the community will support the police cracking down on violence. We are here to offer you positive alternatives." They were able to recruit three hundred new participants for the Ten Point churches' youth programs, and Ray Hammond believes they blunted the new ripple of violence before it became a wave.

Hammond, Rivers, and the rest of the Ten Point Coalition would be impressive even without their police partners (and vice versa). They would have turned around dozens, maybe hundreds, of young people who were headed in the wrong direction. And some decrease in neighborhood violence would probably have attended those victories. But when the work with young people is coupled with constructive law enforcement, a community presence, a strenuous effort to get at illegal firearms, an imaginative approach to probation, and a coordinated attack on outstanding warrants, the result is a story that is truly special.

8

FINDING AMERICA'S HEART

W E LEARNED after the Columbine High School tragedy that many of the neighbors in that affluent suburb did not know one another, and we know that many parents everywhere are so busy that they can't keep up with what their own children are doing. It is so much easier for evil to appear in places where people are unconnected to each other and feel neither warmth nor responsibility. We want to reduce poverty and raise the incomes of millions who are near the brink of poverty, but we also want to improve the quality of life for struggling families, and for all of us. Increased returns from work and a fair safety net are fundamental, but equally fundamental is reweaving a sense of community among so many who are now so isolated.

Most children live in families. Outside rural areas most families live in neighborhoods. Neighborhoods are nested in cities or suburbs. People have other relationships — in religious congregations, at work, and through dozens of other shared interests. All of these ties could be stronger and more rewarding. So many people say they were poor as children but didn't know it. They lived in healthy families that derived some of their health from the neighborhoods and communities of which they were a part.

Strengthening neighborhoods and communities has to be part of an antipoverty strategy, as well as what we pursue for everyone.

The disconnectedness in American society is at all levels: within families, neighbor to neighbor, and in a day-to-day sense of community, locally and nationally. We rise to the occasion when there is a natural disaster. Hurricanes, tornadoes, floods, earthquakes, and fires bring out the best in us. We generously help others to rebuild, and the scars gradually disappear. Then we go back to business as usual.

Yet, if we truly believe we want to be one nation, we are living every day amidst a calamity of greater dimension than any natural disaster. And responding to all who get the short end of the stick in this affluent country is as pressing a challenge. It is shocking that this wealthy nation has fallen so short in reducing poverty and lessening the distance between the rich and the rest of us since we "discovered" poverty a generation ago.

The task of the next decade is to knit into an effective political force everyone who genuinely cares, together with those who with persuasion can be brought into the fold. We have enough money — we just need to decide to use it. An awakening labor movement and a growing progressive wing in the faith community can add strength. Expanding the scope of community organizing will reach some of those not yet part of any progressive politics.

Of course we shouldn't kid ourselves. Many people believe that if people in this wealthy nation don't have a job it's their own fault, and that it's not the government's responsibility to make up for the failure of the market to produce enough earnings from work. To convince this large group that there are serious economic and racial problems that have to be addressed is a tall order.

Then there are the great unknowns. Will the youth of America ever get remobilized? I remember being in Europe in 1958 and explaining to students there that American young people were not politicized. The civil rights movement became visible about a year later, followed by the antiwar movement. I was happily wrong. There is a second unknown, even more important. Will the people who hold the short end of the stick — not just the poor, but everyone who gets an unfairly small slice of the pie — ever get politicized and start expressing their dissatisfaction? The civil rights movement didn't take hold until courageous local people demanded the opportunity to exercise their basic human rights.

A Framework for the Future

WE ARE STARTING a new century. We have a new president and a new Congress. Surely there is no time more appropriate to call on our national leaders (and ourselves) to cut through the politics and resurrect a national commitment to economic justice and fairness. We need direction that honestly states the challenge, and that proposes solutions of a magnitude suitable to the task. We need both national action and national leadership, both concrete policy and a bully-pulpit campaign to enlist everyone. And we need everyone, everywhere. Even if the new president and Congress are not as committed as they should be, there is a big agenda for local action.

We could end poverty, or even set an income floor at a level higher than the poverty line, by giving out money and other aid to supplement wages for workers and guarantee an income for those not working. We can afford to do this. As Charles Murray said when I debated him in early 2000, the fiscal cost would be "a rounding error" in this wealthy country. But it is not a sufficient answer. The heart of the answer is to think in terms of what families need: work that results in a living wage and the preparation and assistance required for success on the job, education and community involvement in the nurturance of children, and safe and healthy neighborhoods in which to conduct the affairs of daily life.

We should commit ourselves to ending poverty and then some, but our strategy for doing so has to go far beyond income supplementation and cash assistance. Work, education, and community renewal have to be at the center of our attention. That was Robert Kennedy's point in the conversation we had on the steps of the bus in Indiana in 1968. Not only do we have to do everything necessary to get the maximum number of people to work at decent jobs, but we have to reform the deeply flawed institutions that are supposed to serve low-income people, be they schools, welfare and employment agencies, public hospitals, housing authorities, or law enforcement. The task of renewing an ethos of community that, combined with education and opportunity, is the best long-range strategy to reduce antisocial behavior, also takes much more than money. That was part of Robert Kennedy's teaching, too.

On the other hand, money is definitely part of the answer, both for households and for improving the institutions that are supposed to serve people. Those who say we can solve poverty by a regimen of behavioral sanctions combined with volunteer activity, private philanthropy, and faith-based commitments are at best misinformed or naive.

Focus just on the question of income from work. Surely part of building stronger communities is the idea of mutuality. When people take responsibility for themselves, society should take responsibility for seeing that they receive a living wage for their work. People who are economically secure are more likely to feel connected to the larger world and more willing to give something back. If the market is going to leave people in the lurch — people who are doing their very best and still not making it — then public funds should be provided to fill the gap. Public policy at all levels of government should address what we might call a social wage — income supplementation by devices like the Earned

Income Tax Credit, and help with health, child care, housing, and higher-education costs. To leave people prey to the unmitigated operation of the market might have been unavoidable when we were less wealthy as a nation, but there is no excuse for it now.

Public policy can have a positive effect on people's incomes in other ways, too. How do we manage the economy? Do we pursue a policy of full employment and tight labor markets, or do we raise interest rates before there is even a hint of inflation on the horizon? This affects the availability of work. There is the question of the minimum wage. As of 1999, the federal minimum wage had less real purchasing power than it did for twenty-eight of the thirty years between 1954 and 1983. There is the possibility of a federal "living wage," like the ordinances adopted in three dozen or so localities around the country, to require that federal contractors pay a minimum of eight to nine dollars an hour. There is the need for vigorous enforcement of antidiscrimination laws (including adequate funds for enforcement). There are the continuing questions of pay equity for women, and paid family and medical leave. And there is the need for reform of the federal laws governing labor organizing to remove encrustations that enable recalcitrant employers to stonewall organizing and put off indefinitely bargaining with recognized unions.

Money, whether in the form of cash assistance, food stamps, health coverage, or housing assistance, is also part of the answer for people who can't find a job or for one reason or another should not be expected to work outside the home. The worst part of the 1996 welfare law was that it destroyed the cash safety net, limited as it was, for poor children and their families. With the debate on its reauthorization about to begin, we need to learn from experience, which has revealed the problems of both those who have found work but at a wage they can't live on and those who despite a full-employment economy are still being left totally behind. The policy details are complicated, but the bottom line is not: we need to restore a safety net to protect children.

A sensible safety net remains indispensable. We should make sure that food stamps, Medicaid, and the more recently enacted CHIP program of health coverage for near-poor children reach everyone eligible. We should invest in jobs programs for people unable to find work, for those who need work experience to assist in the transition to employment, and for those who are able to work only in a partially subsidized environment. The boundaries between those expected to work, those who are functionally disabled or otherwise not in a position to work, and those who are legally disabled present a continuing policy question that will perhaps never be resolved satisfactorily, but the effort to draw workable lines has to go on. We need to end the hypocrisy that says affluent women should stay home with their small children and poor women have to go to work almost immediately.

Nor is a safety net only about welfare. We have to assure that the elderly have the income and support that they need. We need to revisit the limitations on assistance to legal immigrants imposed in a xenophobic panic. Unemployment insurance has deteriorated until it covers only a minority of people out of work. Disability policy needs strengthening to increase employment possibilities for disabled people, and to increase protection for people who are functionally disabled but not covered by existing legal definitions.

Enacting national legislation to assure health coverage for every American, with action in the meantime to get states to offer coverage for the maximum possible number, is a top priority. Making developmental child care available and affordable for all American children, so all children are ready for school and parents can pursue work knowing their children are well cared for, is vital. We need to deal with the mounting shortage of low-income housing. And strengthening access to higher education remains important. All of these are matters of both money and structure. Improving the structure is particularly a matter of community and civic responsibility, although it can be nudged in good directions by national leadership.

All these jobs- and income-related policies will strengthen families. So will other steps like increasing the family friendliness of workplaces, providing home visits to help the parents of newborn children get off on the right path, passing on child-support payments collected by states to the children for whose benefit they are paid, promoting responsible fatherhood, and assuring that families can get legal help and other services they need.

Now is also the time to pursue an issue that is just gaining visibility in the public debate — wealth creation. If the gaps in income are spectacular, the gaps in wealth are more so. For whatever reason, savings among people of color are a special problem. African Americans of the same income level as whites are much less able to afford a home or a college education for their children, and live much closer to the brink of ruin should a financial crisis befall them. Asset development, whether through provision of incentives for savings, individual-development accounts for children, or microenterprise lending, is making its way toward the front burner of public attention. Like many new ideas, each of these differing notions is sometimes promoted as a panacea. None is a magic solution. But all need careful examination and consideration. The problems they propose to address are real.

This has been a long list, but two big categories are still missing — rebuilding a sense of community in places where it is largely lost, and investing in the education of children. Both of these require national funding and policy guidance, and both require local engagement.

Policy must be directed at urban and rural places where the poor live in high concentrations. Measures directed at income and related issues reach the poor everywhere, but extra efforts at family strengthening, job access, school improvement, and basic public safety need to focus on where the poor live in big numbers. Otherwise we will continue to have more people who from one generation to the next fail to escape the circumstances of their birth. Regulation, incentives, and persuasion need to encourage financial institutions of all kinds to lend fairly for business development and housing, and smart economic development strategies for low-income neighborhoods are needed as well.

Some conservatives continue to say that the only way to change behavior that society believes is unacceptable is by getting tough — imposing harsh sentences through the criminal law and narrowly limiting help available to families, especially families headed by single women. Now they have added zero-tolerance policies and high-stakes testing, which too often have the effect of pushing children out of school and stunting possibilities even earlier. Effective but fair and just law enforcement is essential, welfare policy should encourage and support work, and personal responsibility should be expected. But existing law enforcement and welfare policies, joined by the simplistic application of some current education policies, are based on a misunderstanding of the problem and a misjudgment of solutions.

Of the 2 million people held in prisons and jails, 60 percent are African American and Latino, and half a million are coming out of prison and jail every year. Given our attitudes and the legal disabilities imposed on people who have been incarcerated, many of them are not going to be able to reintegrate successfully. This is social dynamite. We need to ask what we can do to reduce the flow into prison. We need drug enforcement policies that introduce a public health perspective and use treatment instead of incarceration wherever possible, and we need youth development policies that minimize the stream of new perpetrators into the criminal justice system.

Similarly, throwing whole families off welfare because they fail to show up for an appointment, or because they look like they should be able to find a job, or when an arbitrary time limit has been reached but they are still in need, places children at great risk. This, too, is social dynamite.

Our best hope for the long term is social inclusion. British Prime Minister Tony Blair has established a social-inclusion unit in his office. We need a similar emphasis. Money, especially money that comes to people from working for a living, is crucial, but so is attention to neighborhood revitalization and re-creating a feeling of community. Inclusion is the best answer to the disproportionate incidence of negative behavior.

A big part of the challenge is to raise children who will be self-sufficient and active participants in our democracy and society. Reform of the public schools through community, state, and (to a far lesser extent) national policy is essential. Equally essential is recognition that the needs of children go beyond the time they spend in school. Outside funding is crucial, but only communities can offer children and older youth activities and opportunities that keep them safe and clear the path to responsible adulthood. A juvenile justice system that makes itself a part of a youth development strategy wherever it can is critical, too.

There may be some who still see the answers solely in terms of passing laws and creating programs or, even more narrowly, in terms of what Congress needs to do. There are others who say everything can be solved by private charity and voluntary action. All of them are wrong. The remedies include public policy at all levels of government, but must also feature both organized and individual private and civic action.

All of us need to look for ways to help. We should help organizations of which we are already a part to find a trail from the problems of individuals they serve to ways in which public policy at every level can make a difference. We should similarly press our church, synagogue, or mosque.

Our help in mentoring or tutoring a young person is fabulous, but is there any way we can help get a hundred more mentors or tutors, or help a group that is trying to improve the whole school that our mentee attends or the whole school system? Our help in seeing that individual children are treated responsively in the world of child welfare and foster care is vital, but could we help a group that is trying to make the whole system work better? Our letters to the editor are great, but can we find people who are organizing in larger numbers to contact the mayor or the city council, or the state government or Congress, to invest more funds or change the law on the issues we care about?

We have to get more people to see the connections. So many people are willing to help but do not see the ways in which bad public policy has exacerbated the problem or ignored it, or have no confidence that public policy could improve things. All of us ought to challenge our own patterns of thinking. If your instinct is to think of public policy, ask not only what you can do to contribute to better public policy but also what you can do to help others individually and what you can do to strengthen helping institutions in the community. If your instinct is in the direction of private action, think not only about how you can do more in that direction but also about why public policy has not alleviated the problems that concern you and what you and others could do to help improve it.

We should ask what we want our government to do. So many of us do not even ask any more. But we should also ask what we want of ourselves. Too many of us do not ask that question either.

The questions remain. Who is America? What is America? This has not been a good decade for inclusive answers to these questions. The nineties produced a devastating cocktail of radical reactionary Republicanism and Clintonian me-first politics, which hardened the lines between the greatly prospering few and the reasonably comfortable majority on the one hand, and the people at the margins on the other.

Still, the message Americans have been sending, both electorally and civically, since the darkest days of the Gingrich period, is that this is not an extremist country. Individual communities have opened their doors and their arms over the years to Vietnamese boat people, Soviet refuseniks, Kosovar refugees, and others. Yet too many in America have shut their eyes and ears to appreciating why millions of its children of all vintages — with ancestry on these shores dating back three hundred years, as well as three years and three dozen years — live in such poor circumstances with such poor chances.

My own journey continues. Since I left the government in 1996 I have added my voice to those pointing out what is actually happening under the new welfare legislation. I am so grateful that I have had the chance to make some difference on poverty issues over the past thirty-five-plus years. It is amazing how the twists and turns of my career have consistently kept me involved in this concern. More than once, professional possibilities that intrigued me but would have taken me in a different direction did not materialize or materialized but did not last. Forces that I did not anticipate have repeatedly kept me involved on these questions of economic justice and fairness. I'm not sure why, but it all adds up, and I'm grateful.

This is a time of particular opportunity. The prosperity of recent years, the ensuing surpluses, the increase in local activism, and the effect of the new welfare law in deflating anger at the poor come together to offer opportunity. More lower-income people seem ready to speak about their needs. More civic leaders seem to understand the need to attend to their public schools, and to issues such as child care, health coverage, and connecting people to jobs.

But changing things takes a long time. Especially if the endeavor is to change how a system or an institution or a bureaucracy works, or how a neighborhood functions, those who need instant gratification should look elsewhere. In this world of instant communication and overnight millionaires, the idea of staying with what has to be a never ending effort against poverty and for economic justice and community may seem particularly anachronistic or at least anomalous.

Nonetheless, I think we are at a better place to make progress and to build a movement than we have been at any time since Robert Kennedy died. He always said we can do better. We still can. Now.

INDEX